Implementing Cisco UCS Solutions

A hands-on guide to implementing solutions in Cisco UCS, as well as deploying servers and application stacks

Farhan Ahmed Nadeem

Prasenjit Sarkar

BIRMINGHAM - MUMBAI

Implementing Cisco UCS Solutions

First published: December 2013

Production Reference: 1181213

Published by Packt Publishing Ltd.
Livery Place
35 Livery Street
Birmingham B3 2PB, UK.

ISBN 978-1-78217-066-2

www.packtpub.com

Cover Image by Abhishek Pandey (abhishek.pandey1210@gmail.com)

Credits

Authors
Farhan Ahmed Nadeem
Prasenjit Sarkar

Reviewer
Anuj Modi

Acquisition Editor
Kevin Colaco

Lead Technical Editors
Mayur Hule
Neeshma Ramakrishnan

Commissioning Editor
Aarthi Kumaraswamy

Technical Editors
Nadeem Bagban
Aparna Chand
Zainab Fatakdawala
Dennis John
Aparna Kumari

Copy Editors
Brandt D'Mello
Dipti Kapadia
Gladson Monteiro
Insiya Morbiwala
Deepa Nambiar
Lavina Pereira

Project Coordinators
Cheryl Botelho
Rahul Dixit

Proofreaders
Bernadette Watkins
Elinor Perry-Smith

Indexer
Tejal R. Soni

Graphics
Disha Haria
Yuvraj Mannari

Production Coordinator
Arvindkumar Gupta

Cover Work
Arvindkumar Gupta

About the Authors

Farhan Ahmed Nadeem has been in the IT field for over 17 years. He has a Master's degree in Electrical Engineering and holds a number of certifications including CCNP/CCNA DC, VCP, CISSP, CCA, and MCSE-EA. Starting with Microsoft certification MCSE-NT in 1997, he always stayed abreast with the latest technologies and server hardware through proactive learning and successful real-world deployments. He has extensive work experience in complex heterogeneous environments comprising various hardware platforms, operating systems, and applications. This exposure gave him broad knowledge in investigating, designing, implementing, and managing infrastructure solutions. He progressively started focusing on virtualization technologies and the Cisco UCS platform and has completed a number of successful UCS deployments with both VMware ESXi and Citrix XenServer hypervisors. When not working with computers, he enjoys spending time with his family.

I am thankful to my friend Prof. Dr. Adeel Akram, who helped me in developing the contents. I am also thankful to my wife and four kids who missed a lot of their weekends while I was working on this project.

Prasenjit Sarkar (@stretchcloud) is a senior member of technical staff at VMware Service Provider Cloud R&D, where he provides architectural oversight and technical guidance for designing, implementing, and testing VMware's Cloud datacenters. He is an author, R&D guy, and a blogger focusing on virtualization, Cloud computing, storage, networking, and other enterprise technologies. He has more than 10 years of expert knowledge in R&D, professional services, alliances, solution engineering, consulting, and technical sales with expertise in architecting and deploying virtualization solutions and rolling out new technologies and solution initiatives. His primary focus is on VMware vSphere Infrastructure and Public Cloud using VMware vCloud Suite. His aim is to own the entire life cycle of a VMware based IaaS (SDDC), especially vSphere, vCloud Director, vShield Manager, and vCenter Operations. He was one of the VMware vExperts of 2012 and is well known for his acclaimed virtualization blog http://stretch-cloud.info. He holds certifications from VMware, Cisco, Citrix, Red Hat, Microsoft, IBM, HP, and Exin. Prior to joining VMware, he served other fine organizations (such as Capgemini, HP, and GE) as a solution architect and infrastructure architect.

I would like to thank and dedicate this book to my mom and dad. Without their endless and untiring support, this book would not have been possible.

About the Reviewer

Anuj Modi has been working in the IT field for more than 11 years, starting out his career as a system administrator. He has worked with leading companies such as Computer Science Corporation (CSC) as Wintel Senior Administrator and Hewlett-Packard (HP) as a technical solutions consultant. Currently, he is working as a unified computing and virtualization consultant with Cisco Systems (Private) Limited, providing consultations on datacenter solutions to customers. He is involved in datacenter assessment, planning, designing, implementing and optimizing infrastructure, and helping customers to build and migrate to the green datacenter of the next generation. He is also involved in the demonstration of Cisco Unified Computing Solution (UCS) value targeting cloud computing, virtualization, unified I/O, datacenter management, and orchestration. He ensures delivery of datacenter architecture and industry standard solutions such as Vblock, FlexPod, VSPEX, VDI, VXI, Nexus 1000v, Virtual Security Gateway (VSG), ASA 1000V, Unified Computing Solution Director (UCSD), and Application Centric Infrastructure (ACI), and helps customers with server consolidation, capacity planning of existing servers, P2V, migration of datacenter, and so on.

www.PacktPub.com

Support files, eBooks, discount offers and more

You might want to visit www.PacktPub.com for support files and downloads related to your book.

Did you know that Packt offers eBook versions of every book published, with PDF and ePub files available? You can upgrade to the eBook version at www.PacktPub.com and as a print book customer, you are entitled to a discount on the eBook copy. Get in touch with us at service@packtpub.com for more details.

At www.PacktPub.com, you can also read a collection of free technical articles, sign up for a range of free newsletters and receive exclusive discounts and offers on Packt books and eBooks.

http://PacktLib.PacktPub.com

Do you need instant solutions to your IT questions? PacktLib is Packt's online digital book library. Here, you can access, read and search across Packt's entire library of books.

Why Subscribe?

- Fully searchable across every book published by Packt
- Copy and paste, print and bookmark content
- On demand and accessible via web browser

Free Access for Packt account holders

If you have an account with Packt at www.PacktPub.com, you can use this to access PacktLib today and view nine entirely free books. Simply use your login credentials for immediate access.

Instant Updates on New Packt Books

Get notified! Find out when new books are published by following @PacktEnterprise on Twitter, or the *Packt Enterprise* Facebook page.

Table of Contents

Preface

Implementing Cisco UCS Solutions is written with a hands-on approach. With actual examples for configuring and deploying Cisco UCS components, this book prepares readers for the real-world deployments of Cisco UCS datacenter solutions.

This book starts with a description of Cisco UCS equipment options and introduces Cisco UCS Emulator, which is an excellent resource for practically learning Cisco UCS components deployment. Subsequent chapters introduce all areas of UCS solutions with practical configuration examples.

You will be introduced to the Cisco UCS Manager, which is the centralized management interface for Cisco UCS. Once the reader establishes elementary acquaintance with UCS Manager, we go deep into configuring LAN, SAN, identity pools, resource pools, and service profiles for the servers. We also present miscellaneous administration topics including backup, restore, user roles, and high-availability cluster configuration. The last few chapters introduce virtualized networking, third-party integration tools, and testing failure scenarios.

If you want to learn and enhance your hands-on skills with Cisco UCS solutions, this book is certainly for you. You will learn everything you need for the rapidly growing Cisco UCS deployments.

What this book covers

Chapter 1, Cisco UCS Physical Architecture and Installing UCS Hardware, covers physical components of UCS solutions including Fabric Interconnects, blade chassis, IOM/FEX modules, mezzanine cards, blade servers, and rack-mount servers. Specifications of different components are provided along with the physical installation and connectivity of all of the components.

Chapter 2, Setting Up Lab Using Cisco UCS Emulator, introduces the UCS Emulator, which is an excellent tool from Cisco to learn UCS even without a physical lab. Different UCS Emulator installation options are discussed, and configuring the UCS Emulator for lab usage is explained.

Chapter 3, Configuring Cisco UCS Using UCS Manager, gives an overview of UCS Manager, which is the core management tool for the UCS platform. Readers get acquainted with the UCS Manager navigation and configuration options using both graphical user interface and command-line interface.

Chapter 4, Configuring LAN Connectivity, explains UCS network connectivity. UCS platform-unique features, including Fabric Interconnect operational modes, pin groups, port channels, virtual PortChannel, and virtual network interface card configuration, are explained along with both northbound and southbound network connectivities from Fabric Interconnects.

Chapter 5, Configuring SAN Connectivity, explains storage connectivity for different SAN protocols supported by the UCS platform. Configuration of protocols including FC, FCoE, and iSCSI is discussed along with an introduction to UCS unique features including FC operational modes, VSANs, and uplink pinning.

Chapter 6, Creating Identity and Resource Pools, introduces identity and resource pools which include UUID, MAC addresses, WWN, and server pools. Identity and resource pools are used for abstracting unique identities and resources for devices such as vNICs; vHBAs and server pools can assign servers in groups based on similar server characteristics.

Chapter 7, Creating and Managing Service Profiles, shows how to create service profiles that provide necessary identities, resources, and configuration to the stateless servers. Readers first learn how to create policies which provide server configuration, and then learn various service profile configuration options.

Chapter 8, Managing UCS through Routine and Advanced Management, introduces the most common and advanced management tasks performed with UCS, from startup and shutdown to logging, upgrading firmware, licensing, and role-based access. These routine management tasks are crucial to understand in order to effectively administer Cisco UCS.

Chapter 9, Virtual Networking in Cisco UCS, explains the integration of Cisco UCS and the virtualization of hypervisor mostly with VMware vSphere and Cisco Nexus 1000v Distributed Virtual Switch.

Chapter 10, Configuring Backup, Restore, and High Availability, covers UCS backup and restore options. This chapter also provides details of high-availability configuration for UCS Fabric Interconnects.

Chapter 11, Cisco UCS Failure Scenarios Testing, discusses various failure scenarios that provide necessary knowledge for UCS troubleshooting for identifying and resolving issues.

Chapter 12, Third-party Application Integration, covers third-party applications including VMware vCenter extension, goUCS automation toolkit, EMC UIM, and so on.

What you need for this book

In order to create a lab without physical equipment and to practice procedures provided in this book, you will need the following:

- A UCS Emulator virtual machine that provides UCS Manager application and emulated hardware.
- A hypervisor that can run the UCS Emulator VM. Options include VM Player, VM Workstation, VM Fusion, vSphere, and HyperV.
- A client machine with an Internet-Explorer- or Mozilla-compatible browser for accessing the UCS Manager application.

Who this book is for

This book is intended for the professionals responsible for Cisco UCS deployments which include systems, network, and storage administrators. Readers should have basic knowledge of the server's architecture, network, and storage technologies. Although not necessary, familiarity with virtualization technologies is also recommended because a majority of real-world UCS deployments run virtualized loads. Even though UCS Fabric Interconnects running the UCS manager software are based on the Nexus platform, knowledge of Nexus OS is not necessary, because a majority of the management tasks are handled in the graphical user interface with very few exceptions using the CLI.

Conventions

In this book, you will find a number of styles of text that distinguish between different kinds of information. Here are some examples of these styles and an explanation of their meaning.

Code words in text, database table names, folder names, filenames, file extensions, pathnames, dummy URLs, user input, and Twitter handles are shown as follows: "All uplink ports are configured as `802.1q` trunks."

Any command-line input or output is written as follows:

```
# show cluster state
A: UP, PRIMARY
B: UP, SUBORDINATE
HA READY
```

New terms and **important words** are shown in bold. Words that you see on the screen, in menus or dialog boxes for example, appear in the text like this: "Click on the **Equipment** tab in the Navigation pane."

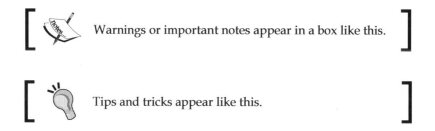

Warnings or important notes appear in a box like this.

Tips and tricks appear like this.

Reader feedback

Feedback from our readers is always welcome. Let us know what you think about this book—what you liked or may have disliked. Reader feedback is important for us to develop titles that you really get the most out of.

To send us general feedback, simply send an e-mail to feedback@packtpub.com, and mention the book title via the subject of your message.

If there is a topic that you have expertise in and you are interested in either writing or contributing to a book, see our author guide on www.packtpub.com/authors.

Customer support

Now that you are the proud owner of a Packt book, we have a number of things to help you to get the most from your purchase.

Errata

Although we have taken every care to ensure the accuracy of our content, mistakes do happen. If you find a mistake in one of our books—maybe a mistake in the text or the code—we would be grateful if you would report this to us. By doing so, you can save other readers from frustration and help us improve subsequent versions of this book. If you find any errata, please report them by visiting http://www.packtpub.com/submit-errata, selecting your book, clicking on the **errata submission form** link, and entering the details of your errata. Once your errata are verified, your submission will be accepted and the errata will be uploaded on our website, or added to any list of existing errata, under the Errata section of that title. Any existing errata can be viewed by selecting your title from http://www.packtpub.com/support.

Piracy

Piracy of copyright material on the Internet is an ongoing problem across all media. At Packt, we take the protection of our copyright and licenses very seriously. If you come across any illegal copies of our works, in any form, on the Internet, please provide us with the location address or website name immediately so that we can pursue a remedy.

Please contact us at copyright@packtpub.com with a link to the suspected pirated material.

We appreciate your help in protecting our authors, and our ability to bring you valuable content.

Questions

You can contact us at questions@packtpub.com if you are having a problem with any aspect of the book, and we will do our best to address it.

1
Cisco UCS Physical Architecture and Installing UCS Hardware

In previous decades, computers evolved at a dramatic pace. Moore's law, which predicted that the density of transistors and integrated circuits would double every two years as computing components kept on shrinking in size while improving in computational capacity, has truly prevailed. This technological evolution led to three distinct generations of computing devices.

We witnessed the era of the following generations:

- Gigantic mainframe computers
- Commoditized personal computers and tower and rack servers (also known as pizza-box servers)
- Blade servers (also known as modular servers)

Mainframes were monolithic systems often with proprietary hardware and software. With their enormous computing power, mainframes were able to run multiple applications; however, their major limitations were cost and many single points of failure. Due to their high cost and management complexity, mainframes remained mainly confined to military use, universities, and some very large organizations.

Tower and rack-mounted servers usually have limited computational resources as compared to mainframes; however, these are very cost effective. Because of the limited resources available on these servers, a one-to-one server-to-application ratio is usually the way to go. Because of this *one server one application* design, rack and tower servers need more rack space, separate cabling, individual power supplies, and more cooling in the datacenter, which makes management of the infrastructure quite complex. However, this second generation of computers is generally very cost effective. This led to the mass adoption of computers everywhere.

The latest trend in the ever evolving computer architecture space is to move away from tower and rack-mounted servers in favor of blade servers. In today's highly demanding enterprise applications, blade server architecture provides excellent features when compared with rack and tower servers. These features include the following:

- Less rack space usage
- Less cabling
- Shared power
- Consolidated I/O
- Easy management
- Excellent heating and cooling

Contemporary datacenters are facing unprecedented growth in computational demands alongside the need for reducing implementation and operational costs. Considering these factors, blade servers are designed to minimize the use of resources and space. Components in a blade chassis are either removed or shared between blade servers.

The minimum form factor of a rack server is 1 **Rack Unit (RU)**. 1 RU is equal to 1.75 inches, and the most common server rack height is usually 42 RU. It is therefore possible to fit only 42 pizza-box servers in a standard rack. With blade servers, it is possible to achieve higher densities of servers per rack.

In a blade server, data connectivity interfaces and power supplies are also shared. Thus, blade servers also require less cabling, and hence less management.

In this chapter, we will discuss physical components of the **Unified Computing System (UCS)** equipment. The list of the topics covered in this chapter is as follows:

- A quick look at the UCS equipment
- Understanding the physical architecture of UCS

- Understanding **Fabric Interconnects (FIs)**
- Cisco UCS 5100 series blade server chassis
- IOM modules
- Blade servers and rack-mount servers
- Getting started with mezzanine cards
- Power capacity and power plugs
- Installing UCS chassis components
- Cabling FI and IOM

Looking at the UCS equipment

With the ever increasing demand on datacenters, vendors started focusing on different aspects of server and networking hardware consolidation; however, most of the ad hoc solutions were based on gluing together the existing products which were not designed grounds up to provide a cohesive infrastructure and failed to address the requirements of the datacenter as a whole. Hence, management of these amalgamated solutions was a nightmare for IT administrators.

Cisco entered into the blade server market with a holistic approach to the blade server design. With a strong background in networking and storage products, Cisco developed a cohesive solution consolidating the computing, network, and storage connectivity components along with centralized management of these resources. The purpose of Cisco UCS is to reduce the **Total Cost of Ownership** (TCO) and improve scalability and flexibility.

Salient features and benefits of the UCS solution include the following:

- Stateless computing
- Rapid provisioning of servers
- Simplified troubleshooting
- Virtualization readiness
- Choice of industry-standard form factors
- Extended memory technology for increased density

Stateless computing

Cisco introduced the idea of stateless computing with its blade server design. Cisco blade servers do not have any initial configuration. **Universally Unique Identifiers (UUIDs)** for blades, **Network Interface Cards (NICs)**, **Media Access Control (MAC)** addresses, storage **World Wide Node (WWN)** numbers, firmware, and BIOS settings are all abstracted from **Unified Computing System Manager (UCSM)**, the management software running on the FIs.

Rapid provisioning of servers

Provisioning of servers dramatically improves as the servers can be provisioned using the UCSM software even before they are physically available. Once the server is physically installed, it will abstract its identity from UCSM. Using server configuration templates, it is therefore possible to create a server template only once and apply the template to hundreds of servers.

Simplified troubleshooting

Replacement of servers also becomes very easy. Since the servers are stateless, as soon as a replacement server is installed, it will abstract all the configuration of the old server and will be available for use. Servers can also be easily migrated for different roles and workloads.

Virtualization readiness

Virtualization in the form of modern bare metal hypervisors is a major breakthrough for optimal utilization of computational resources. Cisco UCS solution supports all major hypervisor platforms including VMware ESX/ESXi, Microsoft Hyper-V, and Citrix Xen server. Support and integration with VMware vSphere solution is very strong. UCSM can be integrated with vCenter to abstract and manage features at the individual **Virtual Machine (VM)** level. By leveraging the benefits of virtualization and increasing the density of the physical server, the UCS solution can scale up to thousands of VMs.

Choice of industry-standard form factors

Cisco UCS servers are available in two categories: B-series blade servers and C-series rack-mount servers. Both form factors are designed using the same industry-standard components and can address different computational requirements. Both B-series blade servers and C-series rack-mount servers are designed using Intel Xeon CPUs. B-series servers are managed through UCSM, whereas C-series servers can either be individually managed or can be integrated to UCSM.

Extended memory technology for increased density

Cisco also introduced a patented extended memory technology for two CPU socket servers to increase the total amount of memory support; this could be more than double the amount of memory as compared to the industry standards for two socket servers. Virtualized workloads can leverage this extra memory to support an even greater density of VMs in a reduced physical footprint, resulting in reduced **Capital Expenditure (CAPEX)** and **Operational Expenditure (OPEX)** costs. Extended memory technology is available in both B-series blade servers and C-series rack-mount servers.

Understanding the physical architecture of UCS

The Cisco UCS solution can be divided into the following three main categories:

- The Cisco UCS FIs
- The Cisco UCS blade servers
- The Cisco UCS rack-mount servers

The Cisco UCS FIs

The Cisco UCS FIs provide network connectivity and management for the connected servers. The UCS FIs run the UCSM control software and consist of the following components:

- 6100 series and 6200 series FIs
- Transceivers for network and storage connectivity
- Expansion modules for both FI series
- UCSM software

The Cisco UCS blade servers

The Cisco UCS blade servers require a mother chassis where these servers can be installed. The UCS blade server solution consists of the following components:

- A blade server chassis, used for installing blades
- B-series blade servers

- IOM modules for connectivity to the FIs
- Transceivers for connectivity to the FIs
- Mezzanine cards for network and storage connectivity

The Cisco UCS rack-mount servers

The Cisco UCS rack-mount servers are standalone servers that can be installed and controlled individually. Cisco provides **Fabric Extenders (FEXs)** for the rack-mount servers. FEXs can be used to connect and manage rack-mount servers from FIs. The UCS rack-mount server solution consists of the following components:

- UCS C-series rack-mount servers
- FEXs for connecting rack-mount servers to FIs

In this chapter we will provide details about hardware options available for both blade servers and rack-mount servers. Most of the field deployments of UCS servers are based on blade servers. Therefore, our main focus will be on blade server configuration in this book. However, if proper connectivity is established between rack-mount servers and FIs, rack-mount servers can also be managed in the same fashion.

The following figure depicts the FIs running the UCSM software, a blade server chassis with IOM modules, and the main components of a blade server:

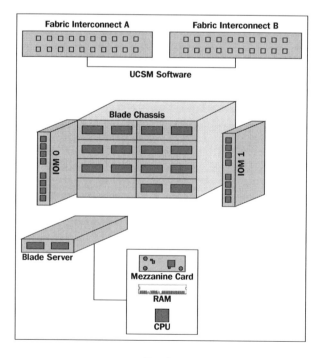

In this chapter, we will go into the details of various UCS components and will focus on their physical specifications and installation in the subsequent sections.

> The Cisco interactive 3D model for Cisco 5100 series chassis and blades is an excellent resource for exploring Cisco UCS components physically. It is also available for iPhone/iPad (search for UCS Tech Specs in the marketplace). More details on this are available at `http://www.cisco.com/en/US/prod/ps10265/ps10279/ucs_kaon_model_preso.html`.

Understanding FIs

An FI is the core component of a UCS solution. FIs are typically configured as highly available clustered pairs in production environments. It's possible to run a single FI-based design as a proof of concept test deployment before actually implementing it in production. FIs provide the following two capabilities:

- Network connectivity to both LAN and SAN
- UCS infrastructure management through the embedded management software, UCSM, for both hardware and software management

FIs are available in two generations, namely Cisco UCS 6100 series and Cisco UCS 6200 series. The core functionality is the same in both generations; however, UCS 6200 series has a newer generation **Application Specific Integrated Circuit** (ASIC), higher throughput, and increased number of physical ports. Both generations can be upgraded to the latest UCSM software.

FIs provide converged ports. Depending on the physical **Small Form Factor Pluggable** (SFP) transceivers and FI software configuration, each port can be configured in different ways. Cisco 6200 series FI ports can be configured as Ethernet ports, **Fiber Channel over Ethernet** (FCoE) ports, or **Fiber Channel** (FC) ports. On the other hand, 6100 series converged ports only support Ethernet and FCoE (they also support FC, but only in the expansion slot).

In production, FIs are deployed in clustered pairs to provide high availability. Cisco-supported implementation requires that clustered FIs be identical. The only possibility for having different FIs in a cluster is during a cluster upgrade.

Larger enterprises may consider deploying the Cisco UCS central software, which can manage multiple UCS domains across globally distributed datacenters.

The following are the specifications of all the available UCS FIs.

The Cisco 6296UP FI

The Cisco 6296UP FI (**UP** represents **Unified Ports**) is a 2 RU device with a maximum of 96 converged ports. Ports can be configured as 1 GB Ethernet, 10 GB Ethernet, 10 GB FCoE, and 2/4/8 GB FC. The specifications of this FI are as follows:

- A maximum of 20 blade server chassis per FI

- A fabric throughput of 1920 Gbps

- A 48-port base unit with three expansion slots (each expansion slot can add 16 ports)

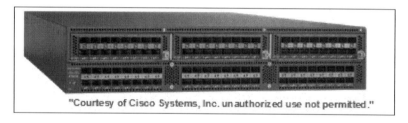

"Courtesy of Cisco Systems, Inc. unauthorized use not permitted."

The Cisco 6248UP FI

The Cisco 6248UP FI is a 1 RU device with a maximum of 48 converged ports. Ports could be configured as 1 GB Ethernet, 10 GB Ethernet, 10 GB FCoE, and 2, 4, or 8 GB FC. The specifications of this FI are as follows:

- A maximum of 20 blade server chassis per FI

- A fabric throughput of 960 Gbps

- A 32-port base unit with one expansion slot that can provide 16 extra ports

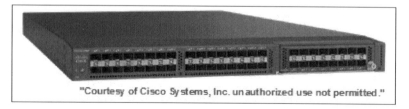

"Courtesy of Cisco Systems, Inc. unauthorized use not permitted."

The Cisco 6140UP FI

The Cisco 6140UP FI is a 2 RU device with a maximum of 48 converged ports. Fixed ports can be configured as 10 GB Ethernet and 10 GB FCoE. Only the first 16 ports can be configured as 1 GB Ethernet. The FC is only supported in the expansion module ports. The specifications of this FI are as follows:

- A maximum of 20 blade server chassis per FI
- A fabric throughput of 1040 Gbps
- A unit of 40 fixed ports with two expansion slots where each expansion slot can provide eight FC ports of 2, 4, or 8 Gbps or six 10 Gbps SFP+ ports

"Courtesy of Cisco Systems, Inc. unauthorized use not permitted."

The Cisco 6120UP FI

The Cisco 6120UP FI is a 1 RU device with a maximum of 20 fixed 10 GB ports. Fixed ports can be configured as 10 GB Ethernet and 10 GB FCoE. Only the first eight ports can be configured as 1 GB Ethernet. The FC is only supported in the expansion module ports. The specifications of this FI are as follows:

- A maximum of 20 blade server chassis per FI
- A fabric throughput of 520 Gbps
- A unit of 20 fixed ports with one expansion slot, which can provide eight 2/4/8 Gbps FC or six 10 Gbps ports

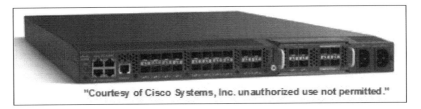

"Courtesy of Cisco Systems, Inc. unauthorized use not permitted."

 Standard pricing of FIs provides a limited number of port licenses. To enable more ports, extra licenses can be purchased per port.

Exploring connectivity transceivers for FIs

A variety of SFP transceivers are available for both FI series. These transceivers provide south-bound IOM connectivity and north-bound network and storage connectivity. They are based on industry-standard SFP+ specifications.

Transceivers can be selected depending on the technology, for example, Ethernet or FC, and also according to the distance requirements. For shorter distances between FIs, IOMs, and north-bound network switches, twinax cables with integrated SFP is an economical alternative as compared to fiber optic SFP.

The most commonly used transceivers include the following:

- **Cisco SFP-10G-SR**: This is a multimode optical fiber 10 Gbps Ethernet SFP that can be used for distances up to 400 meters.

- **Cisco SFP-10G-LR**: This is a single-mode optical fiber 10 Gbps Ethernet SFP that can be used for distances up to 10 Km.

- **Cisco SFP-10G-FET**: This is a low power consuming multimode fiber optic 10 Gbps Ethernet SFP that can be used for distances up to 100 meters.

- **Cisco SFP-H10GB-CUxM**: These are the twinax cables providing low cost 10 Gbps Ethernet connectivity and are available in 1, 3, 5, and 7 meter fixed length configurations. The actual transceivers are named SFP-H10GB-CU1M, SFP-H10GB-CU3M, SFP-H10GB-CU5M, and SFP-H10GB-CU7M according to the length each twinax cable provides.

- **Cisco SFP-H10GB-ACU10M**: This is a 10-meter-long twinax cable providing 10 Gbps Ethernet. At a length of 10 meters, this cable requires active transceivers at both ends.

- **DS-SFP-FCxG-xW**: These are multi-mode and single-mode fiber optic FC transceivers that are available at 2, 4, and 8 Gbps transfer speeds. The actual transceivers are named DS-SFP-FC4G-SW and DS-SFP-FC8G-SW according to the speed and distance covered by the transceiver.

 A detailed list of FI-compatible SFPs is available at `http://www.cisco.com/en/US/prod/collateral/ps10265/ps11544/data_sheet_c78-675245.html`.

Distance and other detailed specifications of the Cisco SFPs are available at `http://www.cisco.com/en/US/prod/collateral/modules/ps5455/data_sheet_c78-455693.html`.

The Cisco UCS 5100 series blade server chassis

The Cisco 5100 series blade server chassis is a vital building block of the Cisco UCS solution. Currently, there is only one generation of UCS blade chassis, which is Cisco UCS 5108. The chassis form factor is 6 RU and it can host the following:

- A maximum of eight half-width blade servers

- A maximum of four full-width blade servers

- Any other combination of half-width blade and full-width blade servers is also possible

A look at the chassis front

The UCS chassis front is used to insert blade servers into the chassis. The front of the chassis also holds UCS power supplies. The UCS chassis front can hold the following hardware:

- Eight half-width empty slots for a maximum of eight half-width blade servers with a removable divider in the middle; this can be removed for installing a maximum of four full-width blades or any other combination of half-width and full-width servers

- Four slots for single power supplies; these slots can be configured as nonredundant, N+1 redundant, and grid redundant

This has been demonstrated in the following image:

A look at the chassis back

The UCS chassis back provides slots for IOM modules, fan units, and power connectors. It provides the following connectors:

- Two slots for IOM modules that act as remote line cards to the FIs
- Eight fan units
- Four power supply connectors

This has been demonstrated in the following image:

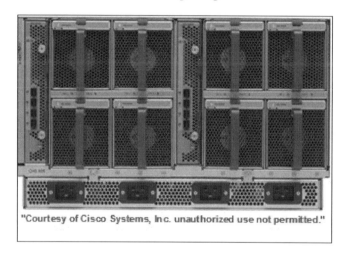

"Courtesy of Cisco Systems, Inc. unauthorized use not permitted."

Environmental requirements

The UCS chassis is designed for the industry-standard rack form factor. The following are the environmental requirements for the UCS chassis:

- An industry-standard, four-post, 19 inch rack or cabinet is required as the chassis cannot be mounted onto a two-post relay rack because of its weight and length
- It requires a 6 RU rack space
- Ensure proper cooling and ventilation for the rack as chassis air flow is front to back and should not be obstructed

- The operating temperature of the UCS is 10 to 35 degrees centigrade
- The acoustic power level is 85 dBA under normal operation
- The weight of an empty chassis is 136 kg, which requires special consideration for floor loading

> Due to the weight and size of the chassis, at least two persons are required to mount it to the rails. It is highly recommended to mount the chassis first and then insert the power supplies, fan units, and blade servers.
>
> The use of a server lift is highly recommended. Chassis side handles are only for moving and adjusting the chassis in the rack.

IOM modules

IOM modules are also known as Cisco FEXs or simply FEX modules. These modules serve as line cards to the FIs in the same way that Nexus series switches can have remote line cards. IOM modules also provide interface connections to blade servers. They multiplex data from blade servers and provide this data to FIs and do the same in the reverse direction as well. In production environments, IOM modules are always used in pairs to provide redundancy and failover.

Apart from data transfers between chassis and FIs, IOM modules provide the following two features:

- **Chassis Management Controller (CMC)**: This monitors chassis components such as fan units, power supplies, and chassis temperature. This also reads chassis component identification data and detects the insertion and removal of blade servers.

- **Chassis Management Switch (CMS)**: This provides fast Ethernet links to the embedded **Cisco Integrated Management Controller (CIMC)** on blade servers for **Keyboard Video Mouse (KVM)** access and **Serial over LAN (SoL)** access and for **Intelligent Platform Management Interface (IPMI)** data to travel from individual blades to FIs for monitoring and management purposes.

The following figure depicts components and connectivity inside an IOM module:

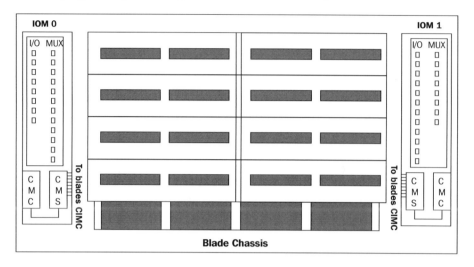

The Cisco 2208XP IOM card

The specifications of the Cisco 2208XP IOM card are as follows:

- Eight 10 Gbps fabric ports for connecting to the FI
- 32 10 Gbps, server-facing ports with FCoE
- 80 Gbps throughput

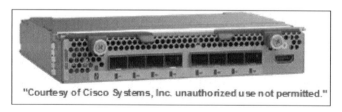

"Courtesy of Cisco Systems, Inc. unauthorized use not permitted."

The Cisco 2204XP IOM card

The specifications of the Cisco 2204XP IOM card are as follows:

- Four 10 Gbps fabric ports for connecting to the FI
- 16 10 Gbps, server-facing ports with FCoE

- 40 Gbps throughput

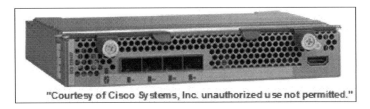

"Courtesy of Cisco Systems, Inc. unauthorized use not permitted."

The Cisco 2104XP IOM card

The specifications of the Cisco 2104XP IOM card are as follows:

- Four 10 Gbps fabric ports for connecting to the FI
- Eight 10 Gbps, server-facing ports with FCoE
- 40 Gbps throughput

"Courtesy of Cisco Systems, Inc. unauthorized use not permitted."

Blade servers and rack-mount servers

While blade servers are the dominant deployment of the UCS solution, Cisco has strategically extended its offering to include the industry-standard rack-mount form factor as well in order to provide users a choice against the competing rack-mount server vendors such as HP, IBM, and Dell.

Learning more about blade servers

Blade servers are at the heart of the UCS solution and come in various system resource configurations in terms of CPU, memory, and hard disk capacity. All blade servers are based on Intel Xeon processors and there is no AMD option available. **Small and Medium Businesses (SMBs)** can choose from different blade configurations as per business needs.

The B22 M3 blade server

The B22 M3 blade server is a new addition to the blade server series. It is a half-width blade server and has been shown in the following image:

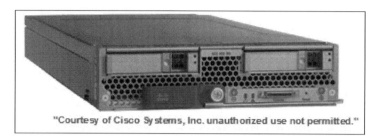

"Courtesy of Cisco Systems, Inc. unauthorized use not permitted."

The specifications of the B22 M3 blade server are as follows:

- Two Intel® Xeon® E5-2400 series processor family CPUs
- A maximum of 192 GB as the total memory capacity with a total of 12 memory slots
- Two drive bays for internal SAS/SATA/SSD hard drives for up to 2 TB of maximum storage capacity with built-in RAID 0,1 controllers
- Up to 80 Gbps of I/O throughput with a supported mezzanine card

The B22 series entry level blade server provides an excellent price-to-productivity balance. It is an excellent choice for IT, web infrastructure, and scale-out applications.

B200 M1/M2/M3 blade servers

B200 M1/M2/M3 blade servers are currently in the third generation. The B200 series is a half-width blade server. The latest B200 M3 series blade server further extends the capabilities of the B200 M2 servers. There are slight differences in the physical construction of M1 and M2/M3. Have a look at the following image for more details:

"Courtesy of Cisco Systems, Inc. unauthorized use not permitted."

The specifications of the latest B200 M3 blade server are as follows:

- Two Intel® Xeon® E5-2600 series processor family CPUs (a single processor is no longer supported with B200 M3)
- A maximum of 768 GB in total memory capacity (using 32 GB **Dual Inline Memory Modules (DIMMs)**) with a total of 24 memory slots
- Two drive bays for internal SAS/SATA/SSD hard drives for up to 2 TB of maximum storage capacity with built-in RAID 0,1 controllers
- Up to 80 Gbps of I/O throughput with a supported mezzanine card

B200 series entry-level blade servers are an excellent choice for web server farms, distributed databases, and CRM applications.

B230 M1/M2 blade servers

B230 M1/M2 series servers differ from B200 series servers in terms of computational capabilities. This is also a half-width blade server with two CPUs; however, the B230 server is based on a slightly different CPU family. The B230 series memory slot density is higher as compared to that of the B200 series blade servers. Have a look at the following image for more details:

"Courtesy of Cisco Systems, Inc. unauthorized use not permitted."

The specifications of the B230 M2 blade server are as follows:

- Two Intel® Xeon® processors of the E7-2800/8800 product family CPUs
- A maximum of 512 GB as the total memory capacity with a total of 32 memory slots
- Two SSD drive bays with a maximum of 600 GB of storage and built-in RAID 0,1 controllers
- Up to 20 Gbps of I/O throughput with a supported mezzanine card

B230 series servers are an excellent choice for virtualized loads and databases in compact form factor.

The B420 M3 blade server

B420 M3 series blade servers are full-width blade servers with the highest memory density ideal for demanding enterprise application deployment.

The specifications of the B420 M3 blade server are as follows:

- Four Intel® Xeon® processors of the E4600 product family CPUs
- A maximum of 1.5 TB as the total memory capacity with a total of 48 memory slots
- Four drive bays for internal SAS/SATA/SSD hard drives for a maximum storage capacity of up to 4 TB with built-in RAID 0,1,5,10 controllers
- Up to 160 Gbps of I/O throughput with supported mezzanine cards

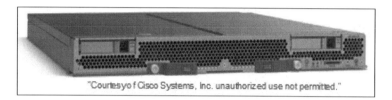
"Courtesy of Cisco Systems, Inc. unauthorized use not permitted."

B440 M1/M2 blade servers

B440 M1/M2 series blade servers are full-width blade servers with four CPUs and high memory density, ideal for enterprise applications deployment.

The specifications of the B440 M2 blade server are as follows:

- Four Intel® Xeon® processors of the E7-4800/8800 product family CPUs
- A maximum of 1 TB as the total memory capacity with a total of 32 memory slots
- Four drive bays for internal SAS/SATA/SSD hard drives for up to 3.6 TB as the maximum storage capacity with built-in RAID 0,1, 5, 10 controllers
- Up to 40 Gbps of I/O throughput with a supported mezzanine card

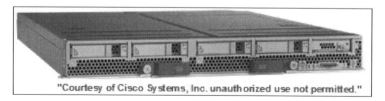
"Courtesy of Cisco Systems, Inc. unauthorized use not permitted."

For a quick comparison of B-series blade servers, please visit
`http://www.cisco.com/en/US/products/ps10280/prod_`
`models_comparison.html`. Select all the servers and click on the
Compare button.

Cisco also had UCS 250 M1/M2 blade servers which were discontinued in
November 2012. You may still see these servers deployed in the field.

Learning more about rack-mount servers

A majority of server vendors manufacture rack-mount servers (also known as
pizza-box servers). Cisco UCS C-series servers are available in the industry-standard
rack-mount form which can be deployed for SMB remote offices and applications
requiring dedicated equipment. Like B-series blade servers, these servers are also
based on Intel Xeon processors and there is no AMD option available.

C-series servers can be managed independently through an **out of band** (OOB)
web interface or can be integrated with the UCSM software. The embedded CIMC
provides the following services:

- Remote KVM to server console

- Remote power management

- Remote virtual media for operating system installation

- Industry-standard IPMI support for monitoring

- Standard SNMP traps for monitoring

Connecting and managing C-series rack servers through UCSM requires a
connection through Nexus 2200 series FEXs, which act as line cards to the FIs.

C-series servers are available in various CPUs, memory, I/O, and storage
configurations to address the needs of differently sized organizations. The following
sections cover the specifications of these servers as available on the Cisco website.

The C22 M3 rack-mount server

The C22 M3 rack-mount server is an entry-level rack-mount server. It is based on the
Intel E2400 CPU product family.

The specifications of the C22 M3 server are as follows:

- Two Intel® Xeon® processors of the E5-2400 product family of CPUs

- A maximum total memory capacity of 192 GB with a total of 12 memory slots

- Up to eight **small form factor (SFF)** or four **large form factor (LFF)** internal storage SAS/SATA/SSD hard disks with an 8 TB (SFF) or 12 TB (LFF) storage capacity and an optional RAID controller
- Two 1 Gbps I/O ports with optional 10 Gbps unified fabric ports
- Two PCIe third-generation expansion slots

The C22 series rack-mount server is an economical choice for SMBs, branch offices, departments for entry level virtualization, and web farms.

"Courtesy of Cisco Systems, Inc. unauthorized use not permitted."

The C24 M3 rack-mount server

The C24 M3 rack-mount server is also an entry level rack-mount server with storage extensibility. It is based on the Intel E2400 CPU product family.

The specifications of the C24 M3 server are as follows:

- Two Intel® Xeon® processors of the E5-2400 product family of CPUs
- A maximum total memory capacity of 192 GB with a total of 12 memory slots
- Up to 24 SFF or 12 LFF internal storage SAS/SATA hard disks with a 24 TB (SFF) or 26 TB (LFF) storage capacity and an optional RAID controller
- Two 1 Gbps I/O ports with optional 10 Gbps unified fabric ports
- Five PCIe third-generation expansion slots

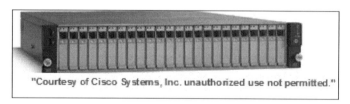

"Courtesy of Cisco Systems, Inc. unauthorized use not permitted."

The C24 M3 series rack-mount server is an economical choice for SMBs, branch offices, departments for entry level virtualization, and web farms.

The C220 M3 rack-mount server

The C220 M3 rack-mount server is based on the Intel E2600 CPU product family.

The specifications of the C220 M3 rack-mount server are as follows:

- Two Intel® Xeon® processors of the E5-2600 product family of CPUs
- A maximum total memory capacity of 512 GB with a total of 16 memory slots
- Up to eight SFF or four LFF internal storage SAS/SATA/SSD hard disks with an 8 TB (SFF) or 12 TB (LFF) storage capacity and an optional RAID controller
- Two 1 Gbps I/O ports with optional 10 Gbps unified fabric ports
- Two PCIe third-generation expansion slots

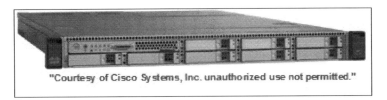

"Courtesy of Cisco Systems, Inc. unauthorized use not permitted."

The C220 M3 series server has great performance and density for distributed database applications and web farms.

The C240 M3 rack-mount server

The C240 M3 rack-mount server is based on the Intel E2600 CPU product family.

The specifications of the C240 M3 rack-mount server are as follows:

- Two Intel® Xeon® processors of the E5-2600 product family of CPUs
- A maximum total memory capacity of 768 GB with a total of 24 memory slots
- Up to 24 SFF or 12 LFF internal storage SAS/SATA/SSD hard disks with a 24 TB (SFF) or 26 TB (LFF) storage capacity and an optional RAID controller
- Four 1 Gbps I/O ports with optional 10 Gbps unified fabric ports

- Five PCIe third-generation expansion slots

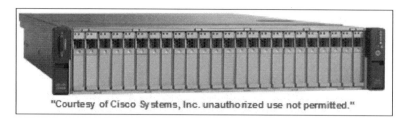

"Courtesy of Cisco Systems, Inc. unauthorized use not permitted."

The C240 M3 series server has great performance along with storage extensibility for distributed database applications and web farms.

The C260 M2 rack-mount server

The C260 M2 rack-mount server is based on the Intel E2800 CPU product family.

The specifications of the C260 M2 rack-mount servers are as follows:

- Two Intel® Xeon® processors of the E7-2800 product family of CPUs

- A maximum total memory capacity of 1 TB with a total of 64 memory slots

- Up to 16 LFF internal storage SAS/SATA/SSD hard disks with a 16 TB (LFF) storage capacity and no RAID controller

- Two **Gigabit Ethernet (GE) LAN on Motherboard (LoM)** I/O ports with two optional 10 Gbps unified fabric ports

- Six PCIe third-generation expansion slots

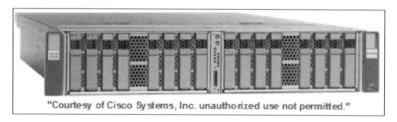

"Courtesy of Cisco Systems, Inc. unauthorized use not permitted."

The C260 M2 series server provides one of the highest densities of computational resources for business-critical applications.

The C420 M3 rack-mount server

The C420 M3 rack-mount server is based on the Intel E4600 CPU product family.

The specifications of the C420 M3 rack-mount server are as follows:

- Four Intel® Xeon® processors of the E5-4600 product family of CPUs
- A maximum total memory capacity of 1.5 TB with a total of 48 memory slots
- Up to 16 LFF internal storage SAS/SATA/SSD hard disks with a 16 TB (LFF) storage capacity and an optional RAID controller
- Two 1 Gbps I/O ports with two optional 10 Gbps unified fabric ports
- Four PCIe third-generation expansion slots

"Courtesy of Cisco Systems, Inc. unauthorized use not permitted."

The C420 M3 series server provides computational resources for business-critical applications such as large databases both in bare metal and virtualized environments.

The C460 M2 rack-mount server

The C460 M2 rack-mount server is based on the Intel E4800 CPU product family.

The specifications of the C460 M2 rack-mount servers are as follows:

- Four Intel® Xeon® processors of the E7-4800 product family of CPUs
- A maximum total memory capacity of 2 TB with a total of 64 memory slots
- Up to 12 LFF internal storage SAS/SATA/SSD hard disks with a 12 TB (LFF) storage capacity and no RAID controller
- Two GE LoM I/O ports with two optional 10 Gbps unified fabric ports

- 10 PCIe third-generation expansion slots with an optional LSI MegaRAID controller in the eleventh slot

"Courtesy of Cisco Systems, Inc. unauthorized use not permitted."

The C460 M2 series server provides exceptional computational resources for business-critical applications such as large databases both in bare metal and virtualized environments.

For a quick comparison of C-series servers, please visit `http://www.cisco.com/en/US/products/ps10493/prod_models_comparison.html`. Select all the servers and click on the **Compare** button to get the results.

Getting started with mezzanine adapters

A huge variety of mezzanine adapters, also known as **Virtual Interface Cards (VICs)**, is available from Cisco for both B-series blade servers and C-series rack servers. Older adapters are of the fixed port type and are not optimized for contemporary virtualized server environments. There are some older third-party network cards also available as an option. Newer adapters are optimized for virtualization and can provide 128 or 256 dynamic virtual adapters. The number of virtual adapters is dependent on the VIC model. These virtual adapters can be configured as Ethernet (vNIC) or fiber channel (vHBA) devices. All virtualization-optimized VICs also support the VM-FEX technology. Our focus will be on those mezzanine adapters that are virtualization optimized.

VICs for blade servers

VICs are available in the form of a mezzanine card. All new VICs provide dynamic vNIC or vHBA interfaces for server-side connectivity.

VIC 1280

The specifications of VIC 1280 are as follows:

- 256 dynamic vNIC (Ethernet) or vHBA (FC) interfaces
- VM-FEX support for virtualized environments
- Hardware failover without driver need
- 80 Gbps network throughput
- Mezzanine form factor
- Compatible with UCS M2 (B230 and B440) and all M3 blade servers

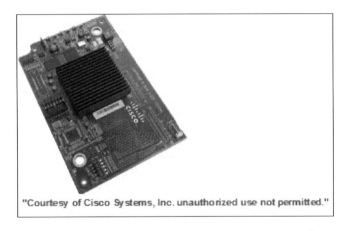

"Courtesy of Cisco Systems, Inc. unauthorized use not permitted."

VIC 1240

The specifications of VIC 1240 are as follows:

- 256 dynamic vNIC (Ethernet) or vHBA (FC) interfaces
- VM-FEX support for virtualized environments
- Hardware failover without driver need
- 40 Gbps network throughput with optional 80 GB throughput using optional port expander in the mezzanine slot
- LoM form factor

- Compatible with all M3 blade servers

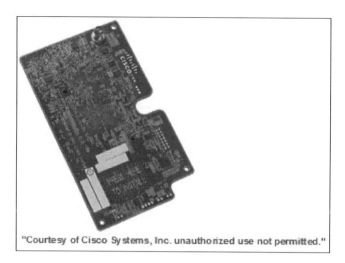

"Courtesy of Cisco Systems, Inc. unauthorized use not permitted."

VIC M81KR

The specifications of VIC M81KR are as follows:

- 128 dynamic vNIC (Ethernet) or vHBA (FC) interfaces
- VM-FEX support for virtualized environments
- Hardware failover without driver need
- 20 Gbps network throughput
- Compatible with UCS M2 blade servers

"Courtesy of Cisco Systems, Inc. unauthorized use not permitted."

VICs for rack-mount servers

VICs are available as PCIe cards as well. All new VICs provide dynamic vNIC or vHBA interfaces for server-side connectivity.

VIC 1225

The specifications of VIC 1225 are as follows:

- 256 dynamic vNIC (Ethernet) or vHBA (FC) interfaces
- VM-FEX support for virtualized environments
- Hardware failover without driver need
- 20 Gbps network throughput
- Compatible with UCS M2 (C460 and C260) and all M3 rack-mount servers

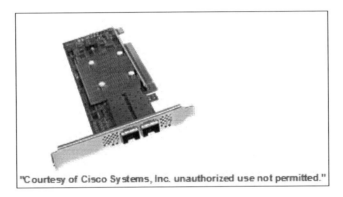

"Courtesy of Cisco Systems, Inc. unauthorized use not permitted."

VIC P81E

The specifications of VIC P81E are as follows:

- 128 dynamic vNIC (Ethernet) or vHBA (FC) interfaces
- VM-FEX support for virtualized environments
- Hardware failover without driver need
- 20 Gbps network throughput

- Compatible with UCS M2 (C460 and C260) and all M3 rack-mount servers

"Courtesy of Cisco Systems, Inc. unauthorized use not permitted."

 For a quick comparison of mezzanine card specifications, please visit
`http://www.cisco.com/en/US/products/ps10277/prod_`
`models_comparison.html#~tab-a.`

Cisco VICs are also famous by their code name, Palo.

Power capacity and power plug types

The UCS 5108 blade chassis comes with options of up to four power supply units. Each is a single phase unit and provides 2,500 watts. Depending on the total number of power supplies in the chassis and input power sources, UCS 5108 can be configured into the following three modes:

Nonredundant mode

Power supply units installed in the system provide adequate power. A power supply failure results in a chassis failure. Load is evenly distributed among power supplies; however, there is no power redundancy.

N+1 redundant mode

In this mode, at least one extra power supply unit is available in the system in addition to the units that are required for providing the power required for the chassis to be operational. The extra power supply unit is in standby mode and the load is evenly distributed among the operational power supply units. In case of single power supply failure, standby power will replace the failed power supply immediately.

Grid redundant mode

In this mode, all the four power supply units must be available in the system and power should be supplied from two different power sources. Power supply units must be configured in pairs. Units 1 and 2 form one pair, and 3 and 4 form the second pair. Ideally, separate physical power cabling from two independent utility grids is recommended to feed each pair of power supply. In case one power source fails, the remaining power supply units on the other circuit continue to provide power to the system.

The power connector inside the UCS blade server chassis is IEC 60320 C19. The connector on the other side of the power cable varies according to the country-specific electrical standards.

 More information regarding power and environmental requirements is available at `http://www.cisco.com/en/US/docs/unified_computing/ucs/hw/site_prep/guide/siteprep_tech_specs.html#wp1064498`.

Installing UCS chassis components

Now that we have a better understanding of the various components of the Cisco UCS platform, we can delve into the physical installation of the UCS chassis, that is, the installation of blade servers, IOM modules, fan units, power supply units, SFP+ modules, and physical cabling.

Care must be taken during the installation of all components as failure to follow the installation procedure may result in component malfunction and bodily injury.

 UCS chassis don'ts

Do not try to lift even an empty chassis alone. At least two persons are required to handle the UCS chassis.

Do not handle internal components such as CPU, RAM, and mezzanine cards without the **Electro Static Discharge** (**ESD**) field kit.

Before the physical installation of the UCS solution, it is also imperative to consider other datacenter design factors including the following:

- Building floor load bearing capacity
- Rack requirements for UCS chassis and FIs
- Rack airflow, heating, and ventilation (HVAC)

Physical installation is divided into the following three sections:

- Blade server component (CPU, memory, hard drives, and mezzanine cards) installation
- Chassis component (blade servers, IOMs, fan units, and power supply units) installation
- FI installation and physical cabling

Blade server installation

Cisco UCS blade servers are designed on industry-standard components with some enhancements. Anyone with prior server installation experience should be comfortable installing internal components using the guidelines provided in the blade server manual and following the standard safety procedures. ESD transient charges may result in thousands of volts of charge building up, which can degrade or permanently damage electronic components.

 The Cisco ESD training course may be referred to at http://www.cisco.com/web/learning/le31/esd/WelcomeP.html.

All Cisco UCS blade servers have similar cover design with a button at the top front of the blade; this button needs to be pushed down. Then, there is a slight variation among models in the way that the cover slides; this could be either towards the rear and upwards or towards self and upwards.

Installation and removal of CPU

The following is the procedure to mount a CPU onto a UCS B-series blade server:

1. Make sure you are wearing an ESD wrist wrap grounded to the blade server cover.

2. To release the CPU clasp, first push it down and then to the side away from the CPU socket.

3. Move the lever up and remove the CPU blank cover. Keep the blank cover in a safe place just in case you need to remove a CPU.

4. Pick up the CPU with the plastic edges and align it with the socket. The CPU can only fit one way.

5. Lower the mounting bracket with the side lever and secure the CPU into the socket.

6. Align the heat sink with its fins in a position allowing unobstructed airflow from front to back.

7. Gently tighten the heat sink screws on to the motherboard.

CPU removal is the reverse of the installation process. It is critical to place the socket blank cover back over the CPU socket. Damage could occur to the socket without the blank cover.

 For UCS B440, air blocker must be installed if you permanently remove a CPU.

Installation and removal of RAM

The following is the procedure to install RAM modules into the UCS B-series blade server:

1. Make sure you are wearing an ESD wrist wrap grounded to the blade server cover.

2. Move away the clips on the side of the memory slot.

3. Hold the memory module with both edges in an upright position and firmly push straight down, matching the notch of the module to the socket.

4. Close the side clips to hold the memory module.

Memory removal is the reverse of the installation process.

 The memory modules must be inserted in pairs and split equally between each CPU if all the memory slots are not populated. Refer to the server manual for identifying memory slot pairs and slot-CPU relationship.

Installation and removal of internal hard disks

UCS supports SFF serial attached **Small Computer System Interface (SCSI)** (SAS) hard drives. Blade servers B200, B240, and B440 support regular thickness (15 mm) hard drives whereas B230 supports thin (7 mm) hard drives.

To insert a hard disk into the B200, B250, and B440 blade servers, carry out the following steps:

1. Make sure you are wearing an ESD wrist wrap grounded to the blade server cover.

2. Remove the blank cover.

3. Press the button on the catch lever on the ejector arm.

4. Slide the hard disk completely into the slot.

5. Push the ejector lever until it clicks to lock the hard disk.

To remove a hard disk press the release button, pull the catch lever outward, and slide the hard disk out.

To insert or release a thin hard drive into or from the B230 server, release the catch by pushing it inside while inserting or removing the hard disk.

 Do not leave a hard disk slot empty. If you do not intend to replace the hard disk, cover it with a blank plate to ensure proper airflow.

Installation of mezzanine cards

UCS B200 and B230 support single mezzanine cards whereas B250 and B440 support two cards. The procedure for installing these cards is the same for all servers, which is as follows:

1. Make sure you are wearing an ESD wrist wrap grounded to the blade server cover.

2. Open the server top cover.

3. Grab the card with its edges and align the male molex connector, the female connector, and the motherboard.

4. Press the card gently into the slot.

5. Once the card is properly seated, secure it by tightening the screw on top.

Mezzanine card removal is the reverse of the installation process.

Installation of blade servers on the chassis

Installation and removal of half-width and full-width blade servers is almost identical with the only difference being the use of one ejector arm for half-width blade servers whereas for full-width blade servers, there are two ejector arms. Carry out the following steps:

1. Make sure you are wearing an ESD wrist wrap grounded to the chassis.
2. Open one ejector arm for the half-width blade servers or both ejector arms for full-width blade servers.
3. Push the blade into the slot. Once firmly in, close the ejector arm on the face of the server and tighten the screw with your hands.

The removal of a blade server is the opposite of the installation process.

> In order to install a full-width blade, it is necessary to remove the central divider. This can be done with a Philips screwdriver to push two clips, one in the downward and the other in the upward direction, and sliding the divider out of the chassis.

Cabling FI and IOM

UCS is an integrated solution that handles both network traffic and management control. All management and data movement intelligence for chassis components and blade servers is present in the FIs and IOM modules (which are line cards for the FIs). Therefore, proper cabling between FIs and IOM modules is an important design consideration.

IOM – FI cabling topology

IOM modules are used to connect blade server chassis to the FIs and act as line cards to them. It is therefore necessary to maintain proper connectivity between IOMs and FIs. Since an IOM module becomes part of the FI, multiple links from a single IOM can only be connected to a single FI and not across to the other FI. Depending on the IOM model, there can be one, two, four, or eight links from IOM to a single FI. These links can be configured in the port channel for bandwidth aggregation. The chassis discovery process is initiated as soon as an IOM is connected to an FI.

In the following figure, on the left-hand side, all links from IOM 0 are connected to a single FI and can be combined into a single port channel. The figure on the right shows a configuration in which links from a single IOM are connected to different FIs. This is an invalid topology, and hence chassis discovery will fail.

 Chassis discovery will also fail if a high availability cluster is not established between FIs.

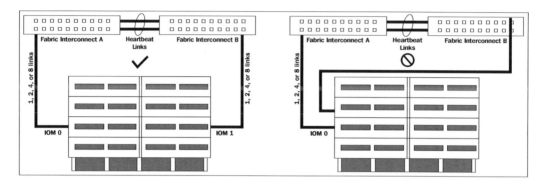

IOM – FI physical cabling

IOMs provide connectivity to the individual blade servers through I/O multiplexer and connectivity to the FI. IOM interface connectivity to blade servers does not require user configuration.

IOM to FI connectivity, however, requires physical cabling. Both IOM and FI have SFP+ slots. There are a variety of possibilities in terms of physical interfaces. Some of the common configurations include the following:

- 10 GB FET SFP+ interface (special optical multimode fiber SFP+ module which can only be used with UCS and Nexus equipment)
- 10 GB CU SFP+ (copper twinax cable)
- 10 GB SR SFP+ (short range multimode optical fiber SFP+ module for up to 300 m)
- 10 GB LR SFP+ (long-range, single-mode optical fiber SFP+ module for above 300 m)

The following figure shows eight connections from IOM 0 to Fabric Interconnect A and eight connections from IOM 1 to Fabric Interconnect B. Depending on the bandwidth requirements and model, it is possible to have only one, two, four, or eight connections from IOM to FI.

Although large numbers of links provide higher bandwidth for individual servers, as each link consumes a physical port on the FI, they also decrease the total number of UCS chassis which can be connected to the FIs.

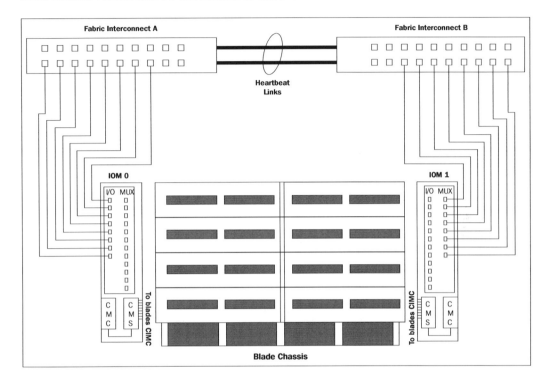

As shown in the preceding figure, IOM to FI only supports direct connection. However, FI to north-bound Nexus switch connectivity can be direct and may use regular **port channel (PC)**, or the connections from a single FI may traverse two different Nexus switches and use **virtual PortChannel (vPC)**.

The following figure shows a direct connection between FIs and Nexus switches. All connections from FI A are connected to the Nexus Switch 1 and all connections from FI B are connected to Nexus Switch 2. These links can be aggregated into a PC.

The following are two other connections that need to be configured:

- **Cluster heart beat connectivity**: Each FI has two fast Ethernet ports. These ports should be connected using a CAT6 UTP cable for cluster configuration

- **Management port**: This is also a fast Ethernet port that can be configured using a CAT6 UTP cable for remote management of the FI

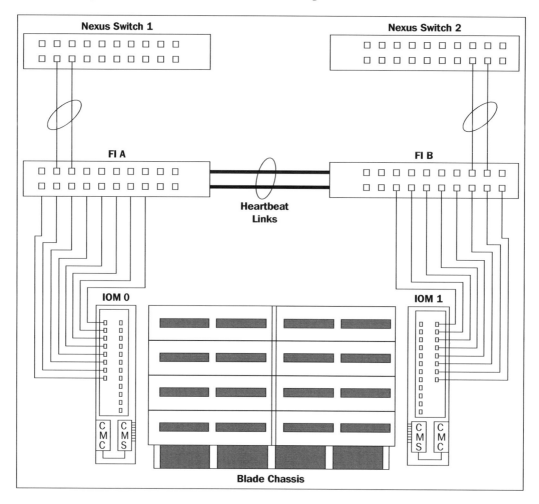

The following figure shows the FI to Nexus switch connectivity where links traverse Nexus switches. One network connection from FI A is connected to Nexus Switch 1 and the other to Nexus Switch 2. Both these connections are configured via vPC. Similarly, one connection from FI B is connected to Nexus Switch 2 and the other to Nexus Switch 1. Both these connections are also configured via vPC. It is also imperative to have vPC on a physical connection between both the Nexus switches. This is shown as two physical links between Nexus Switch 1 and Nexus Switch 2. Without this connectivity and configuration between Nexus Switches, vPC will not work.

Physical slots in Nexus switches also support the same set of SFP+ modules for connectivity that FIs and IOMs do.

A complete list of SFP+ modules is available in *Table 3* at
`http://www.cisco.com/en/US/prod/collateral/`
`ps10265/ps10276/data_sheet_c78-524724.html`.

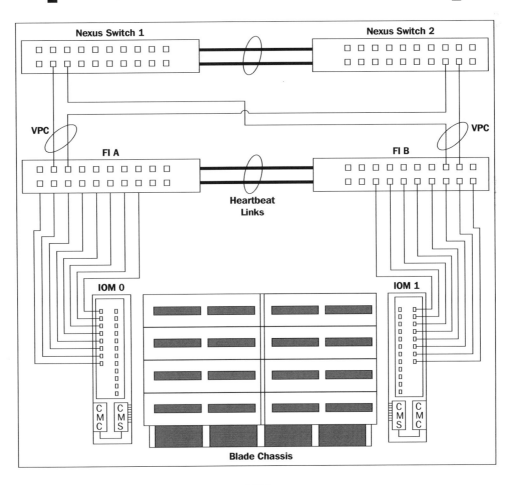

Summary

The Gartner Magic Quadrant report for blade servers, published in 2012, placed Cisco as a market leader along with Dell, HP, and IBM. Cisco has already surpassed Dell from its number three position. According to this report, Cisco's entry into the blade server market is causing re-evaluation among the installed blade server bases. Cisco's clustered FI-based design provides a complete solution for converged data connectivity, blade server provisioning, and management whereas other vendor offerings acquire the same functionality with increased complexity.

Cisco UCS presented a paradigm shift for blade servers and datacenter design and management to the industry. In this chapter, we learned about the UCS solution's integral components and physical installation of the UCS solution.

We learned about the various available options for all the UCS components including FIs, blade chassis, blade servers, rack-mount servers, and the internal parts of the servers.

In the next chapter, we will learn about Cisco UCS Emulator which is an excellent tool for exploring UCSM software.

 The detailed Gartner Magic Quadrant report, 2012, is available at `http://www.gartner.com/technology/reprints.do?id=1-19KZ0QR&ct=120306&st=sb`.

2
Setting Up Lab Using Cisco UCS Emulator

Cisco UCS platform emulator is an excellent tool to demonstrate and practice salient features provided by the UCS platform, in order to attain hands-on experience without setting up a UCS platform lab. UCS emulator could be used to enhance familiarization with the UCS platform and also to provide demos to prospective clients. It mimics the real UCS hardware with a configurable hardware inventory, including multiple chassis with multiple blade servers and multiple rack-mount servers. Working with UCS emulator provides a feeling of real hardware, and allows the user to set up the UCS hardware virtually, while becoming more comfortable with it before configuring the actual UCS hardware. It is an excellent resource for getting hands-on experience with the UCS platform. UCS emulator requirements are so minimal that it can be easily installed in a home-based lab on a standard laptop or desktop.

UCS platform emulator is freely downloadable from the Cisco website. In order to download it, a **Cisco Connection Online (CCO)** login is required, which can be created by anyone interested in learning and working with Cisco technologies. It is available on the Cisco developer's network website (`developer.cisco.com`). You can download the latest emulator package from the developer network, which can be installed under various virtualization platforms. Old archives of previous UCS platform emulator versions are also available for download on the same page.

Using UCS platform emulator, it is possible to import configuration from a live UCS system. Also, a configuration created on the UCS platform emulator can be exported in an XML file format, which can then be imported to a production system. This is extremely helpful for duplicating a production UCS system configuration for troubleshooting, testing, and development purposes.

Cisco UCS Emulator can be downloaded at `http://developer.`
`cisco.com/web/unifiedcomputing/ucsemulatordownload.`

In this chapter, we will interchangeably use the term UCSPE for Unified Computing System Platform Emulator, and UCSM for Unified Computing System Manger.

This chapter will cover the following topics:

- Configuring Cisco UCS emulator
- Configuring Cisco UCS emulator hardware settings
- Launching UCSM using emulator
- UCSPE limitations

Configuring Cisco UCS emulator

Cisco UCSPE is available in an OVA or a ZIP file. It is packaged on CentOS Linux (a Red Hat Enterprise Linux clone operating system). This virtual machine (VM) can run Cisco UCSPE on a standard laptop or desktop computer meeting the minimum system requirements. A UCS emulator application OVA or ZIP file is approximately 500 MB.

System requirements

The minimum system requirements for the installation of UCS emulator are as follows:

- 1.8 GHz CPU
- 2 GB free RAM
- 8 GB free disk space
- Mozilla compatible browser (Firefox or Chrome)
- **Java Runtime Environment (JRE)** 1.6

Hypervisor prerequisites

UCSPE can be installed on the following type 1 and type 2 hypervisor platforms:

- VMware Player 4.0 and above (Windows and Linux version)
- VMware Fusion 4.0 and above for Apple Mac OS
- VMware Workstation 7.0 and above (Windows and Linux version)

- VMware ESXi 4.0 and above
- Microsoft Hyper-V

VMware Player for Microsoft Windows is a free download from VMware. For a basic home-based lab environment, VMware Player is an excellent choice. Users interested in advanced virtualization benefits such as snapshots may download VMware Workstation. Registration on the VMware website is required for the download of VMware Workstation and it is not available for free. Users may also opt to run UCS emulator on VMware ESXi or Microsoft Hyper-V environments if they do not want to install VMware Player, VMware Workstation, or VMware Fusion on their laptop or desktop.

In this chapter, we will be installing the UCS platform emulator on VMware Player 5.0.1 installed on Microsoft Windows 7.

Make sure that the system where VMware Player is installed has enough resources for running the guest UCS platform emulator VM. VMware Player can be installed on a desktop or laptop even with lower specifications, as mentioned in the minimum system requirements for UCS platform emulator. New laptops and desktops generally have more CPU speed than the minimum system requirements. Hard disk storage is very cheap and usually all new systems have it available abundantly. System memory is usually a major consideration. As the UCSPE VM memory requirement is 2 GB, it is recommended that one installs VMware Player on a system with 4 GB of RAM.

VMware Player installation is a typical Microsoft Windows manual-click-next type of installation. It is recommended that you close all the running programs and save your data before installing VMware Player, as the system may require a reboot.

 VMware Player can be downloaded at `https://my.vmware.com/web/vmware/free#desktop_end_user_computing/vmware_player/5_0`.

For downloading UCSPE, log on to the Cisco developer website and download the file in OVA or ZIP format. A simple Google search for UCS emulator download will take you right to the correct section of the Cisco developer network website, where you will be required to enter your Cisco credentials to download the UCSPE.

 VMware Player 5 and VMware Workstation 9 can be installed on Microsoft Windows 8.

Installing UCSPE on VMware Player using a ZIP file

Download and install VMware player from the VMware website by carrying out the following steps:

1. Download the emulator `.zip` file.

2. Extract the downloaded file to an appropriate folder on the local system.

3. In the VMware Player, click on **Open a Virtual Machine** that has been highlighted in the following screenshot:

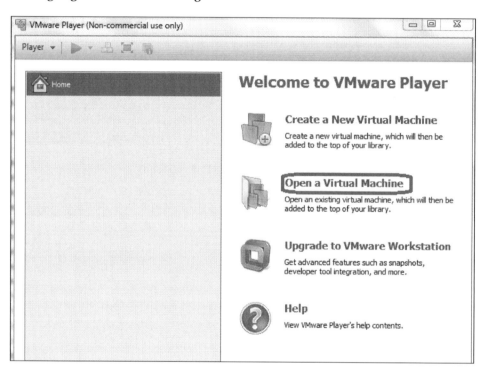

4. Go to the folder where the extracted files have been stored, select the VMX (VMware virtual machine configuration) file, and click on **Open** as highlighted in the following screenshot:

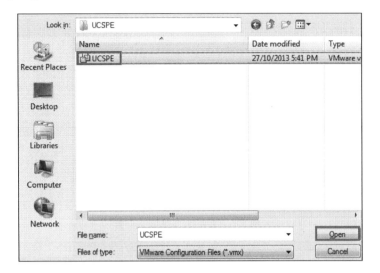

5. Once the VM is shown in the VMware Player inventory, click on **Play virtual machine** as highlighted in the following screenshot:

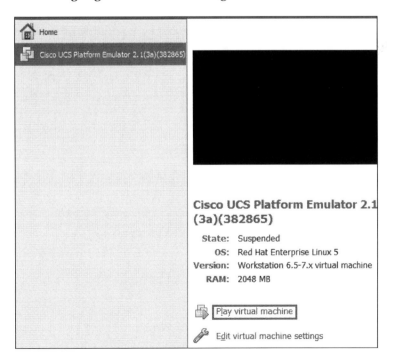

Installing UCSPE on VMware Player using an OVA file

1. Download the .ova file.

2. In the VMware Player, click on **Open a Virtual Machine** and select the .ova file as shown in the following screenshot:

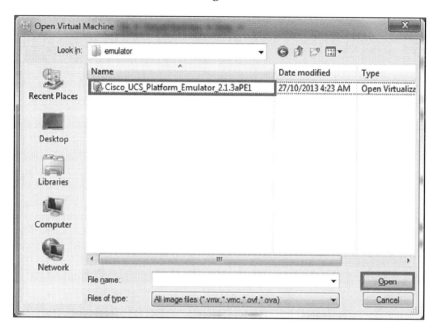

3. The VMware player will detect it as an OVA file, and will query where the UCSPE VM should be extracted. Select an appropriate folder on the local system, and click on **Import** as shown in the following screenshot:

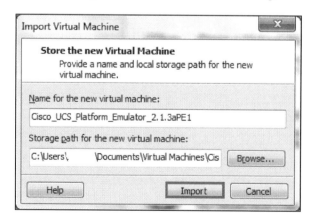

4.   VMware Player will show the OVA import progress, which may take a few minutes as shown in the following screenshot:

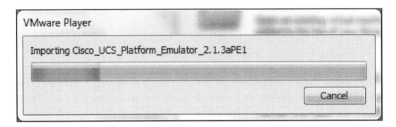

5.   Once the import is complete, VM could be played from the VMware Player by clicking on the **Play virtual machine** button.

 For an older VMware Player or Workstation application, you are required to convert the OVA format UCSPE VM using the VMware OVA conversion tool.

Installing UCSPE on VMware Workstation

The procedure for installing UCSPE on VMware Workstation is identical to the VMware Player installation procedure for both .ova and .zip files. VMware Workstation provides some extra features such as snapshots that are not available in VMware Player. The latest version of VMware Workstation can also be installed on Microsoft Windows 8.

Installing UCSPE on VMware vSphere ESXi

UCSPE VM comes in VMware Workstation VM file format. In order to run the UCSPE VM in vSphere, the VM format should be converted using VMware standalone convertor. VMware standalone convertor is available for free download from VMware for P2V and V2V conversions. Using this convertor, VM could be transferred to a standalone ESXi server directly, or to a vSphere cluster using vCenter.

 In order to run UCSPE using Microsoft Hyper-V, the VMDK file should be converted to VHD format using tools such as **System Center Virtual Machine Manager** (**SCVMM**), or any other supported third-party tools.

Using Cisco UCSPE

UCSPE is packaged on CentOS Linux based VM. Keep in mind that the system boot time is longer compared to regular Linux VM, since UCSPE and UCSM services are initialized before the VM can be used. Once the UCSPE VM is operational, it could be managed through web browsers (Mozilla compatible with JRE), or through VM console CLI session. The most widely supported JRE version is 1.6 and there may be issues with the latest JRE.

For web-based access, type the management IP into the browser as it appears in the VM console. Take a look at the following screenshot for more details on this:

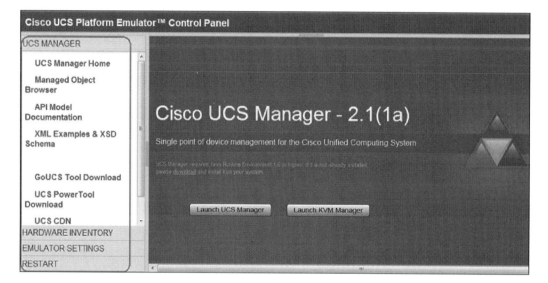

The web interface is divided into two main panes. On the left side is the Navigation pane and on the right side is the main Work pane. The Navigation pane has tabs as shown in the preceding screenshot, and these have been explained in the following table. These are used to manage the UCSPE features, hardware inventory, system reboots, and launching the UCSM software.

Another management option is CLI access which is available from the VM console. CLI access provides driven console interface for making the previously mentioned changes.

The following table summarizes the purpose of the Navigation pane menu tabs:

UCS MANAGER	• Launching UCS Manager
	• Accessing various tools and documentation
HARDWARE INVENTORY	• Displaying and configuring startup inventory
	• Displaying the available hardware catalog
EMULATOR SETTINGS	• Displaying the status summary
	• Management of the IP addresses
	• Configuring fabric high availability
	• Database persistence settings
	• Startup configuration URL for initial inventory
	• Setting up a number of uplink connections and models of Fabric Interconnects
RESTART	• Restarting UCSPE service
	• Rebooting UCSPE VM
	• Shutting down UCSPE VM
	• Performing factory reset to remove any equipment added to the UCSPE

For system hardware changes, **HARDWARE INVENTORY** in the navigation tab is used to add, remove, and modify all the chassis, blade servers, and rack-mount servers. For any hardware changes, a reboot of UCSPE and UCSM service is required. For all system changes requiring a reboot, for example to run a factory reset, the default action selected is **No**, which should be changed to **Yes** in order to perform the action, otherwise the task will not be performed.

The following screenshot shows the **Factory Reset** configuration change and the four steps required to complete this task:

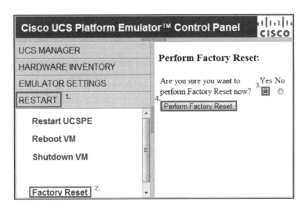

Configuring network settings

UCSPE VM supports **Dynamic Host Control Protocol (DHCP)** and static IP address assignment. The default IP setting is **DHCP** which can be changed to **static**, using the CLI access-to-server interface after the first boot. The DHCP option is easier to configure for obtaining an IP address automatically. For VMware Player and Workstation, if you need to access the UCSPE and UCSM only from the local system, select the network type for the UCSPE VM NICs as **NAT** (NAT is the default option), and a locally accessible IP is automatically assigned. If it is required to access the UCSPE VM from a different computer on the network, it is necessary to change the UCSPE VM network setting to **Bridged** in VMware Player, Fusion, or Workstation. In this scenario, IP address can be assigned by the DHCP server running on the network or the network can be assigned manually.

Perform the following steps to assign an IP manually through the console:

1. Log in to UCSPE VM console `cisco-ucspe login` using the username `config` and password `config`.
2. On the **Select** prompt, enter **a** to select **View & Configure Network Settings**.
3. For **Change settings**, select **y**.
4. For **Use DHCP**, select **n**.
5. Add the IP, subnet mask, and gateway on the next prompts.
6. The interface will reinitialize with the IP settings.

The following screenshot shows the UCSPE console screen configuration options:

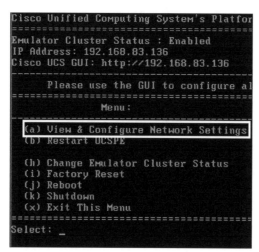

Changing the IP setting will stop and restart the UCSPE and UCSM services.

After the initialization of the UCSPE, the management IP, the default username, and the password are shown on the VM console. This IP, username, and password are used for accessing the VM as shown in the following screenshot:

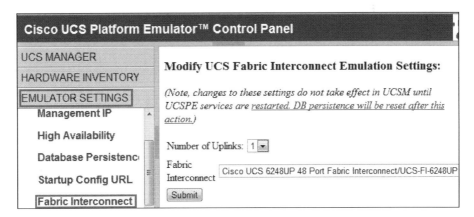

Fabric Interconnect model and network uplinks from the blade server chassis to the Fabric Interconnect are not managed under the **HARDWARE INVENTORY** tab in the Navigation pane. In order to change the Fabric Interconnect model and manage chassis uplinks, click on the **Fabric Interconnect** link under the **EMULATOR SETTINGS** tab in the Navigation pane as shown in the following screenshot:

No network connectivity from Fabric Interconnects to any north-bound switch is possible.

Configuring hardware settings

UCSPE supported hardware is available in **Hardware Catalog**, which can be located under the **HARDWARE INVENTORY** tab in the Navigation pane. This hardware inventory contains all the supported hardware for chassis, blade, and rack-mount servers, and is categorized into **Blades**, **Rack Servers**, **CPU**, **DIMM**, **HDD**, **I/O Adapters**, **Fans**, and **PSU** as shown in the following screenshot:

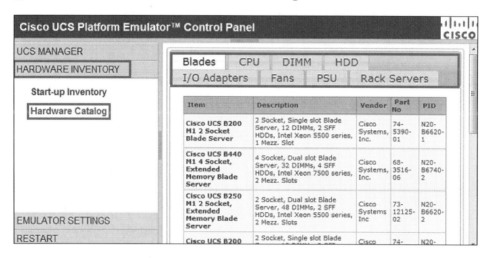

UCSPE is initially configured with one blade chassis including six blades and two rack-mount servers. Additional chassis with blade servers and additional rack-mount servers can be added to UCSPE by configuring items using **Start-up Inventory** under **HARDWARE INVENTORY** in the Navigation pane.

The following menu is used for hardware inventory control:

The following table describes the purpose of each of the preceding icons:

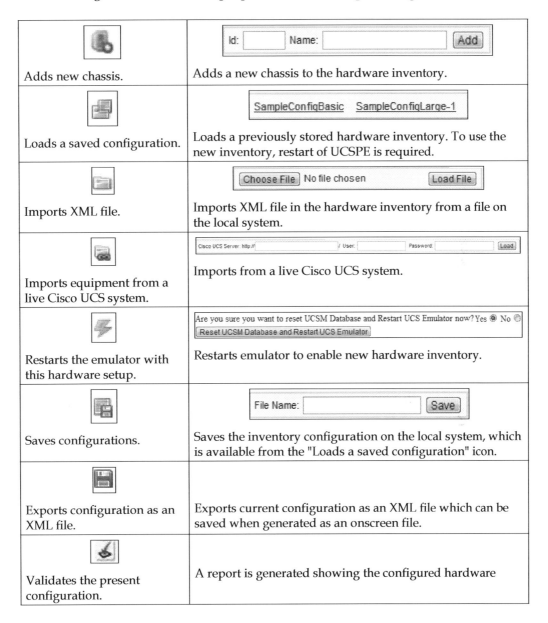

Icon	Description
Adds new chassis.	Adds a new chassis to the hardware inventory.
Loads a saved configuration.	Loads a previously stored hardware inventory. To use the new inventory, restart of UCSPE is required.
Imports XML file.	Imports XML file in the hardware inventory from a file on the local system.
Imports equipment from a live Cisco UCS system.	Imports from a live Cisco UCS system.
Restarts the emulator with this hardware setup.	Restarts emulator to enable new hardware inventory.
Saves configurations.	Saves the inventory configuration on the local system, which is available from the "Loads a saved configuration" icon.
Exports configuration as an XML file.	Exports current configuration as an XML file which can be saved when generated as an onscreen file.
Validates the present configuration.	A report is generated showing the configured hardware

Stash area

Changes to the blade servers such as adding and removing components can be done in the **Stash** area in the working pane of **Start-up Inventory**. It serves as a virtual staging area where servers can be configured, before being deployed to the chassis (B-series blades) or connected to **Fabric Extenders** (**FEXs**) (c-series rack-mount).

The **Stash** area is shown in the following screenshot:

Both blade and rack-mount servers can be added and removed from the hardware inventory using the **Stash** area. This can be accomplished by simply dragging-and-dropping the servers and server components to it.

Components to the individual servers and chassis can also be dragged and dropped directly for addition and removal while the server is in chassis (blade server). In order to modify an existing blade server hardware configuration, it is recommended to eject the server to the **Stash** area and make the changes. The server removed to the **Stash** area will preserve the slot identity.

Drag-and-drop from hardware inventory to the **Stash** area is shown in the following screenshot:

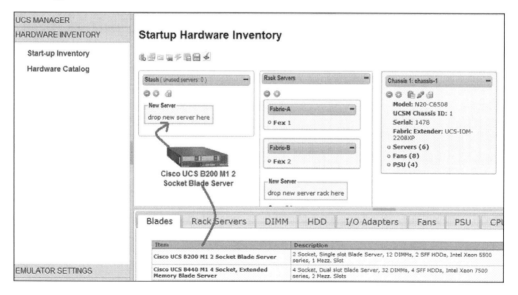

The following icons are used in the **Start-up Inventory** on the work pane of the **Stash** area:

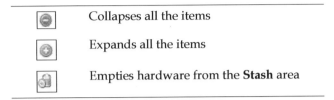

	Collapses all the items
	Expands all the items
	Empties hardware from the **Stash** area

The following table lists the icons used for blade chassis in the **Start-up Inventory** work pane:

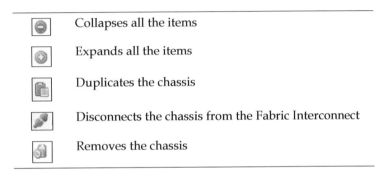

	Collapses all the items
	Expands all the items
	Duplicates the chassis
	Disconnects the chassis from the Fabric Interconnect
	Removes the chassis

Adding a new chassis with blade servers

A new chassis with blade servers could be added in many different ways. The easiest way is to duplicate the current chassis which will create an exact replica, including the blade servers. The blade servers can then be dragged and dropped to the chassis using the **Stash** area. The other method is to manually add the chassis and blade servers.

Adding an empty chassis

1. Click on **Start-up Inventory** in the **HARDWARE INVENTORY** menu tab.

2. Click on the icon for adding a new chassis and provide the chassis ID and chassis name.

3. An empty chassis will be added to the inventory.

4. Add chassis **Fans** by dragging them from the hardware inventory catalog area at the bottom of the page.

5. Add chassis **PSUs** by dragging them from the hardware inventory catalog area at the bottom of the page.

Configuring and adding a blade server to the chassis

Blade servers can be directly added to the blade chassis or **Stash** area. A key point to consider is that the new blade server does not have any components. It is therefore recommended to drag a new server to the **Stash** area, add server components such as CPU, RAM, and others, and move the server to the chassis, which is explained in the following steps:

1. Click on **Start-up Inventory** in the **HARDWARE INVENTORY** menu tab.
2. Click on the **Blades** tab at the bottom of the page.
3. Click-and-hold the mouse's left button, and drag the desired blade server to the **Stash** area.
4. Click on **DIMM, HDD, I/O Adapters**, and **CPU** tabs to drag-and-drop the required components to the server.
5. Repeat step 4 for the required server components.
6. Once the server configuration is complete, drag it to the blade chassis.
7. Repeat the same procedure for all new blade servers.

Configuring and adding a rack-mount server

Rack-mount servers can be added directly to the appropriate rack-mount server area or to the **Stash** area. It is recommended to configure the rack-mount server in the **Stash** area and move the server to the chassis. The FEX 2200 series is automatically included in the rack-mount server area. The following steps explain this procedure in detail:

1. Click on **Start-up Inventory** in the **HARDWARE INVENTORY** menu tab.
2. Click on the **Rack Servers** tab at the bottom of the page.
3. Click and hold the mouse's left button and drag the desired rack-mount server to the **Stash** area.
4. Click on **DIMM, HDD, I/O Adapters, PSU**, and **CPU** tabs to drag-and-drop the required components to the server.
5. Repeat step 4 for the required server components.
6. Once the server configuration is complete, drag it to the **New Server** area and provide an ID for the server.
7. Repeat the same procedure for all new rack-mount servers.

Modifying server components

In order to remove blade servers from chassis, click on the **Eject Server** icon for the server to eject. The ejected server will be moved to the **Stash** area as shown in the following screenshot:

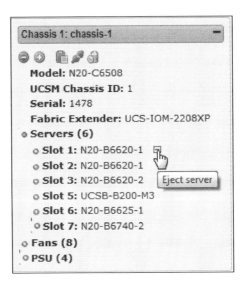

In order to remove the rack servers, click on the **Delete server** icon for the server to be deleted. The deleted server will not be moved to the **Stash** area as shown in the following screenshot:

Removing individual components from servers can be achieved by clicking on the **Remove** icon as shown in the following screenshot:

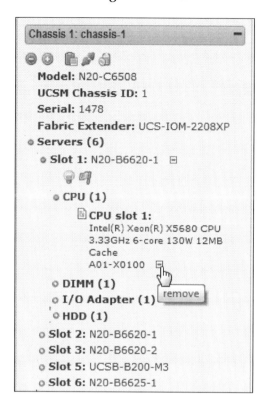

Adding server components could be achieved by dragging-and-dropping components directly to the server. It is recommended to first move the server to the **Stash** area to add or remove components.

Once the required changes to the server inventory are done, it can be saved for future use. In order to immediately use the new system inventory, it is required to restart the UCSPE and UCSM. Once the system is rebooted, you should observe the progress of the UCSPE and UCSM services, which should be started before the system can be used. The system is ready for use once the progress for UCSPE and UCS manager services start is 100%. The following screenshot shows the services in progress:

Launching UCSM using the platform emulator

Launching UCSM from UCSPE is accomplished using a web browser. It is recommended to use Mozilla compliant browsers such as Firefox or Chrome. Java is also required and JRE 1.6 is recommended. In Microsoft Windows, you can check your version of Java from the Java icon present in the control panel. The following steps are needed to be carried out for launching UCSM using platform emulator:

1. Click on the **UCS MANAGER** menu tab in the left navigation window.
2. Click on **Launch UCS Manager** in the right Work pane.

3. At the security prompt, accept the self-signed certificate as shown in the following screenshot:

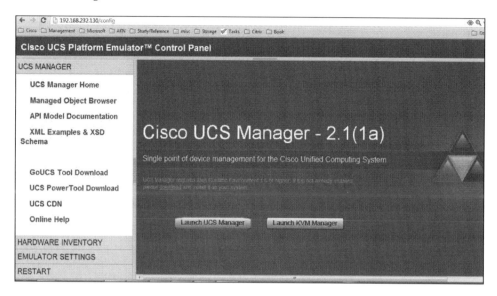

4. In the pop-up **Login** dialog box, type the **User Name** as config, **Password** as config, and click on **Login** as shown in the following screenshot:

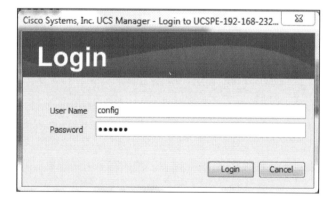

Allow the JRE security-related prompts to trust the application and allow the application to run.

 If you encounter Java compatibility issues while using JRE 1.7, install and use JRE 1.6.

After successful login, UCSM interface will display the hardware currently configured and available from the hardware inventory.

The following screenshot shows a system with default hardware inventory configured in UCSPE:

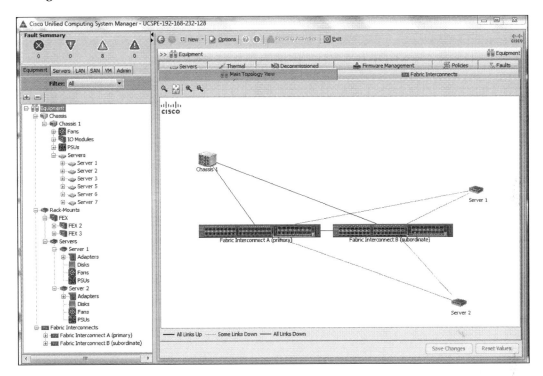

UCSPE limitations

UCSPE is an excellent platform for those looking to gain hands-on experience with Cisco UCS platform and UCSM software without setting up a costly lab. UCSPE provides a profound awareness of all the hardware available for UCS platform, and also provides hands-on configuration experience with the UCSM software.

But, UCSPE has some limitations as compared to the real UCSM software and these are as follows:

- The system cannot be integrated to a directory server (like Active Directory) for user authentication
- Server profiles configured can be assigned to the server, but an OS cannot be installed on the UCSPE servers

- No **Keyboard Video Mouse (KVM)** interface to the servers is available
- Remote monitoring data (syslog, SNMP, call home, smart call home, and so on) cannot be sent out
- High availability of the Fabric Interconnect cluster cannot be simulated

Summary

In this chapter, we learned about the various options available to install UCSPE and also the methods to add, remove, and modify different hardware components. We also launched the UCSM software from UCSPE using a web browser and looked into the user interface elements. In the subsequent chapters, we will be using UCSM running on UCSPE to configure various settings such as server profiles, resource pools, organizations, networking, and storage.

In the next chapter, we will get introduced to UCSM, learn about the **Graphical User Interface (GUI)**, and the options that are available on the tabs and nodes under the two main screen panes, which are used for the configuration and management of UCS hardware and software components.

3
Configuring Cisco UCS Using UCS Manager

In this chapter, we will provide an introduction to **Unified Computing System Manager (UCSM)** and discuss **Graphical User Interface (GUI)** as well as the options that are available in tabs and nodes under the two main screen panes that are used for the configuration and management of UCS hardware and software components. We will look at some global configuration policies that provide information on DNS, **Simple Network Management Protocol (SNMP)**, and power redundancy. We will then look at the basic steps to set up the initial configuration. In subsequent chapters, we will delve deep into individual topics such as policies, identity/resource pools, templates, and service profiles for configuring servers.

We will then discuss **Command Line Interface (CLI)**, which provides the same UCS component configuration as that of GUI. All UCS configurations are possible from both GUI and CLI.

In subsequent chapters, we will extensively use the UCSM GUI mainly for the configuration of various UCS components and policies.

The topics that will be covered in this chapter are as follows:

- Introduction to Cisco UCSM
- Walking through the UCSM interface
- Starting with the initial configuration
- Initial configuration step-by-step
- Global configuration policies
- UCS Manager – Command Line Interface

Introducing Cisco UCSM

Cisco UCSM provides unified management of all hardware and software components for the Cisco UCS solution. UCSM also provides both graphical and command line user interfaces and is embedded into **Fabric Interconnects (FIs)**.

UCSM controls multiple UCS chassis. The number of chassis that can be controlled by UCSM is 20, but the actual number of manageable chassis is dependent upon the model and the number of physical uplinks from each chassis' **Input Output Module (IOM)** or **Fabric Extender (FEX)** module to FIs. UCSM provides unified visibility and management for servers, network, and storage resources. The core functions that UCSM provides are as follows:

- **Identity and resource pools**: UCSM provides identity and resource pools to abstract the compute node identities for the stateless servers whereas traditional servers use the hardware burned-in identities. These identities and resources include **Universally Unique Identifiers (UUIDs)**, **Media Access Controls (MACs)**, **World Wide Node (WWN)** numbers, and physical blade server pools.

- **Policies**: Service policies provide different configurations for UCS servers including BIOS settings, firmware versions, **Virtual Network Interface Cards (vNICs)**, **Virtual Host Bus Adapters (vHBAs)** policies, scrub policies, **Quality Of Service (QOS)**, **Intelligent Platform Management Interface (IPMI)** policies, and so on. A policy once configured can be assigned to any number of blade servers in order to provide the configuration baseline.

- **Templates**: A template is an excellent feature of UCSM that assists on provisioning multiple physical servers, vNICs, and vHBAs with similar hardware configuration through a single source. A template can be configured for each type of server in the environment, different vNICs, and vHBAs as per the business requirement. Templates can be used to create services profiles, vNICs, and vHBAs for the servers very quickly.

- **Service profiles**: Service profile is the principal feature of the UCS platform that enables stateless computing. It combines information and features abstracted from identity and resource pools and server policies. It is a software entity residing in UCSM, which has the specifications of a complete server when associated with a stateless physical hardware server. Service profiles radically improve server provisioning and troubleshooting.

UCSM provides the following benefits:

- **Agility**: With an appropriate initial configuration, UCSM facilitates the system administrator with rapid provisioning of any number of new chassis and blade servers using resource pools, policies, and templates to create service profiles.

- **Flexibility**: UCSM abstracts hardware resources using software configurations. A system administrator can quickly modify vNICs, vHBAs, and other resources using software configurations.

- **Troubleshooting**: Since UCS hardware is stateless, in case of catastrophic failures, servers can be replaced with all the existing identities and configurations without having to deal with lengthy configuration steps.

 With Cisco UCS central software, management can be extended globally to thousands of servers in multiple UCS domains.

UCSM firmware version

The most recent UCSM firmware version available at the time of writing this book was UCSM 2.1. Always check the Cisco website for acquiring the most recent firmware. It is required to have a CCO account and authorization in order to download the UCSM firmware. Older firmware versions are also available in the archive area of the same web page.

Following are the major firmware releases:

- UCSM Version 1.4
- UCSM Version 2.0
- UCSM Version 2.1

For each major release, there are some minor revisions as well. When performing a firmware upgrade, always read the firmware release notes carefully in order to avoid breaking a production environment. For example, if you have configured default SAN zoning (not recommended but configurable in Version 2.0) for production systems running on firmware Version 2.0, upgrading to firmware Version 2.1 will break the SAN access unless proper zoning is configured, as default zoning is not an option in Version 2.1.

Walking through the UCSM interface

UCSM GUI is accessed through a web URL for pointing out the cluster IP or DNS name of the FI. UCSM requires Internet Explorer, Mozilla Firefox, Chrome, and **Java Runtime Environment (JRE)** 1.6.

UCSM GUI is a Java application. Java **web start (WS)** is used to display the UCSM GUI. The UCSM GUI is divided into the following parts:

- **Navigation pane**: On the left-hand side of the screen is the Navigation pane. It provides navigation to all equipment and components such as resource pools, policies, and so on. When a component is selected in the Navigation pane, its details appear on the right-hand side, that is, on the Work pane.

- **Work pane**: On the right-hand side of the screen is the Work pane, which is larger in width compared to the Navigation pane. Tabs in the Work pane can be used to display information about the components, modify the configuration, create new components, launch the KVM console, and observe the status of a finite-state machine. The Work pane also includes a navigation bar at the top.

- **Fault summary area**: The fault summary area is at the upper-left corner on top of the Navigation pane. It provides a summary of all the faults in different colors.

- **Status bar**: At the bottom of the screen, under both Navigation and Work panes, is the status bar that displays the system time and provides information on the logged-in user and the status of the applications. The following screenshot shows different sections of the UCSM GUI:

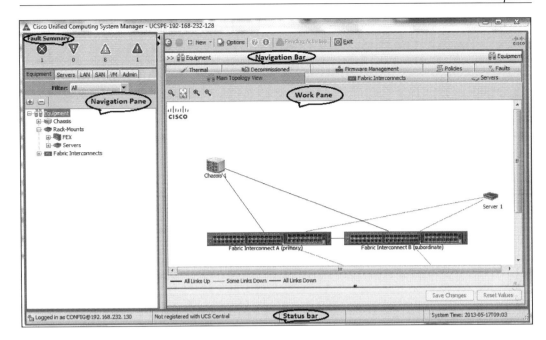

 You may encounter compatibility issues while using Java Version 1.7. If this happens, switch back to the older Java Version 1.6. Multiple JREs can be installed and selected from **Control Panel | Java | Java | View**; select only the appropriate version of Java.

Navigation pane

As discussed previously, the Navigation pane provides navigation to all equipment and components such as resource pools, policies, and so on. The Navigation pane has six main tabs that categorize UCS hardware and software components into physical equipment, servers' software configuration, LAN settings, SAN settings, UCSM administration configuration, and integration with the virtualization platform (usually VMware). These tabs have been shown in the following screenshot. When a tab is selected, it expands to give further information, configuration, and action options in the Navigation pane.

We will now walk through the main configuration options under each tab in the Navigation pane.

The Equipment tab

The Equipment tab provides the view of the physical hardware of the UCS equipment including chassis, blade servers, rack-mount servers, FIs, and other hardware along with connectivity. Any type of failure can be easily detected as it is indicated with a red, orange, or yellow rectangle on that particular piece of equipment as shown in the following screenshot:

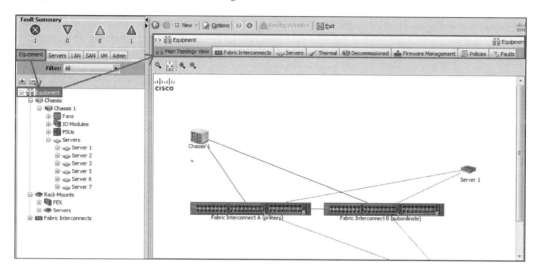

Details about the chassis, servers, and FIs can also be gathered by clicking on the specific equipment. As an example, the following screenshot shows details of the UCS chassis in the Work pane when **Chassis 1** is selected from the **Equipment** tab. Also note the number of options available in the Work pane that provide further details and configuration options.

The main nodes under this tab have been listed as follows:

- **Chassis**
- **Fabric Interconnects**
- **Rack-Mounts**

The Equipment tab has been shown in the following screenshot:

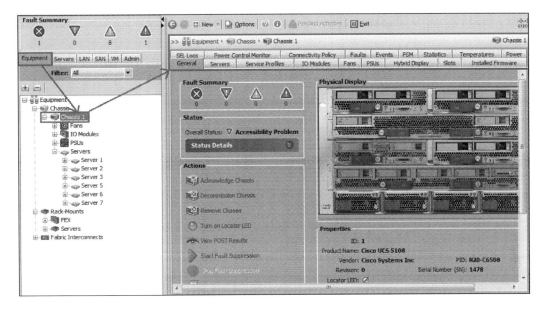

The Servers tab

The Servers tab provides server-related configuration and components, such as service profiles, service profile templates, policies, and pools. All server software configurations are done under this tab by configuring service profiles for physical servers.

The main nodes under this tab have been listed as follows:

- **Service Profiles**
- **Service Profile Templates**
- **Policies**
- **Pools**
- **Schedules**

The Servers tab has been shown in the following screenshot:

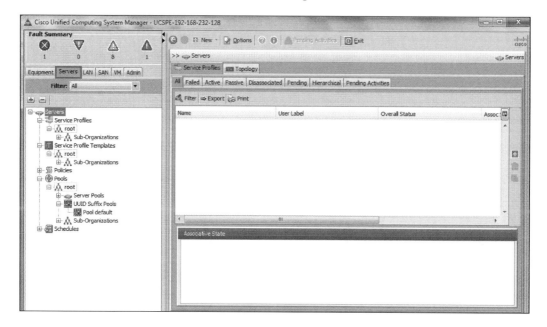

The LAN tab

The LAN tab contains components related to network configuration such as VLANs, vNIC templates, LAN policies, Pin groups, QoS policies, and MAC pools. vNICs created as templates can be assigned to configure virtual server vNICs for service profiles under the **Servers** tab. Network-related policies configured under the **LAN** tab are also assigned to service profiles.

The main nodes under this tab have been listed as follows:

- **LAN Cloud**
- **Appliances**
- **Internal LAN**
- **Policies**
- **Pools**
- **Traffic Monitoring Sessions**

The LAN tab has shown in the following screenshot:

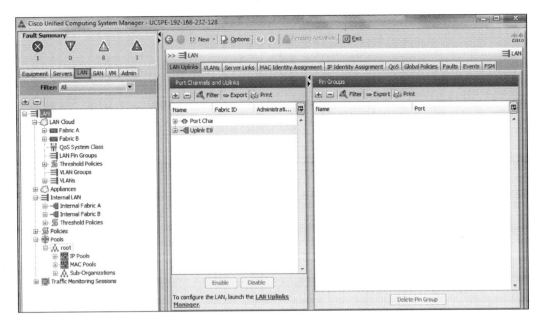

The SAN tab

The SAN tab provides SAN-related information and configuration such as VSANs, policies, zoning configuration, and WWN pools.

The main nodes under this tab have been listed as follows:

- **SAN Cloud**
- **Storage Cloud**
- **Policies**
- **Pools**
- **Traffic Monitoring Sessions**

The SAN tab has been shown in the following screenshot:

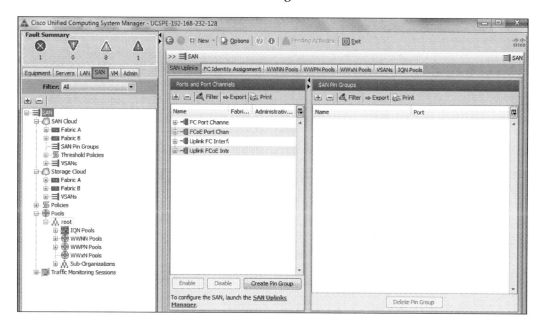

The VM tab

The VM tab provides information on the configuration of the connection between Cisco UCSM and VMware vCenter to configure distributed virtual switches, port profiles, and to view the virtual machines hosted on servers in the Cisco UCS domain. Have a look at the following screenshot for more details:

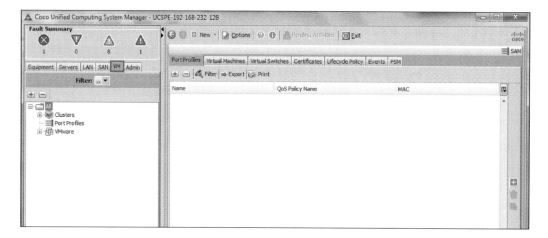

The Admin tab

The Admin tab provides global system administration settings such as faults, events, users, **Role Based Access Control (RBAC)**, external directory services, backup, restore, communication services, and licensing.

The main nodes under this tab have been listed as follows:

- **Faults, Events and Audit Log**
- **User Management**
- **Key Management**
- **Communication Management**
- **Stats Management**
- **Time Zone Management**
- **Capability Catalog**
- **Management Extension**
- **License Management**

The Admin tab has been shown in the following screenshot:

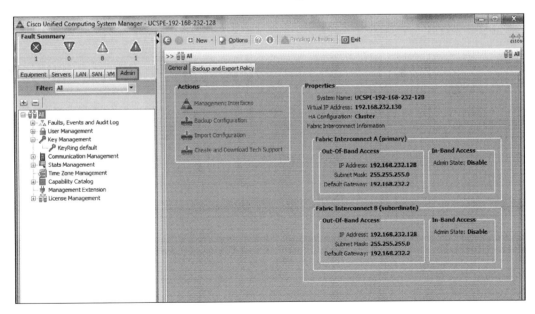

In the Navigation pane, there is a **Filter** drop-down box that can be used to filter the navigation tree to view all the subcomponents or only one, as per our need.

The Fault Summary area

The **Fault Summary** area is at the upper-left corner of UCSM GUI on top of the Navigation pane. This area displays a summary of all the faults that have occurred in the Cisco UCS infrastructure.

Faults are represented by different colored icons. The total number of specific faults is indicated by a small number below each fault icon. If you click on a fault icon in the **Fault Summary** Area, Cisco UCSM GUI changes the view to the **Faults, Events and Audit Log** tab under the **Admin** tab and displays all such similar faults.

Following is the list of alarms displayed in the **Fault Summary** area:

- **Critical alarm**: This is displayed by the red colored icon; this alarm indicates there is a critical fault with a very high probability of services getting disrupted. This requires immediate user intervention for the fix.

- **Major alarm**: This is displayed by the orange colored icon; this alarm indicates there is a fault issue that may affect some services. It also requires immediate user action.

- **Minor alarm**: This is displayed by the yellow colored icon; this alarm indicates there is a minor fault that may partially affect some services. Immediate user action is recommended before the services get adversely affected.

- **Warning message**: This is displayed by the blue colored icon; this alarm indicates there is a minor fault that may affect any of the services. It should be corrected as soon as possible.

Starting with the initial configuration

Before using the UCSM software for the configuration, it is necessary to make sure that the following prerequisites are met:

- Physical cabling of the FIs, specially the L1, L2 dedicated ports for control plane connectivity is working fine

- FI cluster configuration is complete and the cluster status is up

Details on physical cabling and cluster configuration of FIs have been provided in *Chapter 10, Configuring Backup, Restore, and High Availability*.

Although it is possible to use a single FI for data connection as a proof of concept implementation, it is, however, not recommended in the production environment.

Step-by-step initial configuration

Following are the rudimentary steps for the initial configuration of UCSM:

1. First ensure the presence of proper physical cabling between FIs, IOMs, and north-bound switches as explained in *Chapter 1, Cisco UCS Physical Architecture and Installing UCS Hardware*.

2. Access FIs using a serial console as there is no IP assigned to them initially.

3. FI will run an initial configuration wizard that will assign IP and other necessary configurations which are required (detailed steps are provided in *Chapter 10, Configuring Backup, Restore, and High Availability*).

4. Make sure that L1/L2 ports are properly connected between FIs so that when the second FI is powered up, it automatically detects the first FI and configures the cluster settings as part of the initial configuration (detailed steps are provided in *Chapter 10, Configuring Backup, Restore, and High Availability*).

5. Assign cluster IP to get centralized management access of the cluster, also known as **Virtual IP (VIP)**.

6. Once the IPs have been assigned, it is also possible to access FIs through **Secure Shell (SSH)**.

7. Log in to FI and use the following commands to get the status of the cluster as shown in the following screenshot:

```
connect local-mgmt

Show cluster state
```

```
FI55-5-1-A# connect local-mgmt
Cisco Nexus Operating System (NX-OS) Software
TAC support: http://www.cisco.com/tac
Copyright (c) 2009, Cisco Systems, Inc. All rights reserved.
The copyrights to certain works contained in this software are
owned by other third parties and used and distributed under
license. Certain components of this software are licensed under
the GNU General Public License (GPL) version 2.0 or the GNU
Lesser General Public License (LGPL) Version 2.1. A copy of each
such license is available at
http://www.opensource.org/licenses/gpl-2.0.php and
http://www.opensource.org/licenses/lgpl-2.1.php

FI55-5-1-A(local-mgmt)# sh cluster state
Cluster Id: 0xf13c9ab21c5711e2-0xb2df547fee951f44

A: UP, PRIMARY
B: UP, SUBORDINATE

HA READY
FI55-5-1-A(local-mgmt)#
```

8. After confirming the status of the cluster, log in to the UCSM GUI using the cluster VIP IP using a compatible browser as shown in the following screenshot:

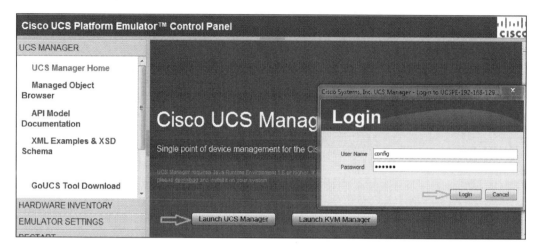

9. Configure the UCS global policies, which will be explained in the next section.

In case it is necessary to reinitialize FI to the default factory setting, use the following commands:

```
connect local-mgmt
erase-config
```

On a primary FI, A is automatically added to the name, and on a secondary FI, B is automatically added to the name; so pay attention to the naming convention.

In this chapter, we will only discuss the configuration of UCS global policies. In subsequent chapters, we will be exploring different configurations using the UCSM application.

Global configuration policies

Most of the policy configurations are assigned to the servers by assigning those policies to service profiles associated with physical servers. There are a few global configuration policies for UCS infrastructure that are not assigned to servers but are necessary for proper functioning of all the components.

These policies include the following:

- **Chassis/FEX Discovery Policy**
- **Power Policy**
- **MAC Address Table Aging**
- **DNS Server**
- **Time Zone Management**
- **SNMP**

These policies are configured under various Navigation pane tabs. We will now look into the configuration of each of these policies.

Chassis/FEX Discovery Policy

This is the first policy needed to be configured so that the UCS chassis is detected by the UCSM software. It has been highlighted in the following screenshot:

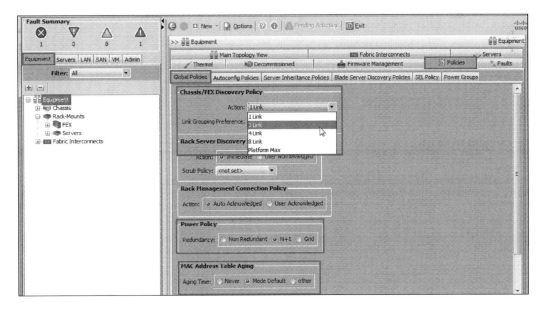

Following are the steps to configure this policy:

1. Log in to the UCSM screen.
2. Click on the **Equipment** tab in the Navigation pane.
3. Select **Policies** from the Work pane and click on **Global Policies**.
4. In the **Chassis/FEX Discovery Policy** area of the Work pane, from the **Action** drop-down menu, select the option with the number of connections that is equal to or less than the actual number of physical connections from IOM/FEX of chassis to the FIs.
5. Click on **OK**.

Power Policy

1. Follow the same steps as you did for Chassis/FEX Discovery Policy and select **Global Policies**.
2. Select the appropriate **Redundancy** option, which is dependent on the total number of power supplies and power feeds to the datacenter.
3. Click on **OK**.

MAC Address Table Aging

1. Follow the same steps as you did for Chassis/FEX Discovery Policy and select **Global Policies**.
2. Select the appropriate **Aging Time** option from the available radio buttons.
3. Click on **OK**.

The other global policies to be configured are under the **Admin** tab in the Navigation pane. Go through the following sections to get an idea of the set of steps required to configure these settings.

DNS Server

Following are the steps to configure this policy:

1. Log in to the UCSM screen.

2. Click on the **Admin** tab in the Navigation pane.

3. Expand **Communication Management**.

4. Select **DNS Management** from the Work pane.

5. Click on **Specify DNS Server** which will pop up another window for providing the IP address of the DNS server.

6. Click on **OK**.

7. Click on **Save Changes** as shown in the following screenshot:

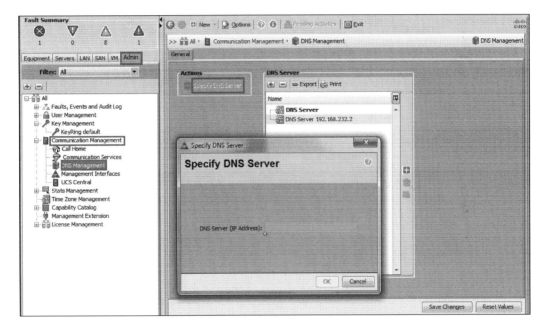

Time Zone Management

Following are the steps to configure this policy:

1. Log in to the UCSM screen.

2. Click on the **Admin** tab in the Navigation pane.

3. Select **Time Zone Management** from the Work pane.

4. Click on **Add NTP Server** which will pop up another window for providing the IP address of the NTP server.

5. Click on **OK**.

6. Click on **Save Changes**.

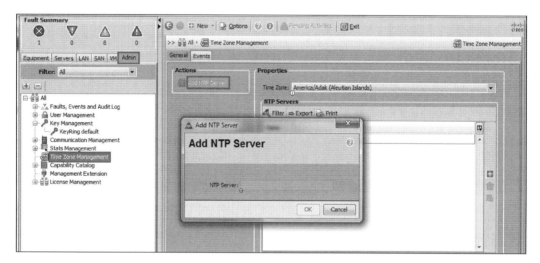

SNMP

Following are the steps to configure this policy:

1. Log in to the UCSM screen.

2. Click on the **Admin** tab in the Navigation pane.

3. Expand **Communication Management**.

4. Select **Communication Services** from the Work pane.

5. In the **SNMP** section, select the **Enabled** radio button for the **Admin State** option as shown in the following screenshot:

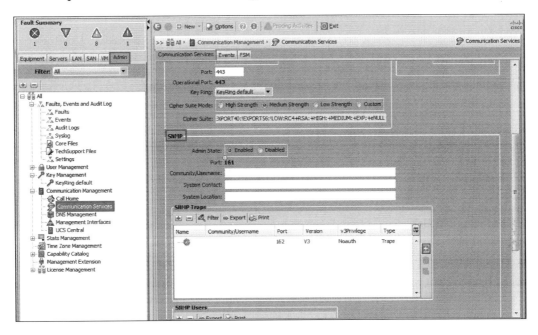

6. Click on the plus sign under the **SNMP Traps** heading; a new pop-up window will appear for configuring SNMP.

7. Provide the **IP Address** value of the remote collection server, SNMP string in the **Community/Username** field, server **Port** value, the server **Version** type, **Type** of data collection, and the authentication option in the **v3Privilege** field.

8. Click on **OK**.

9. Click on **Save Changes**.

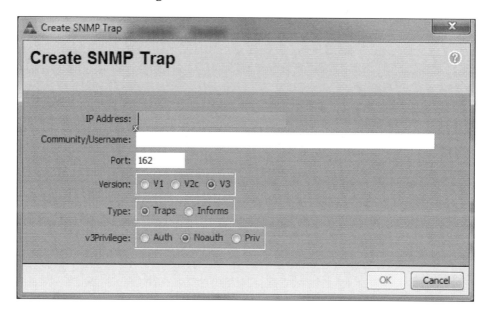

UCS Manager – Command Line Interface

UCSM's command line is different from Cisco's regular IOS and even NXOS (Nexus is the base platform of FIs that runs UCSM). UCSM CLI does provide the same tab completion options as IOS and NXOS. You can either SSH to log in remotely or log in locally through the console access to the FI for getting access to the UCS CLI.

Each UCS component can be configured using the GUI or CLI commands. Each GUI tab and each component present in the infrastructure and represented in the GUI has an equivalent CLI configuration command. You can navigate through various UCS components using the scope command.

Once connected to the CLI, it is also possible to connect to the other advanced CLIs introduced later in the chapter.

Getting help with CLI commands

On the blank command prompt, typing ? lists all the available commands for the mode you are in. It lists all the available keywords and arguments for the command at the current position in the command syntax as shown in the following screenshot:

```
FR60-401-1-A# scope ?
  adapter            Mezzanine Adapter
  chassis            Chassis
  eth-server         Ethernet Server Domain
  eth-storage        Ethernet Storage
  eth-traffic-mon    Ether Traffic Monitoring Domain
  eth-uplink         Ethernet Uplink
  fabric-interconnect  Fabric Interconnect
  fc-storage         FC Storage
  fc-traffic-mon     FC Traffic Monitoring Domain
  fc-uplink          FC Uplink
  fex                FEX (fabric-extender) Module
  firmware           Firmware
  host-eth-if        Host Ethernet Interface
  host-fc-if         Host FC Interface
  license            License
  monitoring         Monitor the system
```

Typing ? with a partially completed command provides the syntax completion option. In this case, ? should be typed without any space as shown in the following screenshot:

```
FR60-401-1-A# scope fc?
  fc-storage       FC Storage
  fc-traffic-mon   FC Traffic Monitoring Domain
  fc-uplink        FC Uplink

FR60-401-1-A# scope fc
```

Accessing the history of CLI commands

UCS automatically saves all the typed commands during a session. You can use the up and down arrow keys in order to step through the commands and the right and left arrow keys to make any modifications before executing.

Accessing other CLIs

It is also possible to connect to other CLI interfaces of individual components, for example, mezzanine adapters, server **Cisco Integrated Management Controllers (CIMCs)**, IOMs, and the underlying Nexus OS. It is usually not required to connect to these CLIs for a normal operation. However, during troubleshooting scenarios, Cisco technicians may ask you to connect to other CLIs. This is done using the `connect` command with the desired CLI option. The options include the following:

- `connect adapter`
- `connect cimc`
- `connect clp`
- `connect iom`
- `connect local-mgmt`
- `connect nxos`

```
FR60-401-1-A#
FR60-401-1-A# connect ?
  adapter       Mezzanine Adapter
  cimc          Cisco Integrated Management Controller
  clp           Connect to DMTF CLP
  iom           IO Module
  local-mgmt    Connect to Local Management CLI
  nxos          Connect to NXOS CLI

FR60-401-1-A# connect
```

Scope commands

UCS scope commands provide hierarchical access to UCS components. The following table lists some of the main categories of this command. Scope categories are mostly self-explanatory and provide access to a major area or component. Under each major category, there are subcategories for specific components. This is equivalent to the hierarchy of different tabs in GUI.

Component	CLI command to access
Chassis	`FI# scope chassis`
	`FI/chassis#`
Fabric interconnect	`FI# scope fabric-interconnect`
	`FI/ fabric-interconnect#`

Component	CLI command to access
Service profile	`FI# scope service-profile` `FI/ service-profile#`
Firmware	`FI# scope firmware` `FI/fimrware#`
Host Ethernet interface	`FI# scope host-eth-if` `FI/host-eth-if#`
Host Fibre Channel interface	`FI# scope host-fc-if` `FI/host-fc-if#`
Virtual NIC	`FI# scope vnic` `FI/vnic#`
Virtual HBA	`FI# scope vhba` `FI/vhba#`
Organization	`FI# scope org` `FI/org#`
Security	`FI# scope security` `FI/security#`
Ethernet uplink	`FI# scope eth-uplink` `FI/eth-uplink#`
System	`FI# scope system` `FI/system#`

Once inside a specific configuration, you can use the following commands to show, add, or delete configurations:

- `show`
- `create`
- `delete`

Use the `exit` command to go one level higher in the hierarchy.

Applying changes

None of the configurations get applied unless the `commit-buffer` command is used. You can make configuration changes, but you do need this final command in order to apply those changes. The `commit-buffer` command is analogous to the **OK**, **Apply**, and **Save** buttons in GUI, which can be used to apply changes.

If you have not used the `commit-buffer` command, it is possible to discard the changes by using the `discard-buffer` command. It is also possible to accumulate multiple configurations and use a single `commit-buffer` command to apply all the changes. You can view the pending commands by entering the `show configuration pending` command in any command mode.

An example configuration using CLI commands

As an example, we will configure the DNS and NTP servers with the IP address 8.8.8.8 for UCSM.

The following command changes the CLI focus to system scope as DNS is a system-wide setting:

```
FI-A# scope system
```

The following command changes the CLI focus to services scope:

```
FI-A /system # scope services
```

The following command creates a DNS server entry:

```
FI-A /system/services # create dns 8.8.8.8
```

The `commit-buffer` command applies the changes and saves the configuration:

```
FI-A /system/services* # commit-buffer
```

The following command changes the CLI focus to system scope as NTP is also a system-wide setting:

```
FI-A# scope system
```

The following command changes the CLI focus to services scope:

```
FI-A /system # scope services
```

The following command creates a DNS server entry:

```
FI-A /system/services # create ntp-server 8.8.8.8
```

The `commit-buffer` command saves the configuration:

```
FI-A /system/services* # commit-buffer
```

Summary

In this chapter, we learned about the UCSM GUI. We looked at how GUI is divided into different panes and sections and the various methods to find the required information or set up the necessary configuration. We briefly described the main tabs in the Navigation pane and some tabs in the Work pane—in subsequent chapters, we will go into the details of Navigation and Work pane tabs. We then went through the initial configuration of UCSM. We walked through the minimum configuration steps. We also learned about CLI UI and learned that its syntax is a bit different than regular IOS or NXOS syntax. We also configured some global policies, which are necessary for UCS components, using the GUI. In subsequent chapters, we will be using UCSM GUI extensively for the configuration of various UCS physical and software objects.

In the next chapter, we will learn about the UCS LAN configuration. We will start using UCSM extensively and will explore different configurations, pools, policies, and so on, related to the LAN configuration.

4
Configuring LAN Connectivity

UCS Fabric Interconnect provides connectivity for Ethernet and storage data traffic. UCS Fabric Interconnect also runs the **Unified Computing System Management (UCSM)** software. UCS Fabric Interconnect hardware is based on the Nexus series of switches and runs NX-OS; however, Fabric Interconnect has some features that are different from a standard Nexus Ethernet switch. In this chapter, we'll focus on Fabric Interconnect Ethernet connectivity to the servers and upstream switches.

In this chapter, we'll discuss the following topics:

- Understanding Fabric Interconnect switching modes
- Introduction to Fabric Interconnect port types
- Configuring northbound connectivity to upstream switches
- Configuring southbound connectivity to IOMs
- Configuring the last piece of the puzzle—vNICs

We'll configure the Fabric Interconnect's downstream (southbound) connectivity to IOMs/**Fabric Extenders (FEXs)** in the blade chassis and upstream (northbound) connectivity to the physical switches. Network configuration is done under the **LAN** and **Equipment** tabs of the UCS Manager software. In this chapter we will thoroughly explore the **LAN** and **Equipment** tabs in the Navigation pane.

Understanding Fabric Interconnect switching modes

UCS Fabric Interconnect supports two types of switching modes: **End Host Mode (EHM)** and standard Ethernet switching mode. The default switching mode is the End Host Mode which eliminates the use of **Spanning Tree Protocol (STP)** on Fabric Interconnect. The standard Ethernet switching is rarely used and it is recommended not to implement this option unless there is a use case.

 Switching mode conversion is a disruptive change requiring Fabric Interconnect reboot and hence should be planned during a scheduled maintenance window.

Ethernet End Host Mode (EHM)

End Host Mode is the default mode of operation for UCS Fabric Interconnect Ethernet connectivity. In this mode, UCS Fabric Interconnect is presented to the northbound LAN switch as an end host with many adapters. STP is not configured on the uplink switch ports. Since there is no STP, all FI ports are in the forwarding state irrespective of the northbound topology. This means that data traffic can use any of the FI uplink ports/port channels. In this mode, Fabric Interconnects are in the Active/Active usage state.

The data traffic flow is accomplished through pinning of host interfaces to the uplink ports. Host interface pinning can be configured dynamically or statically. All uplink ports are configured as 802.1q trunks. No control protocol is used on the uplinks. MAC address learning only happens for southbound server ports and not on uplink ports:

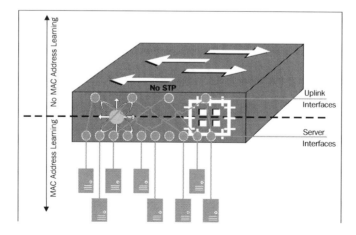

In order to configure or verify End Host Mode for Fabric Interconnects, follow these steps:

1. Log in to UCS Manager.

2. Click on the **Equipment** tab in the Navigation pane.

3. On the **Equipment** tab, click on a **Fabric Interconnect**.

4. The **Status** area in the Work pane shows the current Ethernet mode configuration which is **End Host**.

5. In the **Actions** area of the Work pane, the currently configured Ethernet mode, which in this case is **End Host**, will be shown grayed:

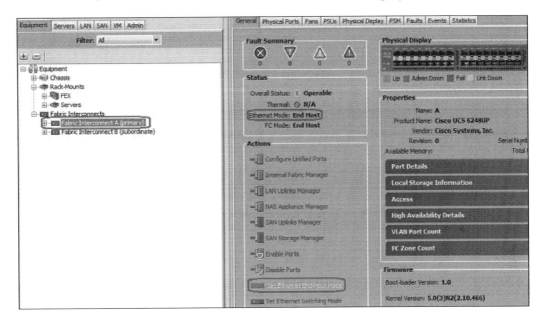

A Fabric Interconnect reboot is required in order to change **Ethernet Mode** from **End Host** to **Switching** and vice versa.

In order to change **Ethernet Mode** from **End Host** to **Switching**, perform the following steps:

1. Log in to UCS Manager.

2. Click on the **Equipment** tab in the Navigation pane.

3. In the **Equipment** tab, click on a **Fabric Interconnect**.

4. In the **Actions** area of the Work pane, the currently configured **Ethernet Mode**, which in this case is **End Host**, will be shown grayed and cannot be selected.

5. Click on **Set Ethernet Switching Mode** in the **Actions** area of the Work pane.

6. Click on **Yes** on the pop-up warning message to restart the Fabric Interconnect:

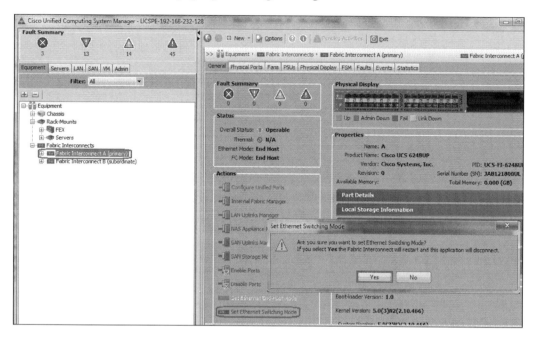

7. After Fabric Interconnect restarts, the **Ethernet Mode** is changed to **Switching**.

 You can also right-click on a **Fabric Interconnect** in the **Equipment** tab in the Navigation pane in order to change the switching mode.

Ethernet switching mode

In this mode, UCS Fabric Interconnect is configured as a standard Ethernet switch with STP configured for loop avoidance. The uplink ports are configured as forwarding or blocking as per the STP algorithm.

In order to verify or configure the switching mode for Fabric Interconnects, perform the following steps:

1. Log in to UCS Manager.

2. Click on the **Equipment** tab in the Navigation pane.

3. In the **Equipment** tab, click on a **Fabric Interconnect**.

4. The **Status** area in the Work pane shows the current **Ethernet Mode** configuration, which is currently **Switch** mode.

5. In the **Actions** area of the Work pane, the currently configured **Ethernet Mode**, which in this case is **Switch**, will be shown grayed:

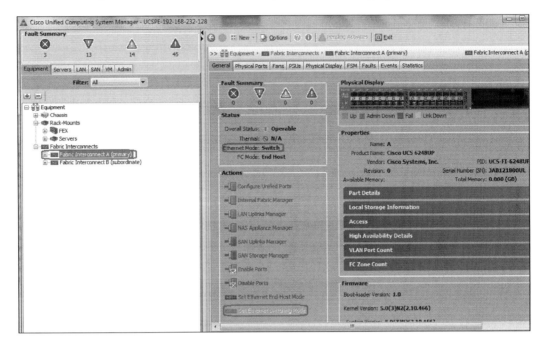

A Fabric Interconnect reboot is required in order to change the value of **Ethernet Mode** from **Switching** to **End Host** and vice versa.

In order to change the value of **Ethernet Mode** from **Switching** to **End Host**, perform the following steps:

1. Log in to UCS Manager.

2. Click on the **Equipment** tab in the Navigation pane.

3. In the **Equipment** tab, click on a **Fabric Interconnect**.

4. In the **Actions** area of the Work pane, the currently configured **Ethernet Mode**, which in this case is **Switch**, will be shown grayed and cannot be selected.

5. Click on **Set Ethernet End-Host Mode** in the **Actions** area of the Work pane.

6. Click on **Yes** on the pop-up warning message to restart Fabric Interconnect:

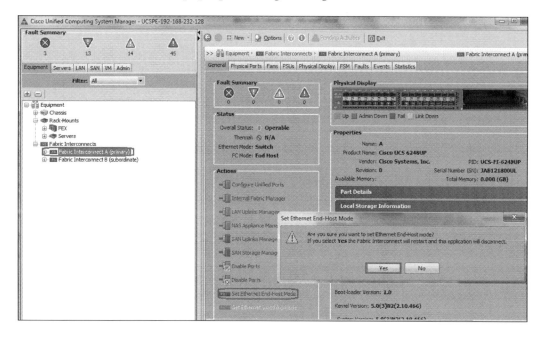

7. After Fabric Interconnect restarts, the Ethernet mode is changed to **End-Host Mode**.

Introduction to Fabric Interconnect port types

By default, all Fabric Interconnect ports are unconfigured. For Ethernet LAN connectivity, Fabric Interconnect ports can be in the following states:

- **Unconfigured**: Port is not configured and cannot be used.

- **Server Port**: Port is configured for southbound connection to an IOM **Fabric Extender (FEX)** module in a blade chassis.

- **Uplink Port**: Port is configured for northbound connection to the upstream Ethernet switch. Uplink ports are always configured as trunk ports.

- **Disabled**: Port is configured either as an uplink or server port and is currently disabled by the administrator.

For 6200 series FI, all ports are unified ports; hence all the ports can also be configured as 1/10 Gig Ethernet, FC, FC uplink, appliance port, or FCoE port. For 6100 series, the FC configurations are only available for expansion module ports.

To define, change, or check the state of a port, expand the **Fabric Interconnect** inventory from the **Equipment** tab in the Navigation pane:

1. Log in to UCS Manager.

2. Click on the **Equipment** tab in the Navigation pane.

3. In the **Equipment** tab, click on a **Fabric Interconnect** and expand ports.

4. Click on a port, and its current configuration will be displayed in the right-hand side working pane.

5. Right-click on a port and select a new configuration for the port from the pop-up menu.

6. Ports can be enabled or disabled from the menu as well:

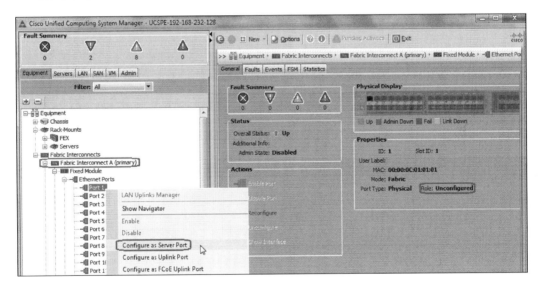

The other option to configure the ports is the LAN Uplinks Manager tool which can be accessed using the following steps:

1. Log in to UCS Manager.

2. Click on the **Equipment** tab in the Navigation pane.

3. In the **Equipment** tab, click on a **Fabric Interconnect**.

4. In the Work area pane, select **LAN Uplinks Manager**:

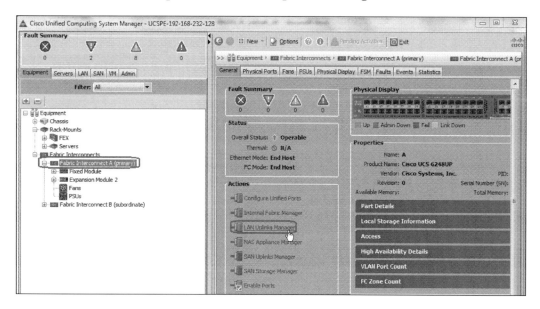

 LAN Uplinks Manager is a pop-up pane that can be used to configure LAN configurations from a single view, which are otherwise configured from different tabs in the Navigation and Work panes. LAN Uplinks Manager shows all ports in various categories. Ports can be configured, enabled, and disabled. Ethernet Port Channels, VLANs, Pin groups, and QoS policies can be created and assigned. Ethernet related events, faults, and FSM status can also be viewed using the tab available at the top in LAN Uplinks Manager.

LAN Uplinks Manager user interface is shown in the following screenshot:

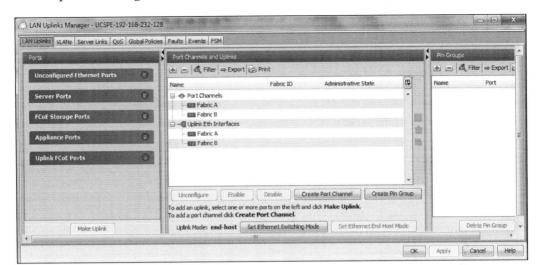

Configuring northbound connectivity to upstream switches

Cisco recommends using Nexus 5K/7K switches for Fabric Interconnect northbound network connectivity because of the features such as **virtual PortChannel** (**vPC**). It is, however, possible to connect Fabric Interconnect to other Ethernet switches as well including Cisco Catalyst series switches and even switches from Cisco competitors as long as those switches use the industry standard protocols.

Majority of UCS field deployments are designed using Nexus 5K/7K switches. Therefore, we will explain the upstream configuration using Cisco Nexus 5K switches.

Configuring upstream switches

Northbound connectivity from Fabric Interconnect can be achieved through a standard uplink, a port channel, or virtual PortChannel configuration. The recommended configuration for the northbound connectivity is through Nexus switches and configuring a vPC.

The vPC configuration aggregates bandwidth and provides redundancy across two physical northbound Nexus switches to each Fabric Interconnect. In vPC configuration, northbound Nexus switches logically appear as a single entity to Fabric Interconnects. A MAC address learned by an individual Nexus switch is shared between both switches.

vPC consists of the following components:

- **Two peer Nexus switches**: One is configured as primary and the other is configured as secondary.

- **vPC domain ID**: This is a logical ID assigned to vPC and should be unique for **Link Aggregation Control Protocol (LACP)** negotiations.

- **vPC peer link**: This is a high throughput link configured between the two Nexus switches for synchronizing the forwarding of information and data movement, if needed.

- **vPC keep alive link**: This is configured between two Nexus switches for sharing heartbeat information.

- **vPC member links**: These are southbound links to Fabric Interconnects:

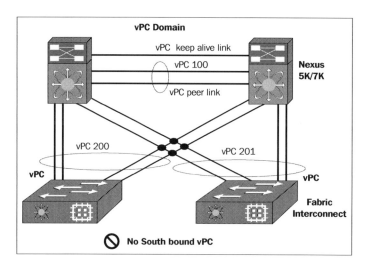

To enable the vPC feature on Nexus switches, use the following commands:

1. The vPC feature is needed to be enabled on Nexus switches. Also enable the LACP feature for port trunking:

```
switch(config)# feature vpc
switch(config)# feature lacp
```

These features should be enabled on both switches.

2. Configure the vPC domain ID:

```
switch(config)# vpc domain 1
```

The domain ID should be configured on both switches.

3. Configure `peer-keepalive`:

    ```
    switch(config-vpc-domain)# peer-keepalive destination x.x.x.x
    ```

    `peer-keepalive` is also configured on both switches where the destination IP is usually the management port IP of the peer switch which is used as a heartbeat link for vPC.

4. Configure the peer link between directly connected ports of both switches:

    ```
    switch(config)# interface ethernet 1/10-11
    switch(config-if-range)# channel-group 100 mode active
    switch(config-if-range)# interface port-channel100
    switch(config-if)# switchport mode trunk
    switch(config-if)# switchport trunk allowed vlan x
    ```

5. Create a port channel on both switches, enable trunk mode, and allow required VLANs:

    ```
    switch(config-if)# vpc peer-link
    ```

    Enable port channel as the vPC peer link.

6. Configure Nexus member ports connecting to Fabric Interconnects:

    ```
    switch(config)#interface ethernet1/1-2
    switch(config-if-range)#channel-group 200
    switch(config-if-range)#interface port-channel200
    switch(config-if)#switchport mode trunk
    switch(config-if)#switchport trunk allowed vlan x
    switch(config-if)#vpc 200
    ```

    Similar configuration is required for vPC 200 on the second Nexus switch connectivity to the same FI.

7. Now configure the second vPC on both switches for connecting to both Fabric Interconnects:

    ```
    switch(config)#interface ethernet1/3-4
    switch(config-if-range)#channel-group 201
    switch(config-if-range)#interface port-channel201
    switch(config-if)#switchport mode trunk
    switch(config-if)#switchport trunk allowed vlan x
    switch(config-if)#vpc 201
    ```

    A similar configuration is required for vPC 200 on the second Nexus switch connectivity to the same FI.

Learning how to configure Fabric Interconnect uplink ports

Fabric Interconnect ports configured as uplink ports are used to connect to northbound upstream network switches. These uplink ports can be connected to upstream switch ports as individual links or links configured as **port channel** (PC) which provides bandwidth aggregation as well as link redundancy.

The Fabric Interconnect port channel configuration is based on LACP. It is also possible to configure a port channel as a vPC where port channel uplink ports from a Fabric Interconnect are connected to different upstream switches.

It is recommended to configure Fabric Interconnect uplink ports in vPC configuration as shown in the following diagram:

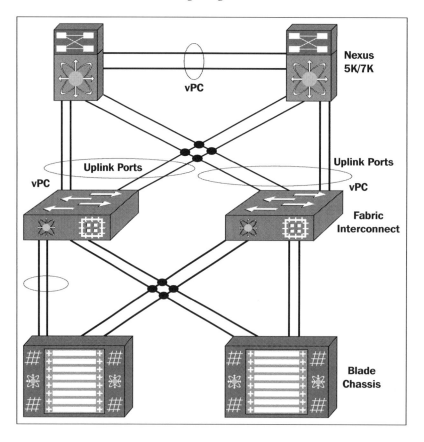

The following are the steps to configure the ports and the port channel for the preceding network topology:

1. Log in to UCS Manager.
2. Click on the **Equipment** tab in the Navigation pane.
3. In the **Equipment** tab, click on a **Fabric Interconnect**.
4. In the Work area pane, select **LAN Uplinks Manager**.
5. Expand **Ports** in the **Fixed Module** or **Expansion Module** (if present).
6. Right-click on a single port or hold the *Ctrl* key and select multiple ports.
7. Select **Configure as Server Port**.
8. A pop-up menu will allow us to configure a new status for the port(s).
9. Select the new port status and click on **Yes**.

Repeat these steps to configure all uplink ports for both Fabric Interconnects.

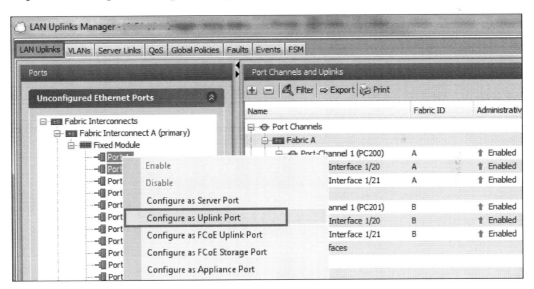

After all uplink ports are configured, a port channel can be created for these ports using the following steps:

1. Right-click on a **Fabric Interconnect** in the middle pane labeled **Port Channel and Uplinks of LAN Uplinks Manager**.

2. Click on **Create Port Channel**.

3. In the pop-up window, assign an ID and a name for the port channel and click on **Next**.

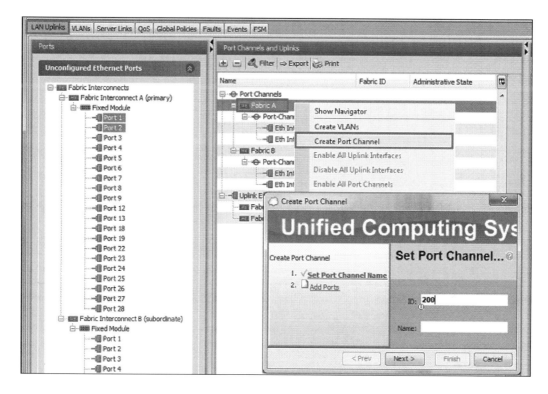

4. In the next window, click on uplink ports that should be added to the port channel and click on the arrow sign to add these ports to the port channel.

5. After adding ports, click on **Finish** to complete the port channel configuration.

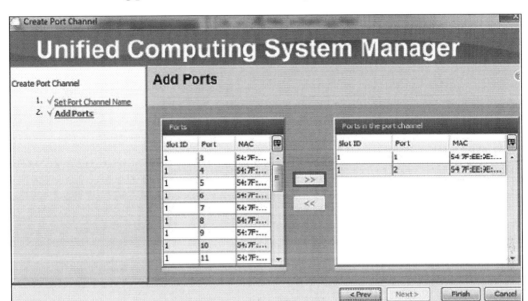

 The port channel name and ID configured on Fabric Interconnect should match the name and ID configuration on the upstream Ethernet switch.

Configuring VLANs

VLAN configuration on Fabric Interconnects can be done either through LAN Uplink Manager or through the **LAN** tab in the Navigation pane. Typically, both Fabric Interconnects have the same VLAN configuration which is called **Global VLAN configuration**. It is possible to configure some VLANs available only on one of the two Fabric Interconnects which is called **FI-specific VLAN configuration**. It is also possible to configure a same VLAN differently on both Fabric Interconnects. Fabric Interconnects also support the creation of private VLANs.

The default VLAN is VLAN 1, which cannot be deleted and is available on both FIs. VLANs can be configured in the range of 1-3967 and 4049-4093. The 3968-4048 and 4094 VLAN IDs are reserved for system use on FIs and cannot be configured.

As the uplink ports on Fabric Interconnects are always trunk ports, UCS Manager automatically manages the allowed VLANs on FI uplink ports whenever a VLAN is created, deleted, or changed. Using USC Manager VLAN wizard, it is possible to create a single VLAN or multiple VLANs, as shown in the following steps:

1. Log in to UCS Manager.

2. Click on the **LAN** tab in the Navigation pane.

3. In the **LAN** tab, right-click on any **Fabric Interconnect** or the **VLAN** tab and click on **Create VLANs**:

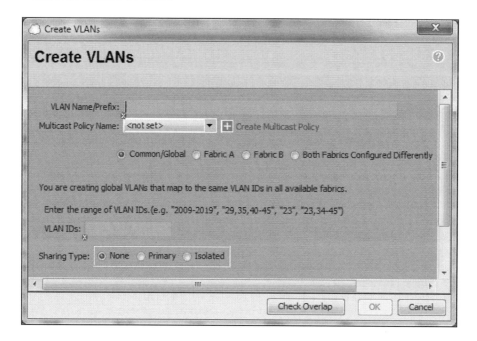

4. In order to configure a single VLAN, assign a VLAN name and ID.

5. Select the VLAN configuration type as **Common/Global** if the same VLAN configuration is required on both Fabric Interconnects.

6. Leave **Sharing Type** as **None**, which is the default selection. This selection can be changed if a private VLAN configuration is required.

7. Click on the **Check Overlap** button in order to verify uniqueness of the VLAN ID.

8. Click on **OK** to create the VLAN.

In order to create a VLAN range, perform the following steps:

1. Open the **LAN** tab in UCS Manager.

2. In the **LAN** tab, right-click on any **Fabric Interconnect** or the **VLAN** tab and click on **Create VLANs**.

3. In order to configure a VLAN range, assign a VLAN prefix and enter the range of VLAN IDs and click on **OK**.

4. VLANs will be created with a combination of prefix and VLAN numbers.

5. On the next window, click on **OK** again after verifying the new VLAN names.

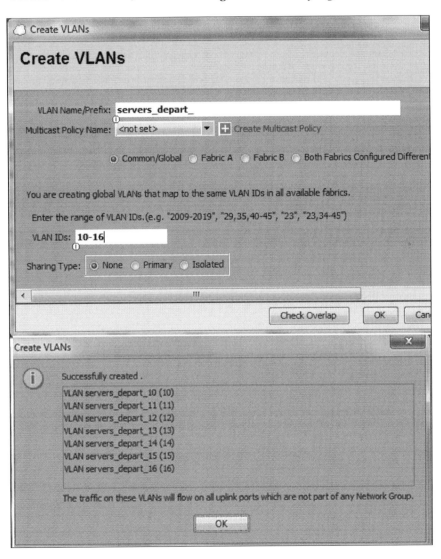

Fabric Interconnects do not participate in **VLAN Trunking Protocol (VTP)**.

Using pin groups

In End Host Mode, Fabric Interconnect does not work as a traditional layer 2 switch. In this mode, UCS Fabric Interconnect is presented to the northbound LAN switch as an end host with many adapters. Traffic from individual server's vNICs is mapped to a specific Fabric Interconnect uplink port or port channel. This mapping of Ethernet traffic is known as LAN pin groups.

Pin groups can be configured as a static or dynamic pin group. The default configuration is dynamic pin groups.

Dynamic pin groups

This is the default pin group setting. In dynamic pinning, Fabric Interconnect automatically binds server vNICs to uplink FI ports. The mapping of server vNICs to uplink FI ports depends upon the total number of active uplinks configured, which could be either 1, 2, 4, or 8 (for older 6100 series FIs, uplinks could only be 1, 2, and 4).

Failure response

Both Fabric Interconnects are in Active/Active mode with respect to Ethernet data traffic movement. Each server is pinned to a single Fabric Interconnect uplink port or port channel. This means that the data traffic from some servers will move using Fabric Interconnect A and for other servers using Fabric Interconnect B.

In case of a northbound uplink or port channel failure where a server is currently pinned to, the server connection will be automatically pinned to another port or port channel on the same Fabric Interconnect. In case of a complete Fabric Interconnect failure, the server will be automatically pinned to any uplink port or port channel on the second Fabric Interconnect provided that the Fabric failover is configured for the vNIC. The Fabric Interconnect will update the northbound switch about this change using **Gratuitous Address Resolution Protocol (GARP)**.

The dynamically pinned server vNIC uplinks are automatically rebalanced after 300 seconds to distribute the data traffic load on both Fabric Interconnects.

No user configuration is required for dynamic pinning. If no static pin groups are configured, dynamic pinning will be automatically used. Dynamic pinning is the recommended configuration and static pinning should only be used for business use cases.

Static pin groups

In static pinning, LAN pin groups are defined by the administrator on Fabric Interconnects using UCSM, which can be assigned to vNICs or vNIC templates. Static pin groups are defined under the **LAN** tab of the UCSM Navigation pane.

The steps for creating a static pin group and assigning to a vNIC are as follows:

1. Log in to UCS Manager.
2. Click on the **LAN** tab in the Navigation pane.
3. In the **LAN** tab, right-click on **LAN Pin Groups** or click on the **+** sign on the right-hand side to create a new global LAN pin group:

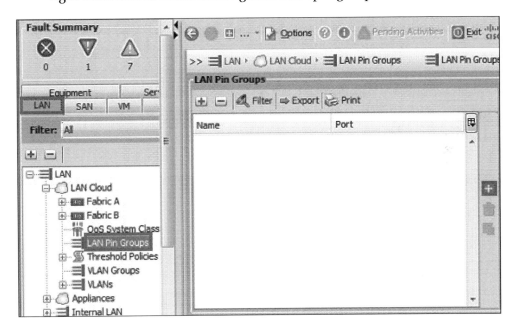

4. In the pop-up window, provide a name for the LAN pin group and bind interfaces (uplink ports or port channels).

5. Click on **OK** to complete the configuration. A pop-up message will inform to make sure that the selected uplinks are in the same layer 2 network:

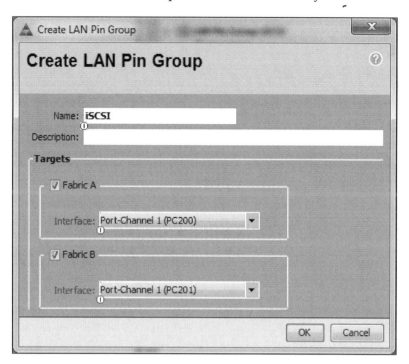

Failure response re-pinning

Each server is statically pinned to a single Fabric Interconnect uplink port or port channel using manual configuration. The administrator will have to make sure the data traffic from servers is equally distributed among Fabric Interconnects.

In case of a northbound uplink, port channel, or Fabric Interconnect failure where a server is statically pinned to, the server connection will be transferred to other Fabric Interconnects where the server will be dynamically pinned to available uplink ports or port channels, provided the Fabric failover is configured for the vNIC.

Configuring southbound connectivity to IOMs

Each Fabric Interconnect is connected to IOMs in the UCS chassis which provides connectivity to each blade server. Internal connectivity from blade servers to IOMs is transparently provided by UCS Manager using 10BASE-KR Ethernet standard for backplane implementations and there is no configuration required.

Connectivity between Fabric Interconnect server ports and IOMs is required to be configured. Each IOM module, when connected with the Fabric Interconnect server port, behaves as a line card to Fabric Interconnect, hence IOMs should never be cross-connected to the Fabric Interconnect. Each IOM is connected directly to a single Fabric Interconnect using the following cabling configuration:

- **Cisco UCS 2100 IOM**: Possible connections are 1, 2, or 4 as there are only 4 ports
- **Cisco UCS 2200 IOM**: Possible connections are 1, 2, 4, or 8 depending on the model, because 2204 provides 4 ports and 2208 provides 8 ports

With UCS 2100 IOMs and older UCS Manager firmware 1.4, it was not possible to create port channels for IOM to FI connectivity. However, starting with UCSM 2.0 and with UCS 2200 series IOMs, it is now possible to create port channels for IOM to FI connectivity as shown in the following diagram:

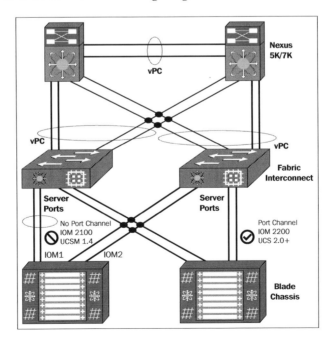

Learning how to configure Fabric Interconnect server ports

Fabric Interconnect ports which should be connected to southbound IOM cards should be configured as server ports.

The following are the steps to configure server ports:

1. Log in to UCS Manager.
2. Click on the **Equipment** tab in the Navigation pane.
3. In the **Equipment** tab, click on a **Fabric Interconnect**.
4. In the Work area pane, select **LAN Uplinks Manager**.
5. Expand **Ports** in the **Fixed Module** or **Expansion Module** (if present).
6. Right-click on a single port or hold the *Ctrl* key and select multiple ports.
7. Select **Configure as Server Port**.
8. A pop-up menu will appear which allows configuring new statuses for the port(s).
9. Select new port status and click on **Yes**.

Repeat these steps to configure all server ports for both Fabric Interconnects:

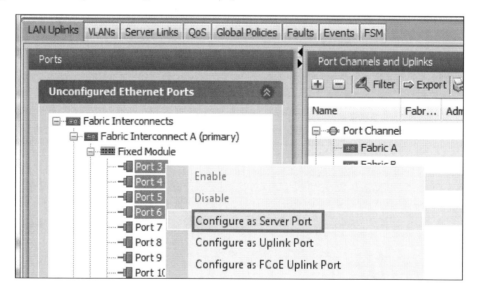

Configuring IOM ports

First, make sure there is physical connectivity between the Fabric Interconnect and IOM. For the IOM ports configuration, global chassis discovery policy, discussed in *Chapter 3, Configuring Cisco UCS Using UCS Manager*, needs to be configured using the following steps:

1. Log in to UCS Manager.

2. Click on the **Equipment** tab in the Navigation pane.

3. In the **Equipment** tab, click on **Equipment**.

4. In the Work area pane, select **Policies** and select **Global Policies**.

5. Under the **Chassis/FEX Discovery** section, click on the down arrow and select the desired number of IOM links in the **Action** field:

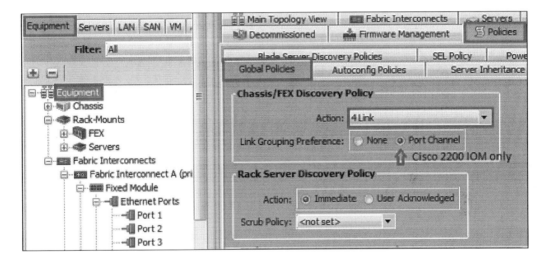

6. For UCS 2200 IOM, you can also select the **Port Channel** option and all IOM connected server ports will be automatically added to a port channel.

7. Click on **Save Changes**.

Configuring the last piece of the puzzle – vNICs

Once the connectivity between northbound uplink switches and southbound IOM is established, we can connect vNICs from blade servers configuring vNICs. It is recommended to create a vNIC template that provides ease of management in the future. A vNIC template can be configured as either of the following:

- **Initiating template**: This vNIC template will provide one-time configuration for the vNICs created using this template. Any subsequent changes to the template are not propagated to abstracted vNICs.

- **Updating template**: This vNIC template will provide initial configuration for the vNICs created using this template. Any subsequent changes to the template will also be propagated to abstracted vNICs. It is recommended to create an updating vNIC template for production environments.

> While updating a template, some changes to the vNIC template setting may trigger an immediate reboot of the associated server depending on the **Maintenance Policies** setting in the **Servers** tab. It is recommended to make **Maintenance Policies** as **User Acknowledge** in order to avoid an immediate reboot of the associated servers.

What is MAC address abstraction?

vNIC MAC addresses can be assigned manually or by configuring a MAC address pool. It is possible to either use the burned-in MAC addresses or abstract MAC addresses from an identity pool with system-defined prefixes. Stateless computing is the salient feature of the Cisco UCS platform; it is therefore recommended to abstract vNIC MAC addresses for server profiles and hence server vNIC MAC addresses from MAC address identity pools instead of using burned-in NIC MAC addresses.

The main benefit of abstracting the MAC identity is that in case of physical server failure, the server profile can be easily associated with the replacement server and the new server will acquire all the identities associated with the old server including the vNIC MAC addresses. From the operating system perspective, there is no change at all.

It is recommended to create vNIC templates with different configurations and create individual vNICs from vNIC templates as per the requirement. Also, define MAC address pools and assign MAC addresses to individual vNICs using MAC address pools.

The following screenshot shows a vNIC template with the MAC address pool server configuration for providing vNIC MAC addresses to server profiles created using a vNIC template.

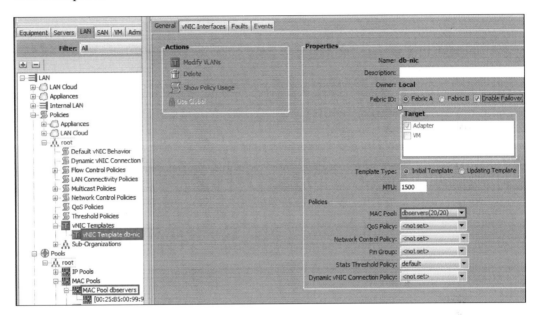

Learning to create vNICs

vNIC is abstracted from the physical mezzanine card. Older Emulex, QLogic, and Intel NIC cards have fixed ports. The Cisco mezzanine NIC card, also known as a **Palo** card or **Virtual Interface Card** (**VIC**), provides dynamic server interfaces. Cisco VIC cards provide up to 256 dynamic interfaces.

vNICs can be created directly into server profiles or by using a vNIC template. Using a vNIC template is the recommended method for configuring the NIC settings once for each template and quickly creating vNICs with the desired configuration. The vNIC configuration settings can be optimized for various operating systems, storage devices, and hypervisors.

The vNIC template can be created by performing the following steps:

1. Log in to UCS Manager.

2. Click on the **LAN** tab in the Navigation pane.

3. In the **LAN** tab, click on **Policies** and expand **vNIC Templates** on the root organization or the suborganization (if created).

4. Right-click on **vNIC Templates** and select **Create vNIC Template** as shown in the following screenshot:

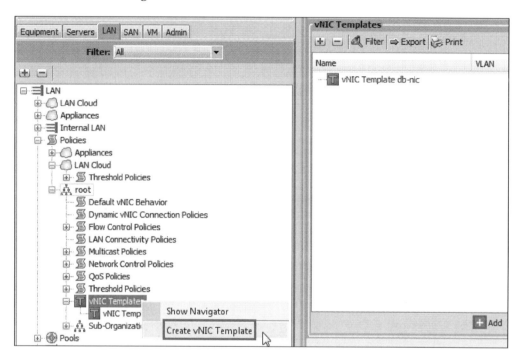

5. A new pop-up window will appear which allows configuring various settings for the vNIC template. These settings are summarized in the following screenshot:

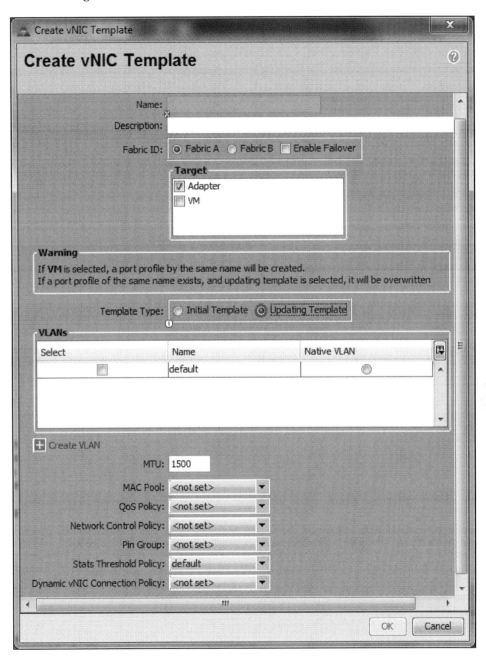

The vNIC configuration options shown in the preceding screenshot are summarized in the following table:

Option	Description
Name	Name for the vNIC template
Description	General description about the purpose of the vNIC
Target	Can be a VM template for VN-Link implementation or an adapter template for creating vNIC for a server profile
Template type	Initiating or updating template
VLANs	Select a VLAN or initiate creation of a new VLAN
MTU	Set the Message Transfer Unit size
MAC Pool	Select a MAC identity pool
QoS Policy	Select a QoS policy
Network Control Policy	Select a network control policy
Pin Group	Select a static pin group
Stats Threshold Policy	Select a statistics threshold policy
Dynamic vNIC Connection Policy	Select a dynamic vNIC connection policy

The vNIC creation for servers is part of the server profile or server profile template creation. Once **Create Service Profile Template** or **Service Profile (Expert)** is started to create a service profile for the blade servers, the vNIC creation is the second step in the configuration wizard. The steps involved in creating a vNIC in Service Profile Template using a vNIC template are as follows:

1. Log in to UCS Manager.
2. Click on the **Servers** tab in the Navigation pane.
3. In the **Servers** tab, click on **Server Profile Templates** and expand the root organization or the suborganization (if created).
4. Right-click on **Service Profile Template** and select **Create Service Profile Template**, as shown in the following screenshot:

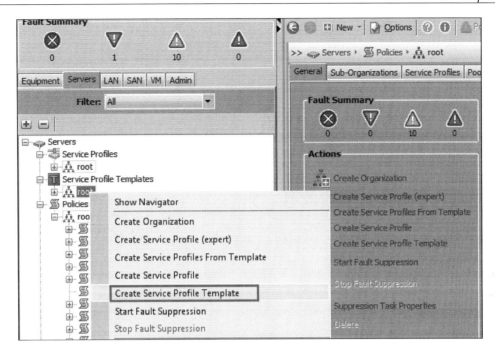

5. In the pop-up window, name the service profile template and click on **Next**.

6. For networking, select the **Expert** option for creation of vNICs and the window display will change:

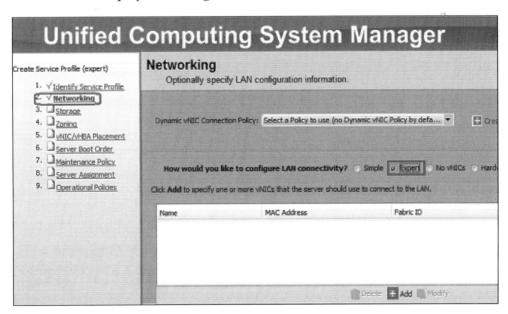

7. Click on **Add** for a new vNIC from the template.

8. In the next window, provide a vNIC name and select the **Use vNIC Template** checkbox. The display will change to select an existing vNIC template.

9. It is also possible to create a new vNIC template on the same window in which the template configuration window appears.

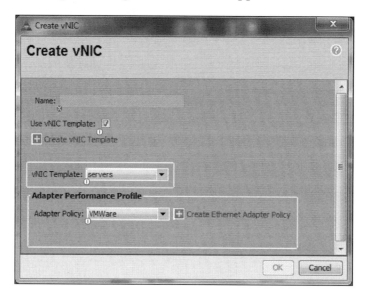

10. Select **OK** to create the new **vNIC** from the existing template.

Summary

In this chapter, we learned about the Fabric Interconnect Ethernet features and how to configure those features. We learned about the Fabric Interconnect switching modes, port types, and port states. We looked into the FI uplink ports and upstream Ethernet switch ports configuration including port channels. We looked into VLANs, pin groups, vNIC MAC address abstraction, and configuration of vNICs for the server profile. We also learned that UCS Fabric Interconnects provide some unique features such as end host mode switching and pin groups which are not available in the standard Ethernet switches. We looked into the Fabric Interconnect to IOM connectivity and also learned how to configure vNIC templates for the server's vNICs.

Now that we understand the network connectivity, we will learn the SAN connectivity in the next chapter, in addition to learning about various options including standard Fiber Channel, FCoE, iSCSI, and NAS appliances connectivity.

5
Configuring SAN Connectivity

In this chapter, we'll start looking at the different types of storage supported by UCS and the benefits of each. We'll provide an overview of Fiber Channel (FC), Fiber Channel over Ethernet (FCoE), and iSCSI. We will look into how UCS integrates with the FC fabric and what the new features available are in UCSM Version 2.1 for configuring zoning on the Fabric Interconnects directly. We'll walk through connecting SAN ports and configuring Service Profiles for single initiator and single target zoning for the SAN. We will also look into SAN pinning, which is similar in concept to LAN pinning, and explain the failure behavior for dynamic and static SAN pinning.

The topics that will be covered in this chapter are as follows:

- Learning storage connectivity options
- Overview of Fiber Channel and iSCSI storage
- Storage connectivity design considerations
- FC Switching mode
- FC port channel and trunking
- Configuring VSAN and zoning
- Configuring FCoE
- Manual and automatic uplink pinning

Learning storage connectivity options

Storage access is a crucial configuration for UCS solutions providing raw storage for both virtualized and non-virtualized servers. Most UCS deployments run virtualized environments where virtual workloads leverage many advanced features of centralized storage accessible through FC, FCoE, and iSCSI protocols. Most UCS blade servers provide very limited direct-attached internal storage space sufficient for installing hypervisors locally and leveraging centralized storage for all virtual servers.

Raw storage is available in three different categories. We will now briefly introduce these main raw storage categories:

- **Direct Attached Storage (DAS)**: This is the storage available inside a server and is directly connected to the system through the motherboard. The cost and performance of this storage depends upon the disks and RAID controller cards inside the servers. DAS is less expensive and is simple to configure; however, it lacks the scalability, performance, and advanced features provided by high-end storages.

- **Network Attached Storage (NAS)**: This storage is usually an appliance providing filesystem access. This storage could be as simple as an NFS or CIFS share available to the servers. Typical NAS devices are cost-effective devices with not very high performance but with very high capacity with some redundancy for reliability.

  NAS is usually moderately expensive, simple to configure, and provides some advanced features; however, it also lacks scalability, performance, and advanced features provided by SAN.

- **Storage Area Network (SAN)**: This storage provides remote raw block-level storage to the connected servers. This type of storage provides maximum reliability, expandability, and performance. The cost of SAN is also very high compared to the other two storage options.

  SAN is the most resilient, highly scalable, and high performance storage; however, it is also the most expensive and complex to manage.

FC and iSCSI are the two main protocols for SAN connectivity. FC has its own standards and protocols provided by IEEE whereas iSCSI runs on top of standard Ethernet protocols. Both FC and iSCSI encapsulate **Small Computer System Interface (SCSI)** protocol commands.

Overview of FC and iSCSI storage

Both FC and iSCSI are used to encapsulate SCSI protocol commands for storage. We will briefly discuss SCSI first.

Overview of SCSI

SCSI (pronounced as "scuzzy") is an industry standard protocol for attaching various I/O peripherals such as printers, scanners, tape drives, and storage devices. The most common SCSI devices are disks and tape libraries.

SCSI has evolved from parallel, daisy-chained SCSI to serially attached SCSI (commonly known as SAS). Older parallel SCSI specifications are defined as Ultra-1, Ultra-2, Ultra-3, Ultra-320, and Ultra-640, whereas the new SAS specifications are defined as SAS 1.0, 2.0, and 3.0. These specifications differ in speed and other performance enhancements. SCSI hard disks are superior in terms of performance and reliability as compared with ATA (PATA and SATA) drives. SCSI drives are commonly used in enterprise-grade SANs because of their reliability and speed.

In SAN world, SCSI is the core protocol to connect raw hard disk storage with the servers. In order to control remote storage with the SCSI protocol, different technologies are used as wrappers to encapsulate these commands. These primarily include FC and iSCSI. In the next sections we'll briefly review these technologies.

Overview of Fiber Channel

The SCSI protocol was initially used inside computers to connect hard disks at a higher speed. Later, SANs were built where storage was separated from the computers and consolidated. The Fiber Channel protocol provided the infrastructure to encapsulate the SCSI traffic and provided connectivity between computers and storage. FC operates at speeds of 2, 4, 8, and 16 Gbps.

Fiber Chanel consists of the following:

- **Hard disk arrays**: They provide raw storage capacity
- **Storage processors**: They manage hard disks and provide storage LUNs and masking for the servers

- **Fiber Channel Switches** (also known as Fabric): They provide connectivity between storage processors and server HBAs

- **Fiber Channel Host Bus Adapters**: They are installed in the computer and provide connectivity to the SAN

Fiber Channel identifies infrastructure components with **World Wide Numbers** **(WWN)**. WWNs are 64-bit addresses which uniquely identify the FC devices. Like MAC addresses, it has bits assigned to vendors to identify their devices. Each end device (like an HBA port) is given a **World Wide Port Number** (**WWPN** or **pWWN**) and each connectivity device (like a Fabric switch) is given a **World Wide Node** **Number** (**WWNN**).

A Fiber Chanel HBA used for connecting to a SAN is known as an **initiator**, and Fiber Channel SAN providing disks as LUNs is known as a **target**.

The Fiber Channel protocol is different from Ethernet or TCP/IP protocols. Hence, it has its own learning curve for professionals with a networking and systems administration background.

Overview of iSCSI

Internet Small Computer System Interface (iSCSI) is SCSI over IP which SCSI commands using the TCP/IP protocol suite. This means that the SCSI commands are encapsulated on top of IP which commonly runs on Ethernet. Fiber Channel SANs typically have a very high cost because the Fiber Channel equipment is specialized. In comparison, iSCSI provides a cost-effective alternative to Fiber Channels because of the low cost of Ethernet equipment; also, the abundance of Ethernet experts as compared to Fiber Channel keeps the administration costs low. iSCSI was subject to lower performance due to the noisy nature of TCP/IP, causing higher protocol overload. Over the years, iSCSI performance and efficiency has improved. In fact, with the latest 10 Gbps implementation and future 40 Gbps/100 Gbps implementation, it is now a serious competitor to Fiber Channel.

iSCSI consists of the following

- **Hard disk arrays**: They provide raw storage capacity.

- **Storage processors**: They manage hard disks and provide storage LUNs and masking for the servers.

- **Ethernet switches**: They provide connectivity between storage processors and server HBAs.

- **iSCSI Host Bus Adapters**: They are installed in a computer and provide connectivity to the SAN. Most operating systems provide software implementation of iSCSI in order to utilize the regular Ethernet NICs, eliminating the need for hardware iSCSI HBAs.

Overview of Fiber Channel over Ethernet (FCoE)

Ethernet is widely used in networking. With some advancement such as **Data Center Ethernet (DCE)** and **Priority Flow Control (PFC)** in Ethernet to make it more reliable for the datacenter, Fiber Channel is now also implemented on top of Ethernet. This implementation is known as FCoE.

In FCoE, Fabric switches can be replaced with standard Ethernet switches which are more cost effective. Also, future development roadmap for Ethernet provides much higher speeds (40 Gbps and 100 Gbps) as compared to a native Fiber Channel. There is rapid adoption of FCoE in the market and chances are that FCoE will be completely extinct from the native Fiber Channel implementation in future.

Storage connectivity design considerations

UCS storage physical connectivity has a slightly different design consideration as compared to LAN physical connectivity. The following are some design considerations for SAN connectivity:

- Northbound storage physical connectivity does not support vPCs like LAN connectivity, where you can have cross-connected vPCs for redundancy.

- Port channels or trunking is possible to combine multiple storage uplink ports that provide physical link redundancy.

- Redundancy of storage resources is handled by the storage itself and varies from vendor to vendor including active-active, active-passive, **Asymmetric Logical Unit Assignment (ALUA)**, and so on.

- Storage can be connected through northbound Cisco Nexus, MDS or third-party Fabric Switches. This is the recommended configuration for better scalability and performance.

- It is possible to connect storage directly to UCS Fabric Interconnects, which is recommended for small implementations because of FI's physical ports consumption and increased processing requirements. Prior to UCSM Version 2.1, it was necessary to have a northbound Nexus or MDS switch to provide zoning configuration.

- Software configuration including VSANs and zoning is required for providing access to storage resources.

The following diagram provides an overview of storage connectivity. In the next sections, we will go through various storage configurations:

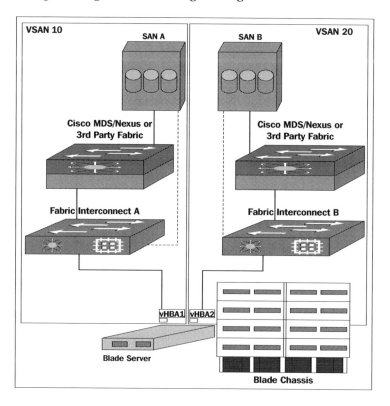

Learning about the FC switching mode

Similar to LAN connectivity, UCS Fabric Interconnects support two types of switching modes: Fiber Channel **End-host mode (EHM)** and Fiber Channel **Switching** mode. The default switching mode is end-host mode where UCS appears as a number of hosts attached to the upstream switch. This is also known as **NPV N Port Virtualization** and requires an NPIV-capable Fabric Switch for providing the Fiber login services.

The other option available is the native Fiber Channel Switching mode where UCS Fabric Interconnect appears as a native Fiber Channel Fabric Switch. Switching between Fiber Channel modes is a disruptive process and hence should be arranged in a scheduled maintenance window.

In order to configure or verify end-host mode for the Fabric Interconnects, perform the following steps:

1. Log in to UCS Manager.

2. Click on the **Equipment** tab in the Navigation pane.

3. In the **Equipment** tab, click on a **Fabric Interconnect**.

4. The **Status** area in the Work pane shows the current FC Mode configuration which is **End Host**.

5. In the **Actions** area of the Work pane, the currently configured FC mode, which in this case is **End Host**, will be shown grayed:

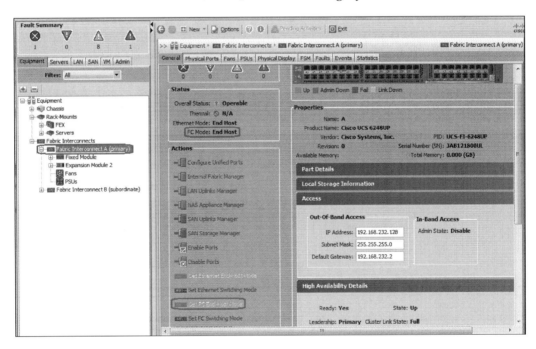

A Fabric Interconnect reboot is required in order to change the Fiber Channel mode from **End Host** to **Switch** and vice versa.

In order to change the **FC Mode** from **End Host** to **Switch**, perform the following steps:

1. Log in to UCS Manager.
2. Click on the **Equipment** tab in the Navigation pane.
3. In the **Equipment** tab, click on a **Fabric Interconnect**.
4. In the **Actions** area of the Work pane, the currently configured **FC Mode**, which in this case is **End Host**, will be shown grayed and cannot be selected.
5. Click on **Set FC Switching Mode** in the **Actions** area of the Work pane.
6. Click on **Yes** on the pop-up warning message to restart the Fabric Interconnect:

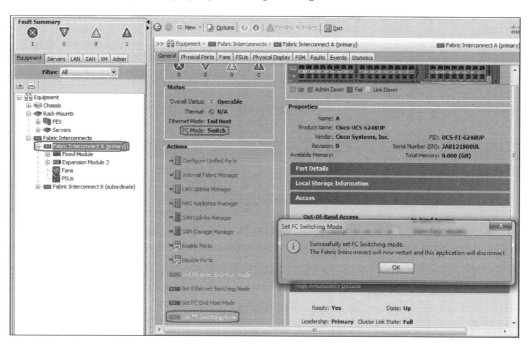

Configuring the FC port channel and trunking

Similar to an Ethernet port channel, a Fiber Channel port channel or trunk can be created to aggregate multiple physical Fiber Channel links into a single logical link to provide higher throughput and redundancy. A maximum of 16 uplink ports can be aggregated in a port channel. Perform the following steps to configure the FCoE port channel:

1. Log in to UCS Manager.
2. Click on the **SAN** tab in the Navigation pane.
3. In the **SAN** tab, expand **SAN** and then **SAN Cloud**.
4. Right-click on **FCoE Port Channel** and click on **Create FCoE Port Channel**:

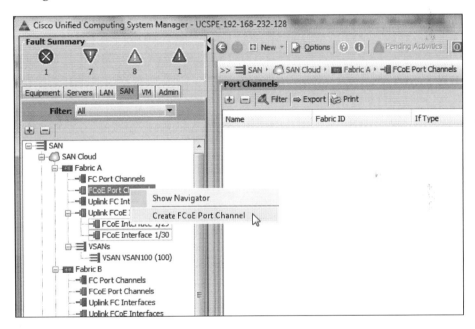

5. In the pop-up window, set the port channel **ID** and **Name**.
6. Click on **Add Ports**.

7. On the next screen, drag appropriate ports to the port channel **Add Ports**.

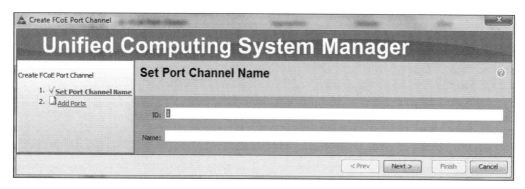

8. Repeat steps for both VSANs.

Configuring VSAN and zoning

Storage connectivity not only requires the configuration of connectivity protocols such as FC, FCoE, and iSCSI, but in case of FC and FCoE SAN connectivity, it is also required to configure zoning to allow access to servers/hypervisors to the SAN LUNs. When using Cisco switches for SAN connectivity, it is also recommended to configure VSANs along with proper zoning. We will now look into zoning and VSANs.

Learning about zoning

Zoning is a conventional SAN security mechanism which is used to restrict storage access between anticipated targets (typically SANs) and initiators (typically servers). There are two main methods to configure zoning: soft zoning and hard zoning. Hard zoning is more secure compared to soft zoning and is the preferred zoning method. SAN Fabric Switches from various vendors might support different zoning configurations, so it is always recommended to consult your SAN admin for proper zoning configuration.

In the previous UCS versions including Version 2.0, while using Cisco switches for SAN connectivity, zoning needed to be configured on the northbound MDS or Nexus (with native FC ports) switches which propagates down to the directly connected Fabric Interconnects. So, even though SAN direct connectivity to Fabric Interconnects was possible, northbound MDS or Nexus switches were necessary for the zoning configuration. Avoiding the northbound switch, one rudimentary configuration was to configure everything in the default zone, which is analogous to allowing access to all and is not recommended because of security concerns.

Prior to the UCS 2.1 upgrade, it was not possible to configure zoning directly on the Fabric Interconnects.

Learning about VSAN

VSAN is a Cisco proprietary security mechanism which can be compared to VLANs for the networks. VSAN can further increase security for storage and servers by allowing only the physical member ports of storage and servers to physically access each other. Like VLANs, if a port on the same Fabric switch is not part of a VSAN, it will not have access to SAN. There are a number of ways that SAN could be connected with UCS servers which include the following:

- **Cisco Fiber Channel MDS switches**: MDS switches are Cisco Fiber Channel SAN connectivity switches. These switches deal with the SAN protocols and are recommended in large-scale environments requiring a dedicated SAN infrastructure.

- **FC module expansion or Unified ports in Cisco Nexus switches**: Cisco Nexus 5000 series switches provide FC module expansion to provide FC ports with SAN connectivity. The newer 5500 series switches have unified ports like the Fabric Interconnects which can be configured as Ethernet, FC, or FCoE. These switches are recommended for medium to large-scale infrastructures.

- **Direct with Fabric Interconnects**: The Fabric Interconnect provides unified ports which can be configured as Ethernet, FC, or FCoE, and hence storage can be directly attached with the Fabric Interconnects. This is recommended for a small-scale deployment.

- **Third-party Fabric switches**: Fabric switches from other vendors like Brocade can also be used to connect storage to Cisco UCS.

Example configuration – connecting SAN directly to Fabric Interconnects

In our example, we will connect the SAN directly with Fabric Interconnects with zoning configured on them. With UCS Version 2.1, it is now possible to configure zoning directly on the Fabric Interconnects using different SAN policies. In our example, we will configure VSAN and zoning directly on the Fabric Interconnects to attach the FCoE directly.

The following diagram shows the physical connectivity between the chassis, Fabric Interconnects, and SAN:

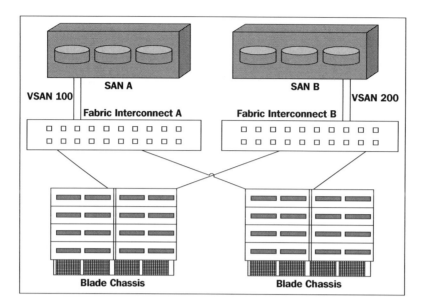

In order to configure VSANs for Fabric Interconnects, perform the follow procedure:

1. Log in to UCS Manager.
2. Click on the **SAN** tab in the Navigation pane.
3. In the **SAN** tab, expand **SAN** and then **SAN Cloud**.
4. Right-click on **VSANs** and click on **Create VSAN**.

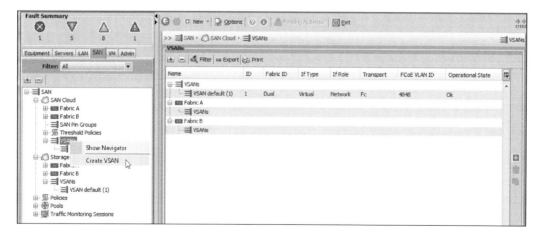

5. In the pop-up window, assign a name to the VSAN.

6. For the **Zoning** section, click on the **Enabled** radio button of **FC Zone**.

7. Attach **Zone** to the Fabric Interconnect **A** or **B**.

8. Assign a VSAN ID and its corresponding VLAN ID. The VLAN ID does not need to be the same number as VSAN ID, however, it is a good practice to keep it so. Also, a VLAN ID used for VSAN mapping cannot overlap with that of an Ethernet VLAN.

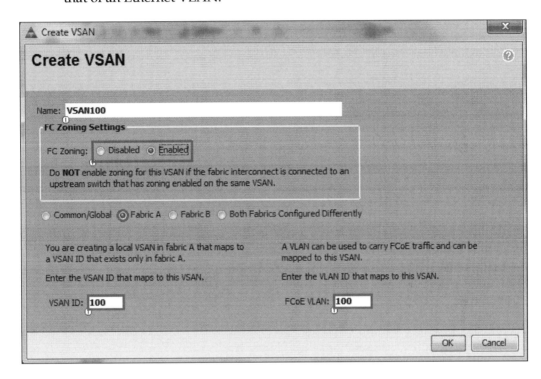

Create the required VSANs and configure ports for the VSAN membership. In our example, we created two VSANs for connecting two separate SAN processes.

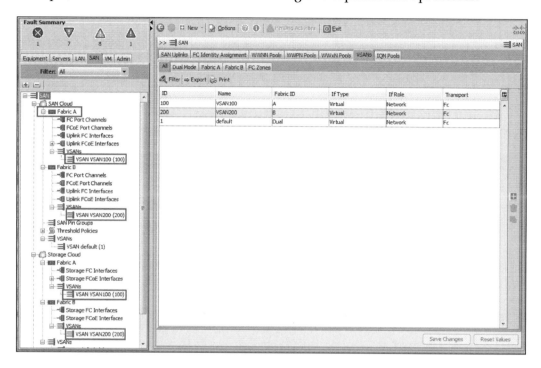

Once the physical connectivity is established, the following will configure the zoning for the servers and SAN:

- **Storage connection policies**: This configures the storage connectivity including the WWPN Target numbers for the SAN
- **SAN connectivity policies configuration**: This configures vHBAs for the servers which will provide WWPN Initiator numbers for the servers

First, we will configure the storage connection policy by performing the following steps:

1. Log in to UCS Manager.
2. Click on the **SAN** tab in the Navigation pane.
3. In the **SAN** tab, expand **SAN** and then expand **Policies**.
4. Right-click on **Storage Connection Policies** and click on **Storage Connection Policy**.

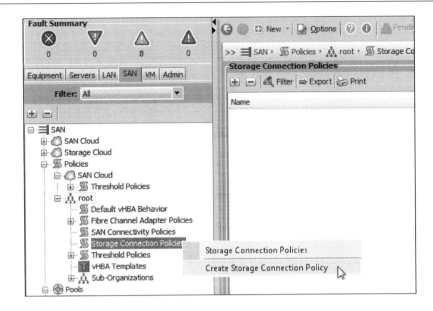

5. In the pop-up window, assign a name to the storage connection policy.

6. Select **Zoning Type**. The recommended and most secure zoning option is the **Single Initiator Single Target**. Consult your storage documentation for zoning recommendations.

7. Click on the **+** sign to define **FC Target Endpoints**. This is the WWPNs of the SAN and this information will be available from the SAN storage processors.

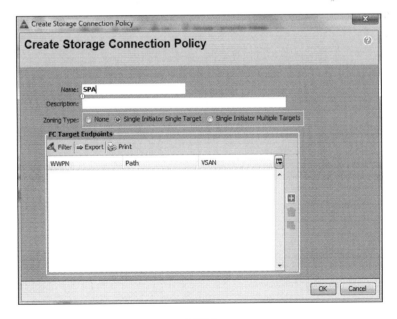

8. On the next screen, manually type the WWPN of the SAN storage processors.

9. Select the Fabric Interconnect **A** or **B** and select a VSAN membership for the storage processors. Click on **OK**:

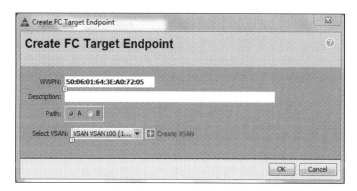

10. Repeat the steps for the second storage processor for the other Fabric Interconnect and VSAN.

Now we will configure the SAN connectivity policy using the following steps:

1. Log in to UCS Manager.

2. Click on the **SAN** tab in the Navigation pane.

3. In the **SAN** tab, expand **SAN** and then expand **Policies**.

4. Right-click on **SAN Connectivity Policies** and click on **Create SAN Connectivity Policy**:

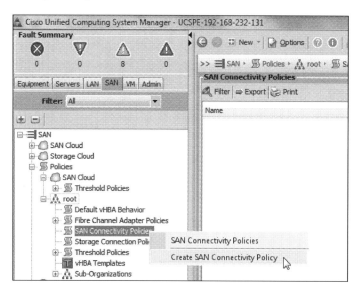

5. In the pop-up window, assign a name to the SAN connectivity policy.

6. Select a predefined World Wide Node Name Pool for the servers or create a new pool by clicking on the + sign close to **Create WWNN Pool**.

7. Click on **Add** to create vHBAs for the servers. vHBAs can be created with a number of different methods. However, as vNICs, the recommended method is to create vHBA templates and then use those templates for creating the vHBAs.

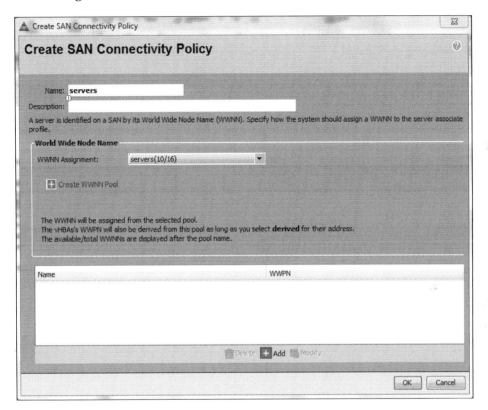

8. Clicking on **Add** in the previous step pops up a new window for the vHBA creation.

9. Provide a name for the vHBA and select **Use vHBA Template** for the creation of the vHBA.

10. Select the required vHBA template and an appropriate **Adapter Performance Profile** for the creation of vHBAs:

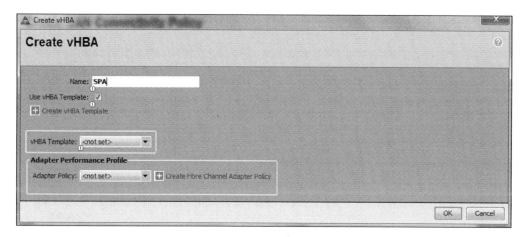

11. New vHBAs will appear in the policy. When this policy is applied during a service profile creation, the vHBAs are automatically created with all configurations for the server:

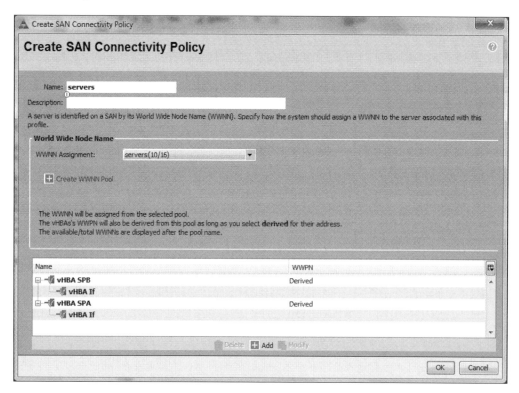

12. Once the SAN connectivity policy is configured, expand it in the Navigation pane. In the Work pane, click on the **vHBA Initiator Groups** tab and create vHBA initiators for both the vHBAs by clicking on the **+** sign on the right-hand side of the Work pane:

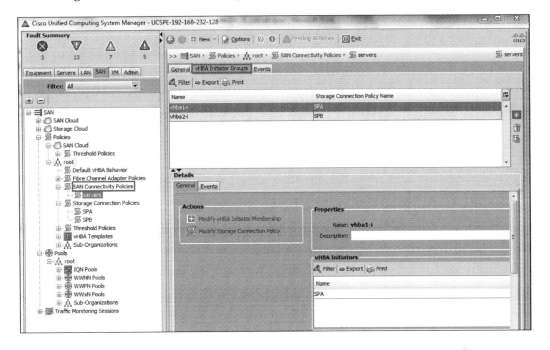

13. In the new window, type a name and a short description for **vHBA Initiator Group**, select a **Storage Connection Policy**. Repeat the steps for the other vHBA initiator groups:

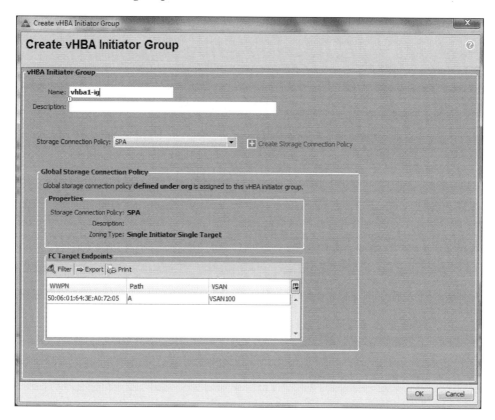

14. New vHBAs will appear in the policy. When this policy is applied during a service profile creation, the vHBAs are automatically created with all configurations for the server.

Zoning is automatically configured for the server vHBAs during the service profile creation using the SAN connectivity policy and storage connection policy. The policies could be applied directly to a service profile or to a service profile template (the procedure for both is the same).

In order to create a service profile or a service profile template, perform the following steps:

1. Log in to UCS Manager.

2. Click on the **Servers** tab in the Navigation pane and click on **Create Service Profile (expert)** or **Create Service Profile Template**.

3. In the third step, where vHBAs for the storage are created, select **Use Connectivity Policy** and click on **Next**:

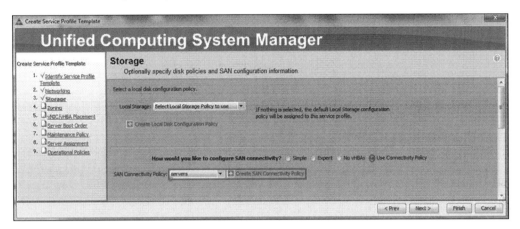

4. This will create the vHBAs for the new server:

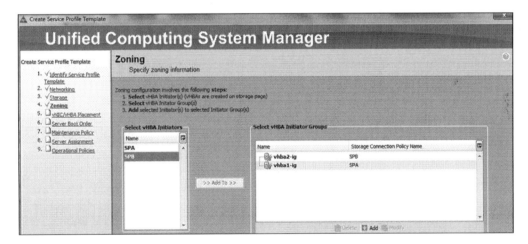

5. Create vHBA initiator groups for both vHBAs.

6. Assign a name to **vHBA Initiator Group**.

7. Assign the previously created storage connection policy. This will associate the FC target endpoint (storage processor WWPN) and VSAN to the vHBA initiator group.

8. Repeat the same steps for the second vHBA initiator group for the second storage processor and VSAN connectivity:

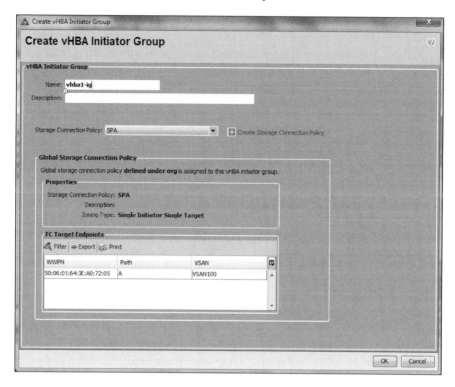

Once the service profile creation is complete, the zoning configuration can be verified by performing the following steps:

1. On the **Servers** tab in the Navigation pane, select **FC Zones** from the Work pane.

2. Click on the **+** sign to expand the information which will provide an initiator to target zone mapping:

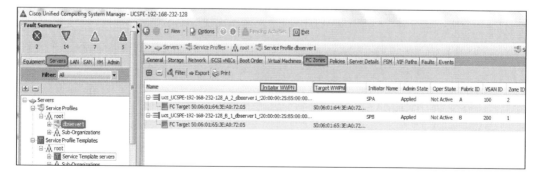

Configuring FCoE

FCoE traffic requires dedicated Ethernet VLANs. FCoE VLANs are dedicated during the VSAN configuration. Starting with UCS 2.0 and later, the FCoE VLAN must not conflict with Ethernet VLANs. UCS 2.1 provides FCoE northbound from FI whereas the previous version of FCoE was only possible up to FI where it should be decoded into native FC.

Configuring FCoE involves selecting the Fabric Interconnect unified ports as FCoE ports. To do this, perform the following steps:

1. Log in to UCS Manager.

2. Click on the **Equipment** tab in the Navigation pane.

3. Expand **Fabric Interconnect** and right-click on any unconfigured unified port and select **Configure as FCoE Uplink Port** or **Configure as FCoE Storage Port**:

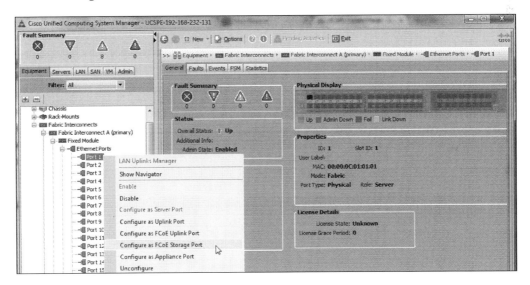

Manual and automatic uplink pinning

Using the end-host mode (NPV), each server is pinned to an uplink port based on Round-robin algorithm. Like Ethernet end-host mode, pin groups can be configured as a static pin group or dynamic pin group. The default configuration is dynamic pin group.

Dynamic pin groups

This is the default pin group setting. In dynamic pinning, the Fabric Interconnect automatically binds server vHBAs to uplink Fabric Interconnect FC/FCoE ports.

Failure response

In case of an uplink failure, server vHBAs are re-pinned to the remaining uplinks of the same Fabric Interconnect. In case of a complete Fabric Interconnect failure, the operating system (Windows, Linux, or hypervisors) relies on its multipath drives (such as MPIO and EMC PowerPath) to re-route I/O for the failed path. If the operating system configuration is missing, Fiber Channel communication will fail until one Fiber Channel uplink is restored on the failed Fabric Interconnect.

This behavior is different from the Ethernet automatic re-pinning and is in accordance with the design goals of SAN connectivity.

Static pin groups

In static pinning, SAN pin groups are defined by the administrator on Fabric Interconnects using UCSM, which can be assigned to vHBAs or vHBA templates. Static pin groups are defined under the **SAN** tab of the UCSM Navigation pane. In case of static pinning, if the uplink goes down, automatic re-pinning will not occur.

The steps for creating a static pin group and assigning to a vHBA are as follows:

1. Log in to UCS Manager.
2. Click on the **SAN** tab in the Navigation pane.
3. In the **SAN** tab, right-click on **SAN Pin Group** or click on the **+** sign on the right-hand side to create a new global SAN pin group:

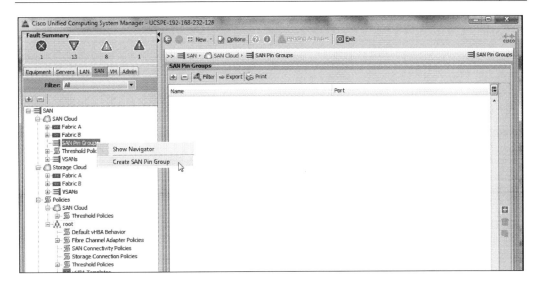

4. In the pop-up window, provide a name for the SAN pin group and bind the interfaces (uplink ports or port channels) to each Fabric Interconnect.

5. Click on **OK** to complete the configuration. A pop-up message will appear to make sure that the selected uplinks are in the same layer 2 network:

Failure response re-pinning

Each vHBA is statically pinned to a single Fabric Interconnect uplink port or port channel using manual configuration.

In case of a northbound uplink, port channel, or Fabric Interconnect complete failure to which a server is statically pinned to, unlike Ethernet pinning, the server connection will not be transferred to the other Fabric Interconnect for dynamic re-pinning, and as discussed, the multipath I/O driver of the operating system running on the server will be responsible for recognizing the path failure. If the multipath configuration is missing in the OS, communication will be stopped until the link is restored.

Summary

In this chapter, we learned about different storage connectivity protocols including Fiber Channel and iSCSI. We looked into configuring FCoE and zoning directly on the Fabric Interconnect's storage connectivity which involves some SAN policies configuration. iSCSI is SCSI over IP, and requires vNICs and Ethernet for connectivity and no special configuration is required other than what was explained in *Chapter 4, Configuring LAN Connectivity*. Finally we looked into SAN pin groups which have the same concepts as LAN pin groups, but have a slightly different failure behavior.

In the next chapter, we will look into Identity and Resource Pools which provide resources such as UUIDs, MAC addresses, WWNN, and WWPN numbers for the service profiles for the servers.

6
Creating Identity and Resource Pools

Computers and their various peripherals have some unique identities such as **Universally Unique Identifiers (UUIDs)**, **Media Access Control (MAC)** addresses of **Network Interface Cards (NICs)**, **World Wide Node Numbers (WWNNs)** for **Host Bus Adapters (HBAs)**, and others. These identities are used to uniquely identify a computer system in a network. For traditional computers and peripherals, these identities were burned into the hardware and, hence, couldn't be altered easily. Operating systems and some applications rely on these identities and may fail if these identities are changed. In case of a full computer system failure or failure of a computer peripheral with unique identity, administrators have to follow cumbersome firmware upgrade procedures to replicate the identities of the failed components on the replacement components.

The **Unified Computing System (UCS)** platform introduced the idea of creating identity and resource pools to abstract the compute node identities from the **UCS Manager (UCSM)** instead of using the hardware burned-in identities. In this chapter, we'll discuss the different pools you can create during UCS deployments and server provisioning. We'll start by looking at what pools are and then discuss the different types of pools and show how to configure each of them.

The list of topics that will be covered in the chapter is as follows:

- Understanding identity and resource pools
- Learning to create a UUID pool
- Learning to create a MAC pool
- Learning to create a WWNN pool
- Learning to create a WWPN pool
- Understanding the server pool
- Learning to create server pool membership and qualification policies

Understanding identity and resource pools

The salient feature of the Cisco UCS platform is stateless computing. In the Cisco UCS platform, none of the computer peripherals consume the hardware burned-in identities. Rather, all the unique characteristics are extracted from identity and resource pools, which reside on the **Fabric Interconnects (FIs)** and are managed using UCSM. These resource and identity pools are defined in an XML format, which makes them extremely portable and easily modifiable. UCS computers and peripherals extract these identities from UCSM in the form of a service profile. A service profile has all the server identities including UUIDs, MACs, WWNNs, firmware versions, BIOS settings, and other server settings. A service profile is associated with the physical server using customized Linux OS that assigns all the settings in a service profile to the physical server. In case of server failure, the failed server needs to be removed and the replacement server has to be associated with the existing service profile of the failed server. In this service profile association process, the new server will automatically pick up all the identities of the failed server, and the operating system or applications dependent upon these identities will not observe any change in the hardware. In case of peripheral failure, the replacement peripheral will automatically acquire the identities of the failed component. This greatly improves the time required to recover a system in case of a failure.

Using service profiles with the identity and resource pools also greatly improves the server provisioning effort. A service profile with all the settings can be prepared in advance while an administrator is waiting for the delivery of the physical server. The administrator can create service profile templates that can be used to create hundreds of service profiles; these profiles can be associated with the physical servers with the same hardware specifications. Creating a server template is highly recommended as this greatly reduces the time for server provisioning. This is because a template can be created once and used for any number of physical servers with the same hardware.

Server identity and resource pools are created using the UCSM. In order to better organize, it is possible to define as many pools as are needed in each category. Keep in mind that each defined resource will consume space in the UCSM database. It is, therefore, a best practice to create identity and resource pool ranges based on the current and near-future assessments.

For larger deployments, it is best practice to define a hierarchy of resources in the UCSM based on geographical, departmental, or other criteria; for example, a hierarchy can be defined based on different departments. This hierarchy is defined as an organization, and the resource pools can be created for each organizational unit. In the UCSM, the main organization unit is root, and further suborganizations can be defined under this organization. The only consideration to be kept in mind is that pools defined under one organizational unit can't be migrated to other organizational units unless they are deleted first and then created again where required.

The following diagram shows how identity and resource pools provide unique features to a stateless blade server and components such as the mezzanine card:

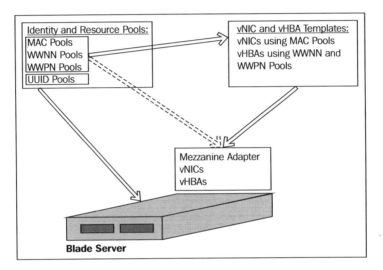

Learning to create a UUID pool

UUID is a 128-bit number assigned to every compute node on a network to identify the compute node globally. UUID is denoted as 32 hexadecimal numbers. In the Cisco UCSM, a server UUID can be generated using the UUID suffix pool. The UCSM software generates a unique prefix to ensure that the generated compute node UUID is unique.

Operating systems including hypervisors and some applications may leverage UUID number binding. The UUIDs generated with a resource pool are portable. In case of a catastrophic failure of the compute node, the pooled UUID assigned through a service profile can be easily transferred to a replacement compute node without going through complex firmware upgrades.

Following are the steps to create UUIDs for the blade servers:

1. Log in to the UCSM screen.
2. Click on the **Servers** tab in the navigation pane.
3. Click on the **Pools** tab and expand **root**.
4. Right-click on **UUID Suffix Pools** and click on **Create UUID Suffix Pool** as shown in the following screenshot:

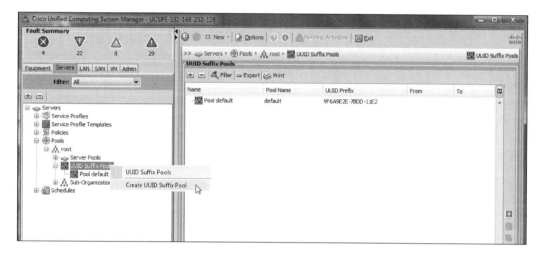

5. In the pop-up window, assign the **Name** and **Description** values to the UUID pool.
6. Leave the **Prefix** value as **Derived** to make sure that UCSM makes the prefix unique.
7. The selection of **Assignment Order** as **Default** is random. Select **Sequential** to assign the UUID sequentially.

8. Click on **Next** as shown in the following screenshot:

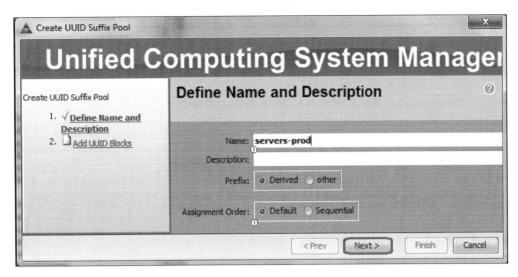

9. Click on **Add** in the next screen.

10. In the pop-up window, change the value for **Size** to create a desired number of UUIDs.

11. Click on **OK** and then on **Finish** in the previous screen as shown in the following screenshot:

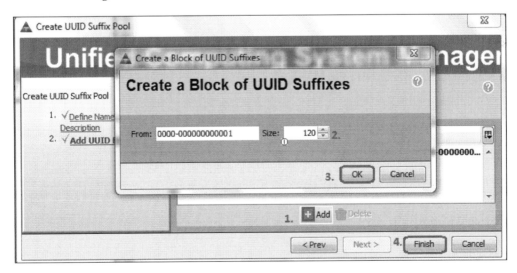

12. In order to verify the UUID suffix pool, click on the **UUID Suffix Pools** tab in the navigation pane and then on the **UUID Suffixes** tab in the work pane as shown in the following screenshot:

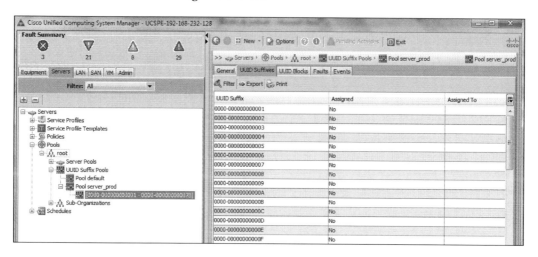

Learning to create a MAC pool

MAC is a 48-bit address assigned to the network interface for communication in the physical network. MAC address pools make server provisioning easier by providing scalable NIC configurations before the actual deployment.

Following are the steps to create MAC pools:

1. Log in to the UCSM screen.
2. Click on the **LAN** tab in the navigation pane.
3. Click on the **Pools** tab and expand **root**.

4. Right-click on **MAC Pools** and click on **Create MAC Pool** as shown in the following screenshot:

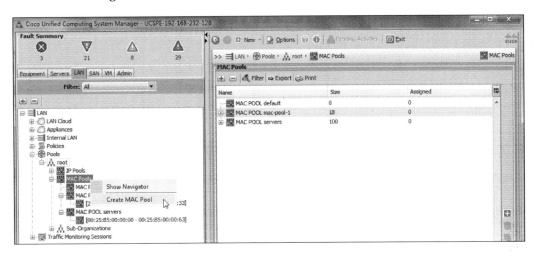

5. In the pop-up window, assign the **Name** and **Description** values to the MAC pool.

6. The selection of **Default** as the **Assignment Order** value is random. Select **Sequential** to assign the MAC addresses sequentially.

7. Click on **Next** as shown in the following screenshot:

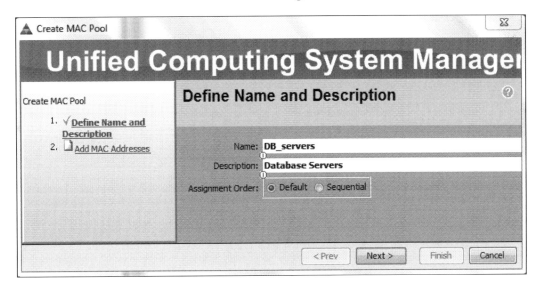

8. Click on **Add** in the next screen.

9. In the pop-up window, change **Size** to create the desired number of MAC addresses.

10. Click on **OK** and then on **Finish** in the previous screen as shown in the following screenshot:

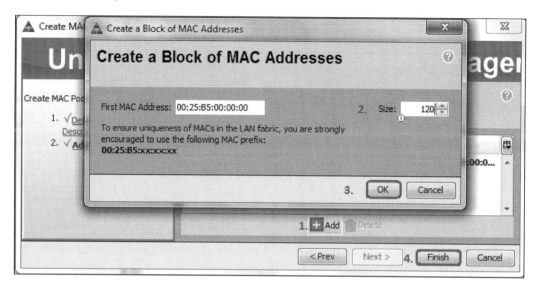

11. In order to verify the MAC pool, click on the **MAC Pools** tab in the navigation pane and then on the **MAC Addresses** tab in the work pane as shown in the following screenshot:

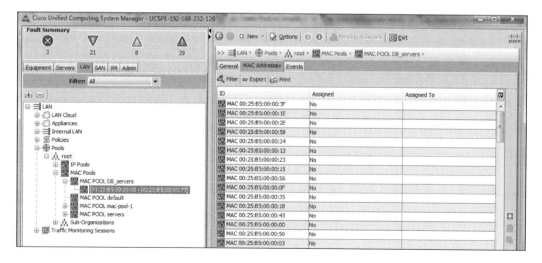

Learning to create a WWNN pool

WWNN is a 64-bit address assigned to **Fiber Channel (FC)** devices. In UCS, WWNN is assigned to the mezzanine card installed in a blade server because a mezzanine card can have more than one port (vHBA). Each port (vHBA) created from the mezzanine card acquires a unique **World Wide Port Number (WWPN)**. (WWPN has been described in the next section.)

Following are the steps to create WWNN address pools:

1. Log in to the UCSM screen.
2. Click on the **SAN** tab in the navigation pane.
3. Click on the **Pools** tab and expand **root**.
4. Right-click on **WWNN Pools** and click on **Create WWNN Pool** as shown in the following screenshot:

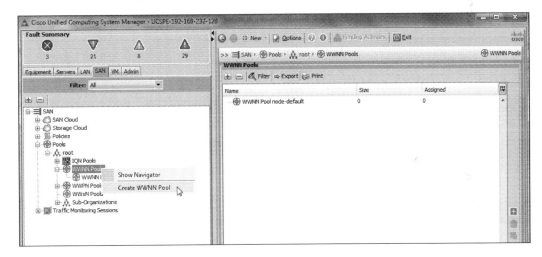

5. In the pop-up window, assign the **Name** and **Description** values to the WWNN pool.
6. The selection of **Default** as the **Assignment Order** value is random. Select **Sequential** to assign the WWNNs sequentially.

7. Click on **Next** as shown in the following screenshot:

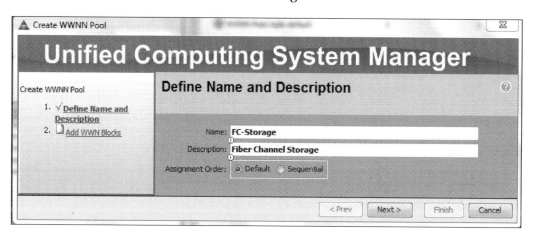

8. Click on **Add** in the next screen.

9. In the pop-up window, change **Size** to create the desired number of WWNN addresses.

10. Click on **OK** and then on **Finish** in the previous screen as shown in the following screenshot:

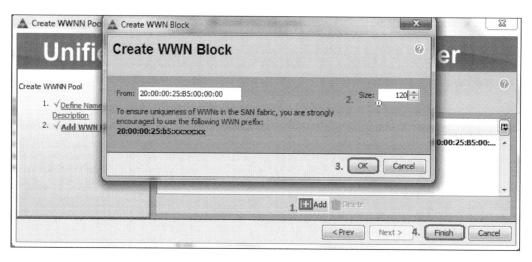

11. In order to verify the WWNN pool, click on the **WWNN Pools** tab in the navigation pane and then on the **General** tab in the work pane as shown in the following screenshot:

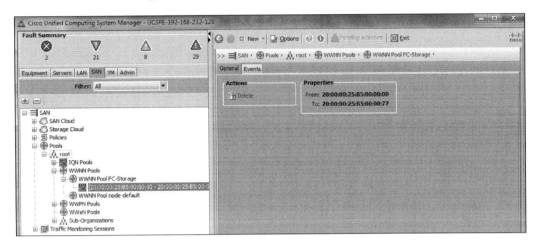

Learning to create a WWPN pool

Similar in format to WWNN, WWPN is a 64-bit address assigned to individual vHBAs in servers. The WWNN for the vHBAs in a blade server is always the same, whereas WWPN is always unique.

Following are the steps to create WWNN address pools:

1. Log in to the UCSM screen.
2. Click on the **SAN** tab in the navigation pane.
3. Click on the **Pools** tab and expand **root**.

4. Right-click on **WWPN Pools** and click on **Create WWPN Pool** as shown in the following screenshot:

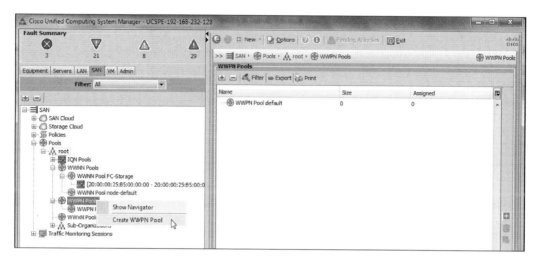

5. In the pop-up window, assign the **Name** and **Description** values to the WWPN pool.

6. Selection of **Default** as the **Assignment Order** value is random. Select **Sequential** to assign WWPNs sequentially.

7. Click on **Next** as shown in the following screenshot:

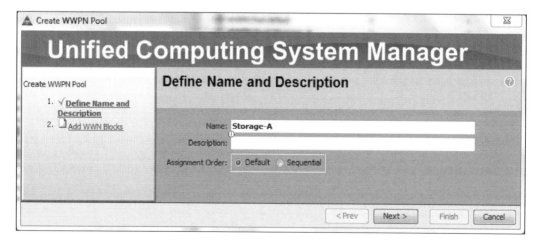

8. Click on **Add** in the next screen.

9. In the pop-up window, change **Size** to create the desired number of WWPN addresses.

10. Click on **OK** and then on **Finish** in the previous screen as shown in the following screenshot:

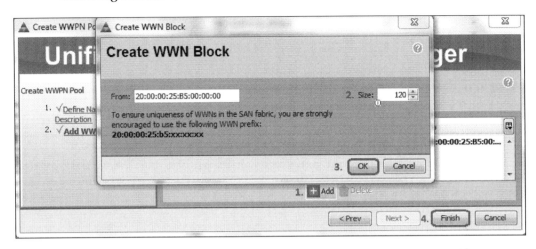

11. In order to verify the WWPN pool, click on the **WWPN Pools** tab in the navigation pane and click on the **General** tab in the work pane as shown in the following screenshot:

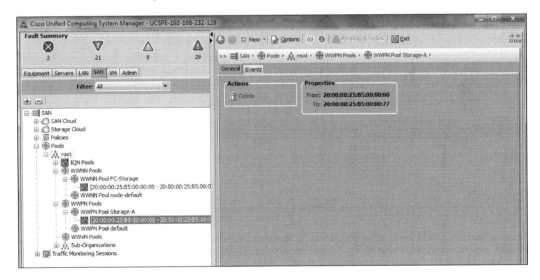

To ensure the uniqueness of WWNN and WWPN pools, only use WWN numbers from 20:00:00:00:00:00:00:00 to 20:FF:FF:FF:FF:FF:FF:FF or from 50:00:00:00:00:00:00:00 to 5F:FF:FF:FF:FF:FF:FF:FF. To ensure the uniqueness of the Cisco UCS WWNNs and WWPNs in the SAN fabric, it is recommended to use the prefix in a pool as 20:00:00:25:B5:XX:XX:XX.

Making your identity pools meaningful

Although not a requirement, it is beneficial to implement some naming hierarchy when creating MAC, WWNN, and WWPN identity pool addresses. This naming hierarchy could be very helpful in troubleshooting scenarios such as network traces and SAN zoning. We will take an example of a MAC pool to implement a simple naming hierarchy. Using these guidelines, you can create the naming hierarchy for any pool.

Cisco MAC pools have the 00:25:B5:XX:XX:XX format, where 00:25:B5 is the Cisco organizational identifier. Now, we have the other six hexadecimal numbers in which we can implement the naming convention.

In our example, we will use the following convention. You can always come up with other suitable guidelines according to your environment:

- Use one hexadecimal number to represent your site or location
- Use one hexadecimal number to represent the cabinet where the chassis is located
- Use one hexadecimal number to represent the primary FI
- Use one hexadecimal number to represent the server operating system

In the following diagram of an example, we can easily identify the server, which is located at the primary site in cabinet one, the chassis number as 3, and the operating system running on the server as Windows:

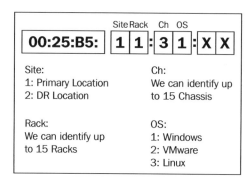

Understanding server pools

Server pools are used to organize servers based on specific criteria such as CPU family, amount of RAM, type of mezzanine card, power, and others. Each server is associated with a unique service profile to receive all the settings. A server pool can be associated with a service profile. UCSM automatically selects an available server in the server pool and associates it with a service profile.

Server pools can be manually populated or they can be autopopulated using server pool policies. Server pools make the servers available for association with service profiles. It is possible to have a server in more than one server pool at the same time.

In order to create and manually populate the server pool, carry out the following steps:

1. Log in to the UCSM screen.

2. Click on the **Servers** tab in the navigation pane.

3. Click on the **Pools** tab and expand **root**.

4. Right-click on **Server Pools** and click on **Create Server Pool** as shown in the following screenshot:

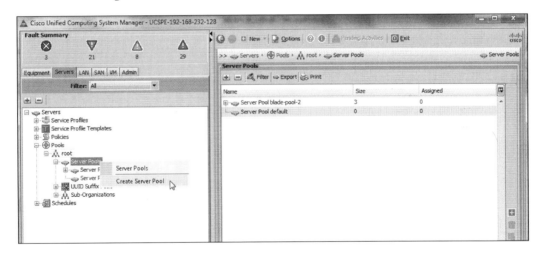

5. In the pop-up window, assign the **Name** and **Description** values to the server pool.

6. Click on **Next** as shown in the following screenshot:

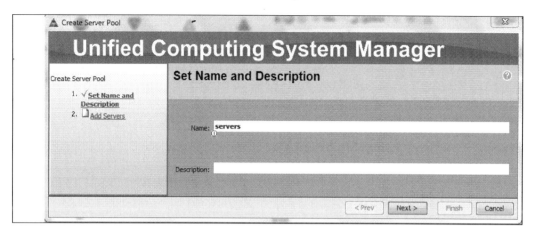

7. Add servers to the pool by selecting the servers provided on the left side and adding them to the list of **Pooled Servers** on the right side.

8. Click on **Finish** after adding servers to the pool as shown in the following screenshot:

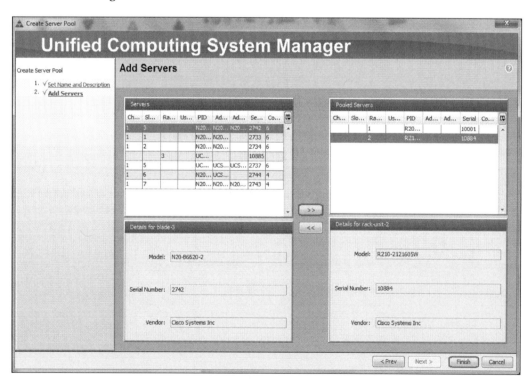

Learning to create server pool membership and qualification policies

Server pools can be automatically populated with servers that match the specifications based on the defined policy settings using **Server Pool Policy Qualifications** and by applying these qualification policies using **Server Pool Policies** under the **Servers** tab in the navigation pane.

First, we will discuss how to create server qualification policies using the options available in the **Server Pool Policy Qualifications** policy.

The steps to create this policy are as follows:

1. Log in to the UCSM screen.
2. Click on the **Servers** tab in the navigation pane.
3. Click on the **Policies** tab and expand **root**.
4. Right-click on **Server Pool Policy Qualifications** and click on **Create Server Pool Policy Qualification** as shown in the following screenshot:

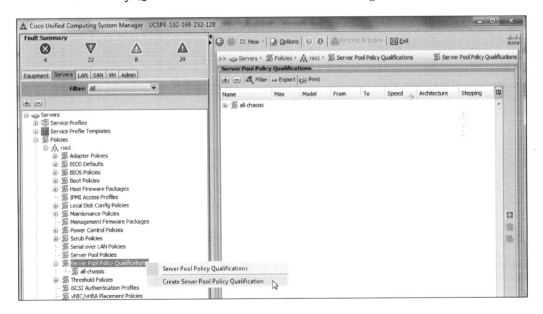

5. In the pop-up window, assign the **Name** and **Description** values to the server pool policy qualifications.

6. In the left pane, click on the options to define the new server pool policy qualifications as shown in the following screenshot:

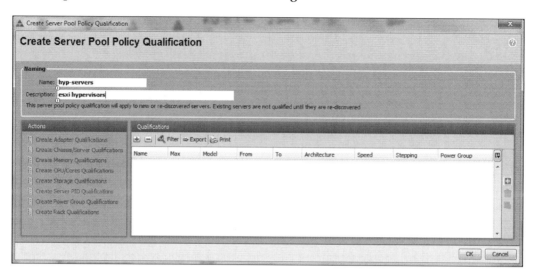

7. The first option in the left pane is **Create Adapter Qualifications**. This setting defines the type of adapters a qualifying server must have. Select the **Type** of the adapter from the drop-down list. It is also possible to select a unique adapter based on the **Process Identifier (PID)** and capacity, which could be from 1 to 65535 as shown in the following screenshot:

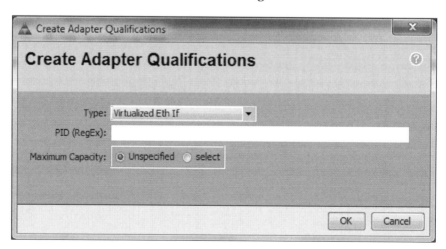

8. The second option is **Create Chassis/Server Qualifications**. This setting defines the **First Chassis ID** and **Number of Chassis** values for the total number of chassis to be included in the pool, starting with the **First chassis ID** value as shown in the following screenshot:

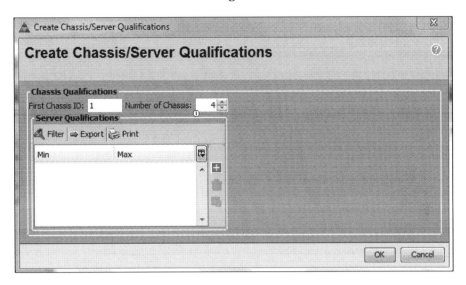

9. Click on the plus sign to select the server slots in each qualified chassis.

10. Select the values for **First Slot ID** and **Number of Slots**, which is the total number of server slots to be included, starting with **First Slot ID**.

11. Click on **Finish Stage** as shown in the following screenshot:

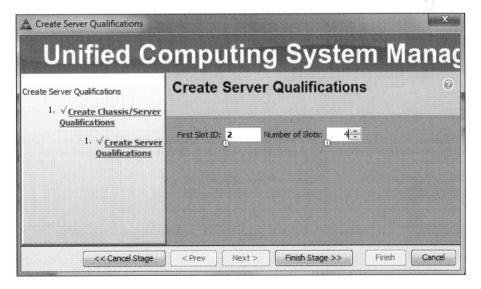

12. The minimum and maximum slot ID will be automatically populated in the previous screen.

13. Click on **Finish** to complete the policy creation as shown in the following screenshot:

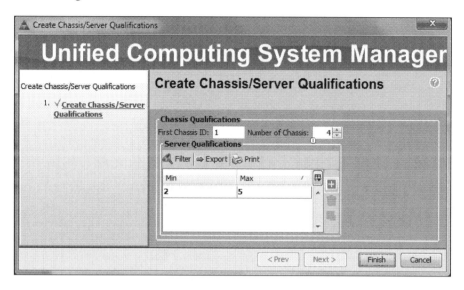

14. The third option is **Create Memory Qualifications**. This option defines the memory characteristics of the servers for qualification. The options include clock speed **Clock (MHz)**, **Latency (ns)**, minimum and maximum memory size **Min Cap (MB)** and **Max Cap (MB)**, data bus **Width**, and data bus width measurement **Units** as shown in the following screenshot:

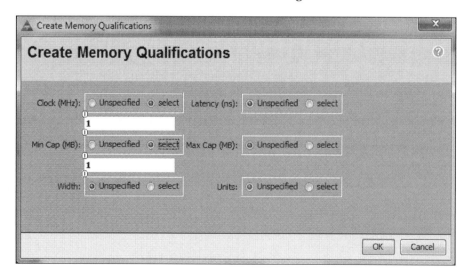

15. The fourth option is **Create CPU/Cores Qualifications**. This option defines the CPU characteristics of the servers for qualification. The options include **Processor Architecture, PID (RegEx), Min Number of Cores, Max Number of Cores, Min Number of Threads, Max Number of Threads, CPU speed (MHz)**, and **CPU Stepping** as shown in the following screenshot:

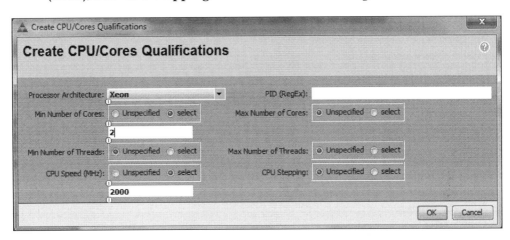

16. The fifth option is **Create Storage Qualifications**. This option defines the storage features of the qualifying servers. The options include the **Diskless** disk status, the **Number of Blocks** value in the disk, **Block Size (Bytes)**, minimum/maximum storage capacity across all disks **Min Cap (MB)** and **Max Cap (MB)**, minimum storage capacity per disk **Per Disk Cap (MB)**, and number of **Units** as shown in the following screenshot:

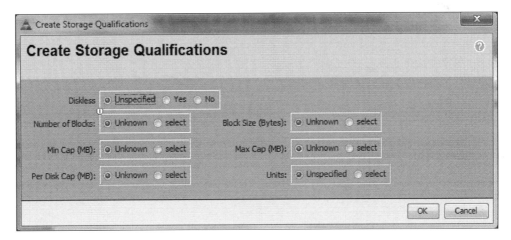

17. The sixth option is **Create Server PID Qualifications**. This is a regular expression string that the server PID must match in order to qualify as shown in the following screenshot:

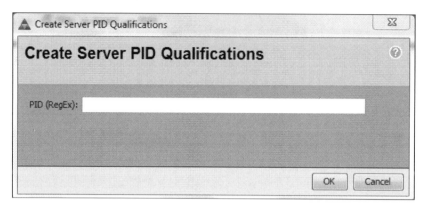

18. The seventh option is **Create Power Group Qualifications**. This policy could match a server based on the server **Power Group** value as shown in the following screenshot:

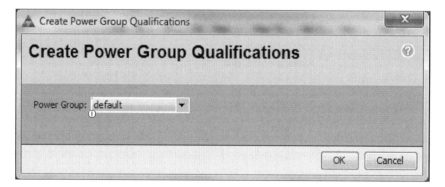

19. The last option is **Create Rack Qualifications**. This option is only applicable if there are some rack-mount servers managed by the UCSM. The **First Slot ID** value is the first server to be included, and the **Number of Slots** value defines the total number of servers to be included starting from the first slot ID as shown in the following screenshot:

Once we have defined the desired **Server Pool Policy Qualification** policies, we can use the **Server Pool Policies** tab to associate qualifying servers to be automatically added to an already created empty server pool.

In the following example, we will create a CPU qualification policy and assign it to a server pool:

1. Log in to the UCSM screen.

2. Click on the **Servers** tab in the navigation pane.

3. Click on the **Policies** tab and expand **root**.

4. Right-click on **Server Pool Policy Qualifications** and then click on the **Server Pool Policy Qualifications** option.

5. In the pop-up window, assign the **Name** and **Description** values to the **Server Pool Policy Qualifications** policy.

6. In the left pane, click on the **Create CPU/Core Qualifications** policy to define the CPU features for the qualifying servers. We created a CPU qualification policy as shown in the following screenshot:

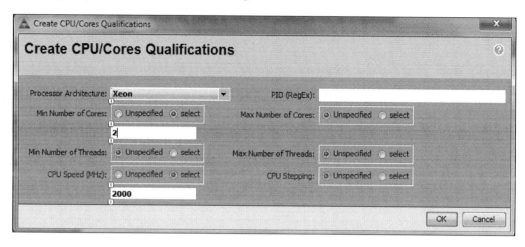

7. Click on **OK** to finish the creation of server pool policy qualifications.

8. Right-click on **Server Pool Policies** in the navigation pane and click on **Create Server Pool Policy**.

9. In the pop-up window, assign the **Name** and **Description** values to it. Select the **Target Pool** value from the drop-down menu, which is already defined, and the **Qualification** policy already created in step 6 (in this case, **CPU**) as shown in the following screenshot:

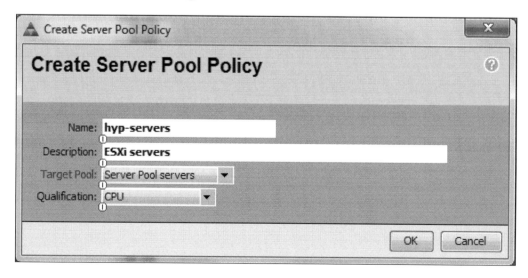

Summary

In this chapter, we learned about creating different identity and resource pool options available with the UCS platform. We learned that by leveraging identity and resource pools, the UCS platform makes server deployments highly scalable, flexible, and portable. Well-organized resource and identity pools in different organizations in UCS not only provide security and role-based access for larger organizations based on geographical, departmental, or any other criteria, but are also the basic building blocks for contemporary multitenancy cloud service environments.

So far, we have learned about LAN configuration, SAN configuration, server policies, and identity and resource pools, which are the building blocks for creating service profiles. In the next chapter, we will use the LAN configuration, SAN configuration, server policies, and identity and resource pools for configuring the service profiles that abstract all the necessary configurations for the stateless physical blade servers.

7
Creating and Managing Service Profiles

Cisco UCS service profile provides the necessary platform for abstracting fundamental building blocks such as BIOS settings, firmware, storage, and networking settings for the servers. Combined with the simplified architecture and reduced infrastructure management, service profiles provide the stateless nature of Cisco UCS platforms. A service profile provides all identities and configurations to a UCS server necessary for the installation of the operating system, making the system unique on the network.

In the previous chapters, we learned about different components of UCS solution including LAN configuration, SAN configuration, and identity and resource pools creation. These individual components provide all resources and configurations to a blade server in the form of service profiles.

In this chapter, we'll explain the role of service profiles in the UCS platform. We'll look into creating various policies for the UCS server's configuration. We'll discuss the difference between standard and expert mode service profiles. Finally, we'll take a deep dive into creating service profiles as well as service profile templates and show the granular configuration options of each.

The list of topics that will be covered in the chapter are as follows:

- Overview of service profiles
- Different ways of creating a service profile
- Creating a service profile template

- Configuring the server BIOS policy
- Configuring the Adapter policy
- Configuring the Scrub policy
- Configuring the QoS policy
- Configuring the Local Disk policy
- Configuring IPMI
- Walking through the service profile creation – expert mode

Overview of service profiles

A service profile is the principal feature of the UCS platform that enables stateless computing. Service profiles radically improve server provisioning and troubleshooting. Servers can be provisioned in software even before the delivery of physical hardware; in case of hardware failure, it can be replaced by associating the existing software service profile of the failed server without going through any painstaking firmware upgrade procedures.

UCS Manager abstracts a service profile from the configurations available under the following categories:

- **Identity and resource pools**: As explained in *Chapter 6, Creating Identity and Resource Pools*, identity and resource pools provide silos for computing node-unique characteristics such as MAC addresses, WWNs, and UUIDs. These identities uniquely recognize systems on the network. UCS servers abstract these physical identities from software pools available from UCS Manager instead of using burned hardware identities.

- **Service policies**: Service policies, which will be explained later in this chapter, provide different configurations for the UCS servers including BIOS settings, firmware versions, adapter policies, scrub policies, IPMI policies and so on.

A service profile combines information and features abstracted from identity and resource pools and server policies. It is a software entity residing in UCS Manager that provides a complete server role when associated with a stateless physical hardware server. Service profile information and association is depicted in the following diagram:

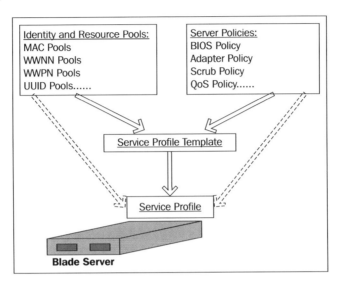

The preceding diagram shows how a service profile provides all features and identities to the physical server by extracting those identities, resources, and policies from different configurations in the form templates, pools, and policies. It is possible to create a service profile directly from pools and policies; however, it is recommended to create service profile templates which could be applied to any number of similar servers, reducing the management effort.

Different ways of creating a service profile

Cisco UCS Manger provides the following three options for creating a service profile:

- Creating a basic service profile
- Creating a service profile expert mode
- Creating a service profile from a service profile template

These service profile creation methods provide various levels of abstraction, flexibility, and scalability in terms of features and configuration options. We will discuss each option in detail.

Creating a basic service profile

This is the most basic option for creating a service profile using the burned-in physical identities. A service profile configuration is completed on a single page wizard providing a basic server configuration. This option can be used to configure a server quickly without applying many advanced policies. For production environments, this option is seldom applicable for server configurations.

Perform the following steps to configure the service profile using this method:

1. Log in to UCS Manager.

2. Click to expand the **Servers** tab in the navigation pane.

3. Click to expand the **Service Profiles** tab and expand **Root**.

4. Right-click on **Root** and on the pop-up menu that appears, click on **Create Service Profile**:

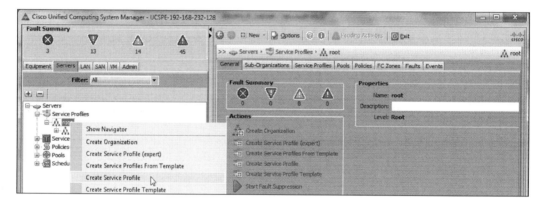

5. In the pop-up screen, provide a name and a short description to the service profile.

6. Create two Ethernet vNICs, two Storage vHBAs, select a boot order, and provide a service profile association on the next page.

7. Click on **OK**, which completes the service configuration.

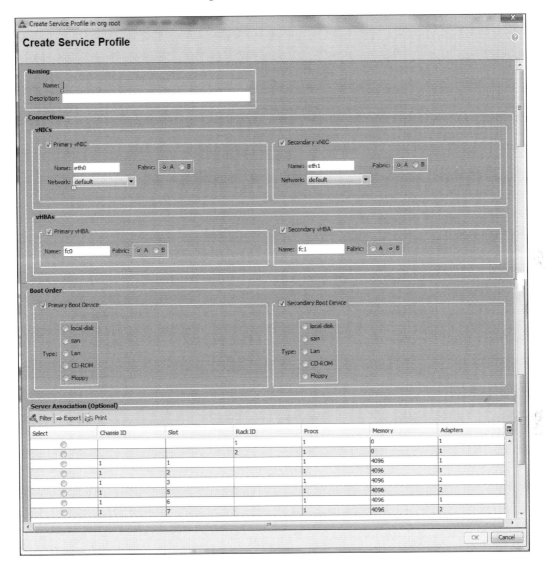

Creating a service profile in the expert mode

Creating a service profile in the expert mode utilizes all UCS features and creates a rich service profile with abstracted identities and advanced policies.

Perform the following steps to configure the service profile using the expert mode:

1.   Log in to UCS Manager.

2.   Click to expand the **Servers** tab in the navigation pane.

3.   Click on the **Service Profiles** tab and expand **Root**.

4.   Right-click on **Root** and on the pop-up menu that appears, click on **Create Service Profile (expert)**. This will start a wizard to configure different options, as shown in the following screenshot:

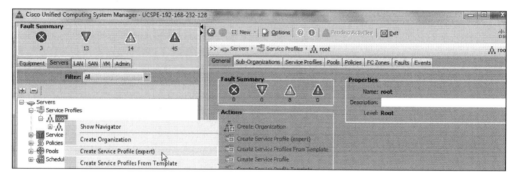

5.   Provide a name and a short description to the service profile. On the same screen, also select a UUID pool for assigning a unique identity to the server or click on the **+** sign to create a new UUID pool if needed. Click on **Next**.

6.   On the subsequent screens, configure processor features, vNICs, vHBAs, storage zoning, boot order, maintenance policy, and operational policies, and finally associate the profile with the server.

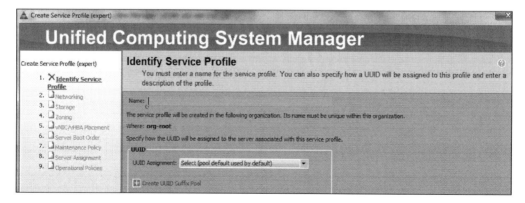

7. We will provide details of the expert mode service profile creation steps, which we have briefly described here, in a subsequent section in this chapter after explaining how to configure various policies.

Creating a service profile from a service profile template

A service profile template is an excellent feature of UCS Manager which assists in provisioning multiple physical servers with similar hardware configuration through a single profile source. A template can be configured once for each type of the server in the environment and can be used to create multiple service profiles for the servers with same specifications very quickly.

The procedure to create service profile templates follows the same steps as of creating a service profile in the expert mode. In production environments, a service profile template is highly recommended as it facilitates consistent server provisioning with ease and also reduces the chances of human errors occurring due to repeated manual profile creation steps.

We will provide detailed procedures for creating and applying a service profile template in the final section of this chapter after explaining how to configure policies and providing a walkthrough of service profile creation using the expert mode.

Configuring policies

UCS Manager allows creation of a number of policies that can be consumed by service profiles associated with servers. When applied through the association of a service profile, these policies provide necessary features and configurations to the physical servers. Policies can be configured for BIOS configuration, firmware versions, adapter configuration, QoS configuration, local disk configuration, boot order configuration, server data scrubbing, server power utilization, and other operational and maintenance configurations.

Configuring the server BIOS policy

BIOS policy lets you configure a server's BIOS settings including CPU, memory, PCI cards, boot, and other options. Perform the following steps to configure the BIOS settings policy:

1. Log in to UCS Manager.

2. Click to expand the **Servers** tab in the navigation pane.

3. Click to expand the **Policies** tab and expand the **Root** tab.

4. Right-click on **BIOS Policies** and on the pop-up menu that appears, click on **Create BIOS Policy**.

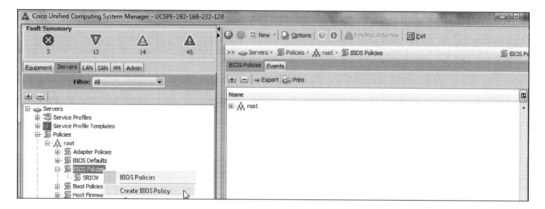

5. In the pop-up screen on the **Main** tab, assign a value for **Name**, and click on the **Reboot on BIOS Settings Change** checkbox if the server needs to reboot automatically on any BIOS change. It is also recommended to properly configure the maintenance policy in order to achieve the desired reboot response from the server.

6. Cisco suppresses the POST messages with a Cisco splash screen. It is recommended to make **Quiet Boot** disabled in order to see boot messages.

7. **POST Error Pause** should be enabled if it is required to pause the system in the event of critical error. If this setting is disabled, the system will try to boot up.

8. The **Resume Ac On Power Loss** field settings show self-explanatory power state settings.

9. If **Front Panel Lockout** is enabled, it will block the power and will reset buttons on the front panel of the server; now, the server can only be rebooted or powered on or off from the CIMC. Click on **Next**.

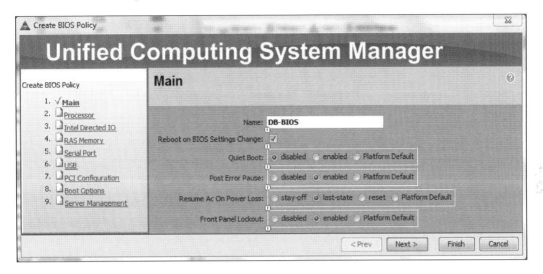

10. The next screen shows the **Processor** settings. A number of CPU settings are available, and it is recommended to check the operating system platform related best practices for CPU settings. As a general recommendation for virtualization, enable **Virtualization Technology VT** and disable **Turbo Boost**, **Enhanced Intel Speedstep**, and all C-States. **Turbo Boost** with enhanced Speedstep and C-State manages CPU power consumption by slowing down or stopping the CPU cores, which may not be handled accurately by the OS. Again, always consult the OS platform recommendation.

11. Click on **Next**.

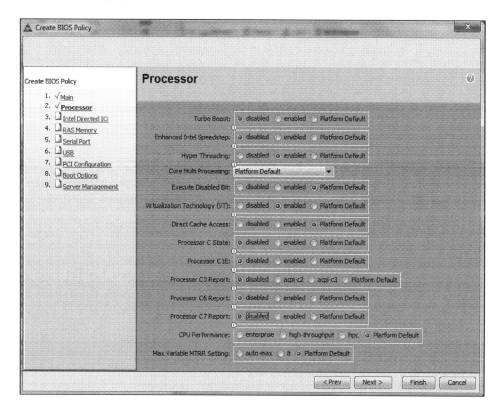

12. **Intel Directed IO** settings are pertinent to the processor features used to facilitate virtualization tasks. Configure the recommended settings for your hypervisor platform or leave it as **Platform Default**:

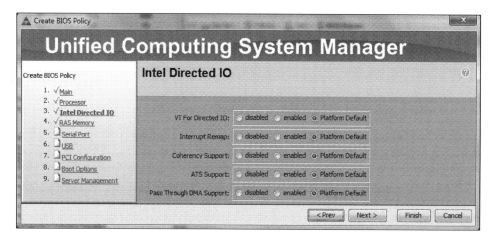

13. **RAS Memory** is a configuration for the memory. Memory RAS configuration options include the following:

  ○ **Maximum performance**: System performance is optimized

  ○ **Mirroring**: System reliability is optimized by using half the system memory as backup

  ○ **Lockstep**: For similar DIMM pairs, the lockstep mode minimizes memory access latency

  ○ **Sparing**: System reliability is enhanced with reserved memory providing redundancy in case of memory module failure

14. The other two memory configuration options are **NUMA** (Non Uniform Memory Access) and low voltage **LV DDR Mode**.

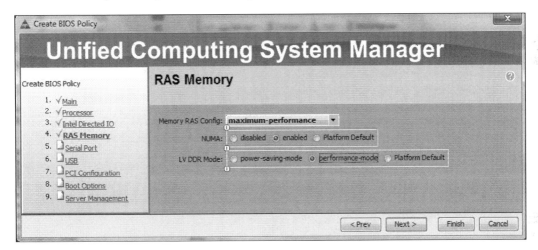

15. The **Serial Port** configuration enables or disables a server serial port:

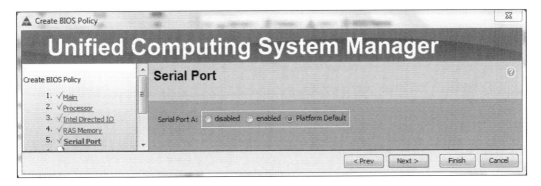

16. The **USB** configuration provides options for the Server USB ports:

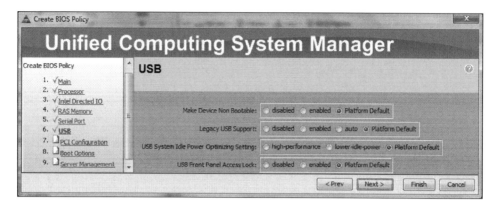

17. **PCI Configuration** checks the operating system requirements for the configuration details or leaves it as **Platform Default**:

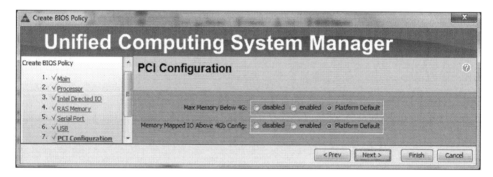

18. The **Boot Options** configuration can also be left with the **Platform Default** setting to automatically use the default settings for the server platform:

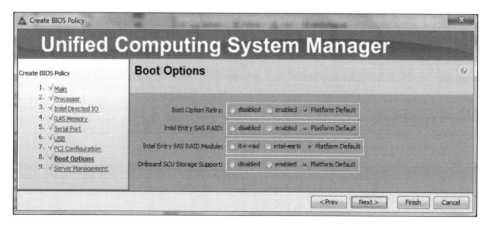

19. **Server Management** BIOS options provide **System Error (SERR), Processor Bus Parity Error (PERR)**, OS Boot Watchdog timer, and Server Console redirection configurations. Again, these settings can be left as **Platform Default** if you are unsure about the configuration:

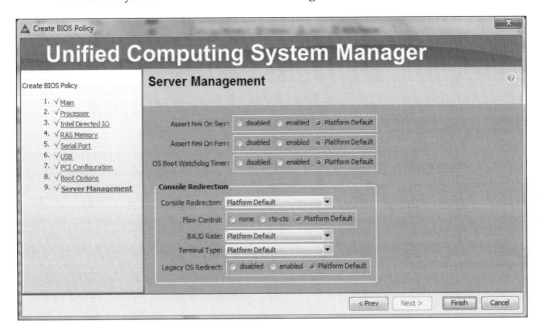

20. Click on **Finish** to complete BIOS settings.

 UCS Manager also provides BIOS Defaults Policy which can be configured to provide platform-default settings for each server's BIOS.

Configuring adapter policies

UCS has some predefined adapter policies for the most popular operating systems including the hypervisors. The settings in these predefined policies are for optimal adapter performance. Separate adapter policies for Ethernet Adapters, Fiber Channel adapters, and iSCSI adapters are available. Select the appropriate policy for the OS/hypervisor. Perform the following steps to configure adapter policies:

1. Log in to UCS Manager.
2. Click to expand the **Servers** tab in the navigation pane.
3. Click on the **Policies** tab and expand **Root**.

4. Click on **Adapter Policies** to expand and select the appropriate policy:

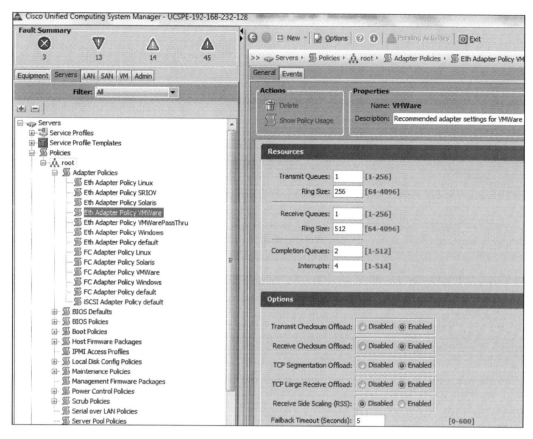

Configuring scrub policies

A scrub policy defines the behavior of a server when it is disassociated from a service profile in terms of BIOS settings and the installed OS on the server. A scrub policy could be very useful for erasing servers for security compliance:

1. Log in to UCS Manager.

2. Click to expand the **Servers** tab in the navigation pane.

3. Click on the **Policies** tab and expand **Root**.

4. Right click on **Scrub Policies** and when the pop-up menu appears, click on **Create Scrub Policy**.

5. Assign a name and a short description to the scrub policy.

6. Set **Disk Scrub** to **Yes**, if it is required to erase all data from the server hard disk, otherwise leave it to **No**.

7. Set **BIOS Scrub** to **Yes** if it is required to serve BIOS, otherwise leave it to **No**:

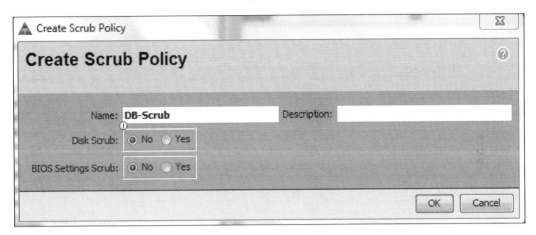

Configuring QoS policies

The **Quality of service (QoS)** policy can be configured to implement network traffic prioritization based on the importance of the connected network; for example, you can implement different QoS policies for application traffic and management traffic. In the following example, we will configure a QoS policy with platinum priority with the help of the following steps:

1. Log in to UCS Manager.

2. Click to expand the **LAN** tab in the navigation pane.

3. Click on the **Policies** tab and expand **Root**.

4. Right-click on **QOS Policies,** and on the pop-up menu that appears, click on **Create QOS Policy**:

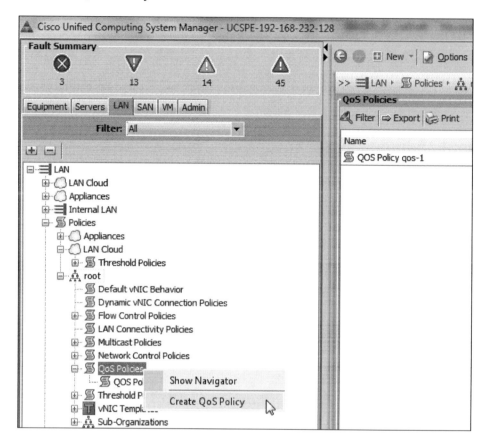

5. Assign a name to the QOS policy.

6. Select **Platinum**, **Gold**, **Silver**, or **Bronze** for vNIC priorities but do not select **Best Effort** which is reserved. Select **FC** for Fiber Channel vHBAs.

7. **Burst (Bytes)** determines the traffic burst size. Default is 1040, minimum is 0, and maximum is 65535.

8. The **Rate** field determines the average rate of traffic, and the default is **line-rate**, which should not be changed.

9. The **Host Control** field defines whether UCS controls the class of service or not:

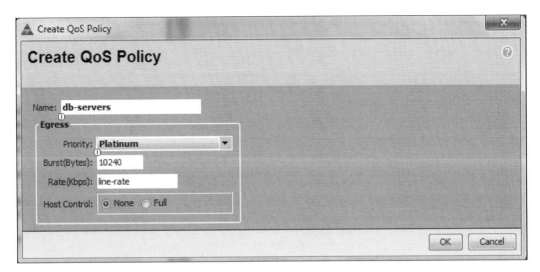

Local disk configuration policies

This policy is used for local disks' RAID configuration. Based on the number of local disks and RAID controller model, different RAID options include 0, 1, 5, 6, and 10. Perform the following steps to configure this policy:

1. Log in to UCS Manager.

2. Click to expand the **Servers** tab in the navigation pane.

3. Click on the **Policies** tab and expand **Root**.

4. Right-click on **Local Disk Config Policies**, and on the pop-up menu that appears, click on **Create Local Disk Configuration Policy**:

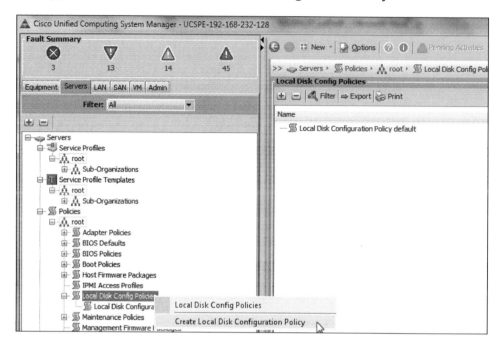

5. Assign a name and a short description to the local disk configuration policy.

6. Select a **RAID** level from the pop-up menu.

7. Select the **Protect Configuration** checkbox in order to preserve the local disk configuration even if the service profile is disassociated.

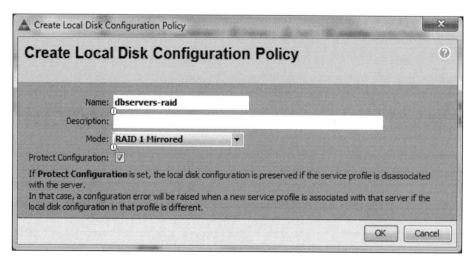

Maintenance policies

The maintenance policy is a very important policy that controls the server's response to any changes in the service profile. Many service profile changes need a reboot of the server to take effect, it is therefore recommended to configure this policy with user acknowledgment settings for production environments so that servers could be rebooted in a controlled change management window:

1. Log in to UCS Manager.

2. Click to expand the **Servers** tab in the navigation pane.

3. Click on the **Policies** tab and expand **Root**.

4. Right-click on the **Maintenance Policies** tab and on the pop-up screen that appears, click on **Create Maintenance Policy**:

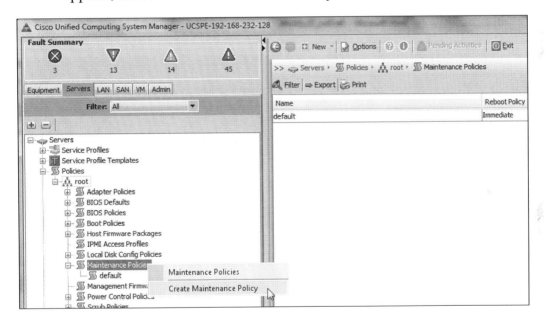

5. Assign a name and a short description to the maintenance policy.

6. Setting a value for **Reboot Policy** is critical. **Immediate** means the server will be instantaneously rebooted for changes that require a reboot, which is not a recommended setting for production servers. **User Ack** means that any change that requires a server reboot will be held until the user's acknowledgment. This setting allows scheduling a maintenance window and rebooting the server following proper procedures. **Timer Automatic** allows you to schedule a maintenance window and automatically reboot the server at a specific time without an administrator's intervention.

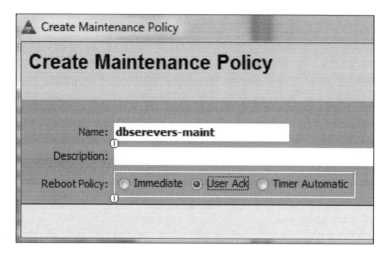

Configuring IPMI

Intelligent Platform Management Interface (IPMI) is open standard technology for monitoring the server's hardware sensors. IPMI runs directly on Baseboard Management Controller (BMC). It is, therefore, necessary to create an IPMI profile with a username, password, and the desired level of access which could be read-only or read/write, and assign the IPMI profile to the blade server for direct management using IPMI commands.

Perform the following steps to configure the IPMI profile:

1. Log in to UCS Manager.
2. Click to expand the **Servers** tab in the navigation pane.
3. Click on the **Policies** tab and expand the **Root** tab.

4. Right-click on **Root** and on pop-up menu that appears, click on **IPMI Access Profiles**:

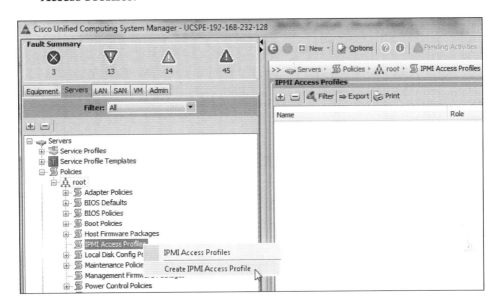

5. Assign a name and a short description to the service profile, and select an already created UUID pool. If there is no existing UUID pool, click on the + sign to create the UUID pool.

A walkthrough of the service profile creation – expert mode

As we discussed at the beginning of this chapter, there are three methods to create a service profile. The quickest method is to create a basic service profile using a single configuration page. This method, however, does not make use of advanced UCS features such as policies and templates and therefore, a basic profile is not recommended for production servers. For production environments, it is recommended to use the expert mode creation method for service profiles that leverages advance UCS features, and provides a detailed identity to the servers where this service profile is applied. It is highly recommended to create service profile templates using the expert mode so that, in the future, servers with similar specifications can be added without a lot of administrative effort. We will now walk through the service profile creation – the expert mode – using the identity and resource pools along with policies. Note that the sections and steps discussed are similar for the creation of both the service profiles in the expert mode and service profile templates. Service profile expert mode or service profile template creations are lengthy processes. We will explain these steps according to the sections in the configuration wizard. Perform the following steps to configure the service profile using the expert mode method.

Identifying the service profile

In the first section, provide a name and identify a UUID pool for the server identity. Perform the following steps to do so:

1. Log in to UCS Manager.
2. Click on the **Servers** tab in the navigation pane.
3. Click to expand the **Service Profiles** tab and expand **Root**.
4. Right-click on **Root** and on the pop-up menu that appears, click on **Create Service Profile (expert)**.
5. Assign a name and a short description to the service profile and select an already created UUID pool. If a UUID pool does not exist, click on the + sign to create a new UUID pool.

6. Click on **Next**.

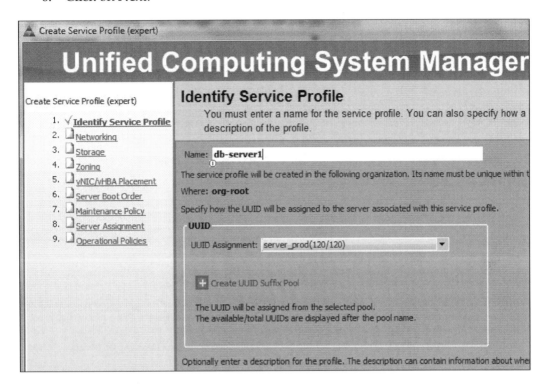

Configuring the networking settings

Perform the following steps to configure the networking settings:

1. On the **Networking** page, configure the networking settings. You may select or create a new dynamic vNIC connection policy. There are multiple options available for the network configuration:

    ○ **Simple**: The **Simple** option will create two vNICs. Existing VLAN IDs can be assigned to those vNICs or VLAN IDs can be created using the + sign.

    ○ **Expert**: The **Expert** mode can be used to create any number (depending upon the Mezzanine card model) of vNICs and iSCSI adapters. vNICs can be configured manually or vNIC templates can also be created.

    ○ **No vNICs**: No vNICs will be created. vNICs can be added to a service profile later.

- ○ **Hardware Inherited**: This option creates two vNICs using the burned-in identities. This is the same as creating vNICs in a basic service profile creation.

- ○ **Use Connectivity Policy**: Use this option to select a LAN connectivity policy.

2. We will utilize the **Expert** mode in our example configuration. Click on **Expert** from **LAN connectivity**. This option will change the page options as shown in the following screenshot:

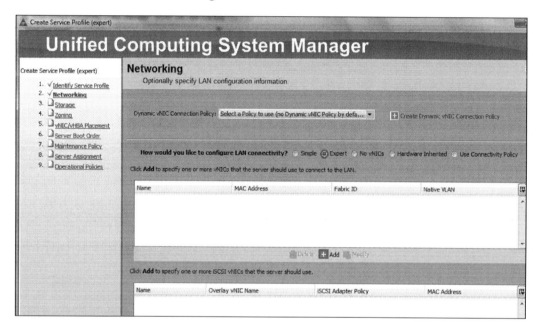

3. Click on the + sign to add a new vNIC.

4. On the pop-up page, you may either manually create the vNIC by assigning a MAC Address Pool, Fabric ID, VLAN membership, and various policies such as QoS and Adapter Policy, or use an existing vNIC template if a vNIC template already exists. If a vNIC template does not exist, you can quickly create a new vNIC template by clicking on the + sign on the same page.

5. In this example, we will use an existing vNIC template. Click on the checkbox **Use vNIC Template**.

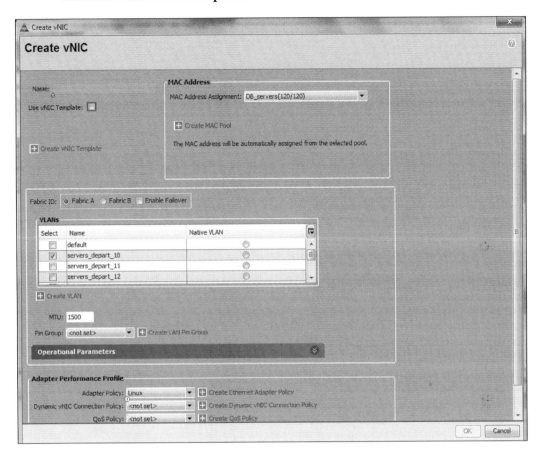

6. Clicking on the checkbox will change the screen. On the next screen, assign a name to vNIC, select an existing vNIC template to abstract vNIC configuration, or create a new vNIC template by clicking on the + sign. You can also assign an existing adapter policy for traffic optimization or create a new adapter policy as shown in the following screenshot:

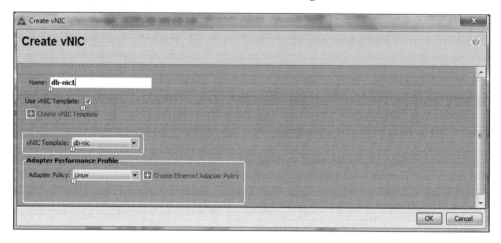

7. Repeat steps 3 to 6 in order to create as many vNICs as you require.

 It is recommended to select different primary Fabric Interconnects for data connectivity, while creating vNIC templates, which ensures load distribution for data traffic.

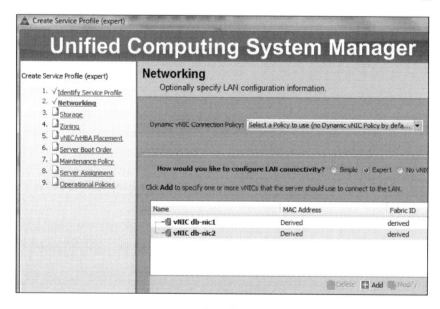

Configuring the storage connectivity

Now we will configure the storage which includes both local storage and SAN connectivity vHBAs. The steps are as follows:

1. After configuration of vNICs, click on **Next**.

2. Now configure a local storage, which may use an existing local disk configuration policy.

3. In this example, we will be selecting an existing local disk configuration policy for the configuration of local storage, and if a policy does not exist, we can create a new policy by clicking on the + sign. In this example, we assigned a pre-configured local disk configuration policy named **dbservers-raid** for RAID configuration of local disks.

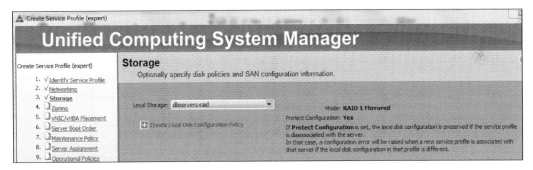

4. The second option on this page is to configure vHBAs. Similar to vNICs, there are the following multiple options for creating vHBAs:

    ○   **Simple**: The **Simple** option will create two vHBAs. Existing VSAN IDs can be assigned to those vHBAs or VSAN IDs can be created using the + sign. You also need to assign a WWNN pool or create an new WWNN pool using the + sign

    ○   **Expert**: The **Expert** mode can be used to create any number (depending upon the Mezzanine card model) of vHBA adapters. vHBAs can be configured manually or vHBA templates can also be created.

    ○   **No vHBA**: No vHBAs will be created. vHBAs can be added to a service profile later.

    ○   **Hardware Inherited**: This option creates vHBAs using the burned-in identities. This is the same as creating vHBAs in a basic service profile creation.

    ○   **Use Connectivity Policy**: Use this option to select a SAN connectivity policy.

5. In this example, we will use the **Expert** mode to create vHBAs. Selecting the **Expert** mode will change the screen configuration options.

6. Select an existing **WWNN pool** for WWNN number assignments or create a new WWNN pool by clicking on the + sign.

7. Click on the + sign near **Add** to create a new vHBA. A new pop-up page will provide options for configuring the vHBA:

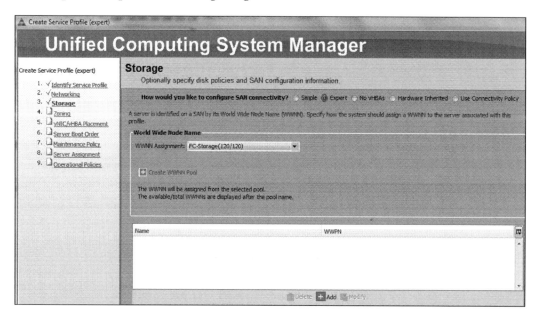

8. On the pop-up page, you may either manually create the vHBA by assigning a WWNN Address Pool, Fabric ID, VSAN membership, and various policies such as QoS and Adapter Policy, or use an existing vHBA template. You can also quickly create a new vHBA template by clicking on the + sign on the same page.

9. In this example, we will use an existing vHBA template. Click on the **Use vHBA Template** checkbox.

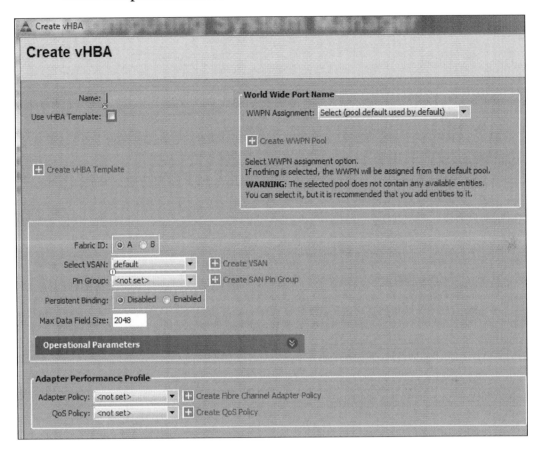

10. Clicking on the checkbox will change the screen. On the next screen, assign a name to vHBA, select an existing vHBA template to abstract vHBA configuration, or create a new vHBA template by clicking on the + sign. You can also assign an existing adapter policy for traffic optimization or create a new adapter policy.

11. Repeat steps 7 to 10 to create more vHBAs for the service profile.

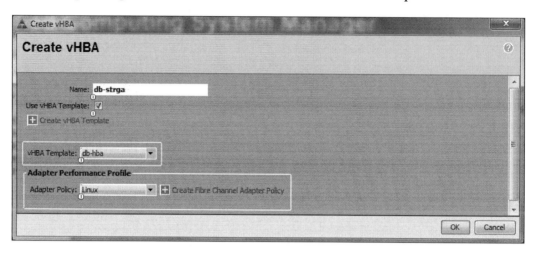

12. In this example, we configured two vHBAs. You may configure the required number of vHBAs as per the requirements of your environment. Click on **Next** after the vHBAs creation:

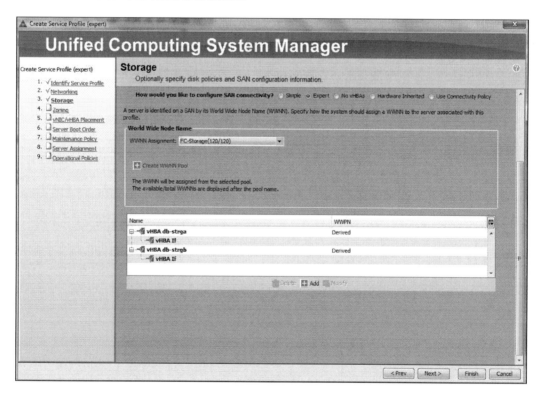

Configuring zoning

On the **Zoning** page, configure the zoning information. The page shows vHBAs (initiators) on the left-hand side of the pane and zones (initiator groups) information on the right-hand side of the pane. Select each vHBA (initiator), and add it to an existing zone vHBA initiator group by clicking on the **>>Add to >>** sign.

Previous versions of UCS Manager supported default zoning. Default zoning allows using a single zone for all vHBAs, which is not the recommended setting from a security perspective. UCSM 2.1 does not support default zoning.

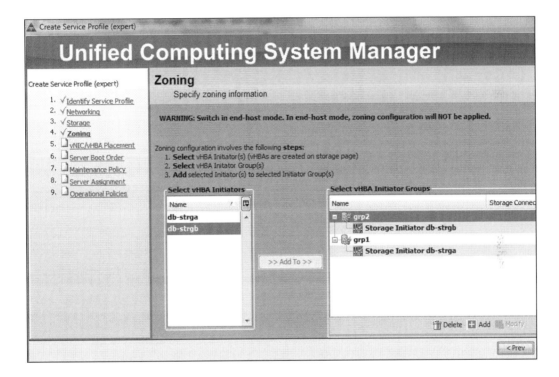

vNIC/vHBA placement

On the **vNIC/vHBA Placement** screen, vNIC/vHBA placement order is configured. The default configuration is the **Let System Perform Placement** order. Other options include using a placement policy or manually ordering the placement of vNICs and vHBAs. Click on the + sign to create a new placement policy if needed:

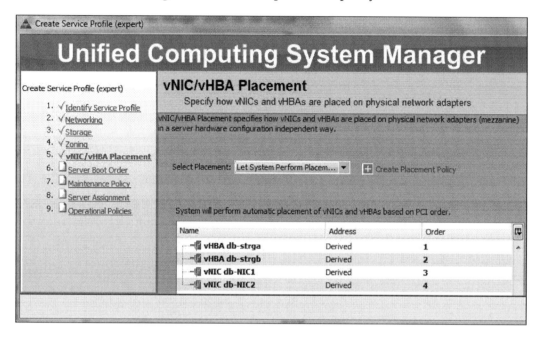

Server Boot Order configuration

The next configuration is of **Server Boot Order**. An existing boot policy can be used to populate the boot sequence, or a new boot policy can also be created by clicking on the + sign. It is also possible to manually create the boot sequence by double-clicking on the boot devices available on the left-hand side of the pane. When manually populated, the boot devices order can also be changed using the move up and down buttons at the bottom of screen. In this example, we have used the preconfigured **Default Boot Policy**:

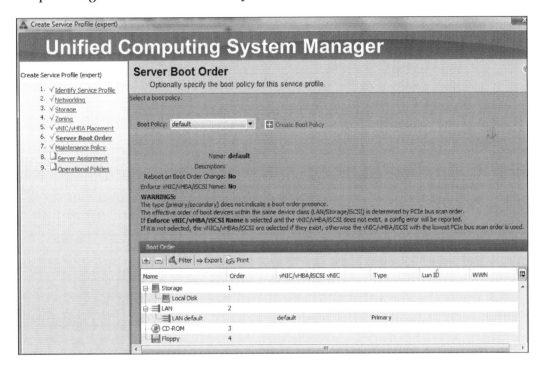

Configuring the server maintenance policy

The next configuration is the **Maintenance Policy** selection. If no preconfigured policy is selected, the default policy is used, which is configured for immediate reboot after any change. Options for a maintenance policy are to select an existing maintenance policy or create a new one by clicking on the + sign. For production environments, it is strongly recommended to create a maintenance policy with the **User Acknowledge** setting. With this maintenance policy, UCS Manager prompts a user to acknowledge the reboot. Hence, the server can be easily scheduled for a reboot during the planned maintenance window. In this example, we are using an existing maintenance policy which has the **User Acknowledge** setting. At the bottom of the screen, the maintenance policy configuration is displayed, which in this example is **User Ack**:

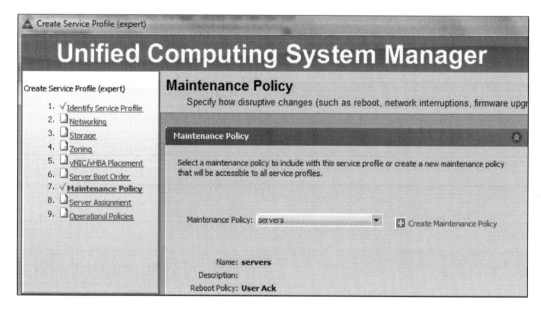

Configuring a SAN boot policy

In many environments, it is common practice to use diskless servers, and boot the hypervisor or OS directly from SAN. UCS makes it very simple to configure a SAN boot policy for direct SAN boot. Make sure you have already configured appropriate vHBAs, and perform the following steps to configure a SAN boot policy for the server:

1. In the **Server Boot Order** tab of template configuration wizard, click on the **+** sign beside **Create Boot Policy**:

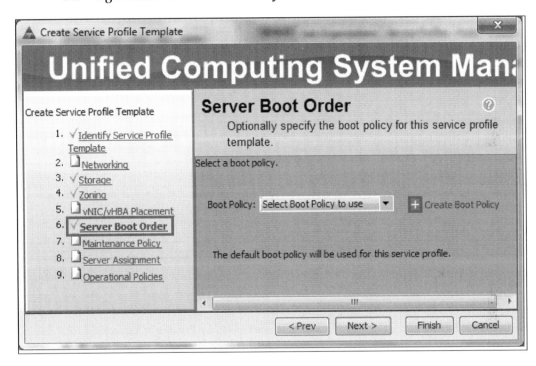

2. On the next pop-up window, provide a name and description for the new policy, expand the **vHBAs** section and click on **Add SAN Boot**:

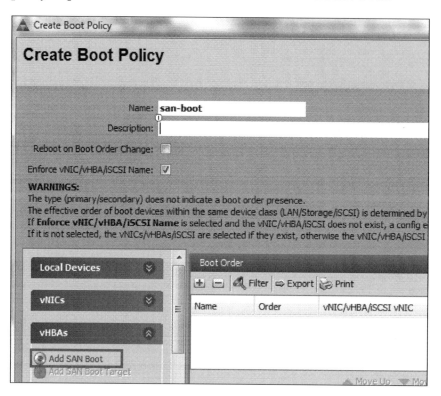

3. On the pop-up window, provide the name of the appropriate vHBA configured. Repeat the steps for primary and secondary vHBAs:

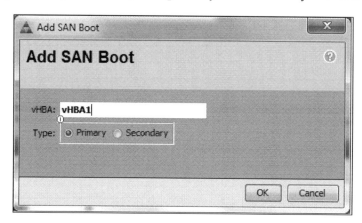

4. After adding vHBAs, **Add SAN Boot Target**, which was initially greyed out, will be highlighted. Click on **Add SAN Boot Target**:

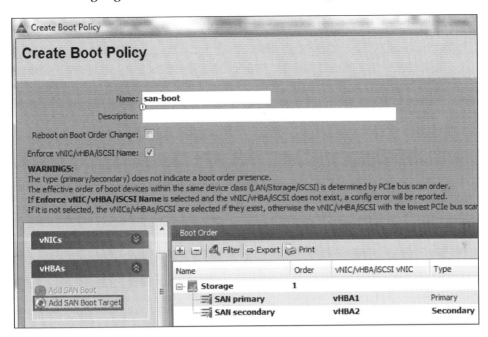

5. On the pop-up window, add values for **Boot Target LUN, Boot Target WWPN**, and **Type** as **Primary** or **Secondary**. Contact the SAN administrator to get the appropriate information about the boot LUN designated for the SAN boot:

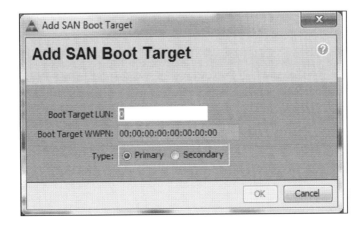

Associating service profiles

Perform the following steps to associate the service profiles with server pools:

1. On the **Server Assignment** screen, you can assign the service profile to a server pool if a server pool already exists or you can create a new server pool for assignment by clicking on the + sign. It is also possible to not put the server in any pool, and a service profile can be manually associated with a physical server. The second option is to select a server specification based on a server pool qualification policy, such as CPU and RAM for a server pool membership.

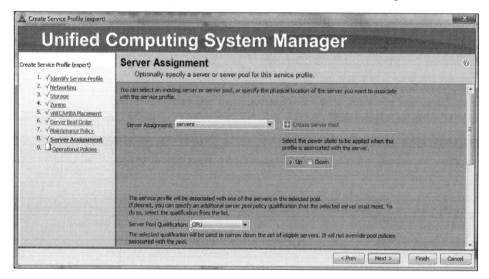

2. The third option available on the **Server Assignment** page is the selection of the host firmware package. Use the + sign to create a host firmware package if it not created already:

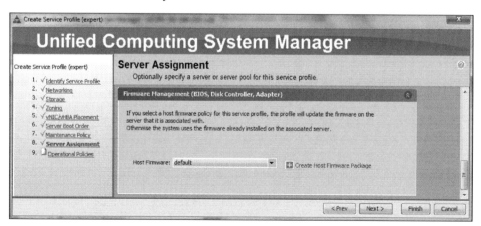

Operational policies

The last page is the **Operation Policies** page and has a number of configurations. Policies that are configured on this page are as follows:

- **BIOS Policy**: Configure BIOS settings
- **External IPMI Management Configuration**: IPMI configuration
- **Management IP Address**: Configure a static IP or an IP Pool
- **Monitoring Configuration (Thresholds)**: Configure monitoring thresholds
- **Power Control Policy Configuration**: Configure Blade Power control
- **Scrub Policy**: Configure data scrub settings

Now we will configure the operational policies one-by-one:

1. The first policy is the **BIOS Configuration** policy. You may select an existing BIOS policy or you can create new BIOS policy by clicking on the + sign. If no BIOS policy is selected, default values from BIOS defaults of the platform will be used:

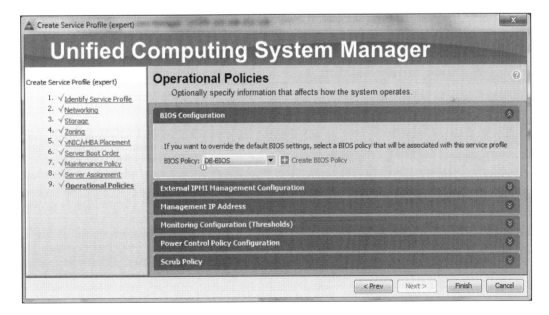

2. The next policy is the **IPMI and Serial over LAN (SoL)** configuration. Select an existing IPMI user access profile or create a new IPMI access profile by clicking on the **+** sign. If serial over LAN redirection for the server is required, configure a new SoL policy or select an existing one:

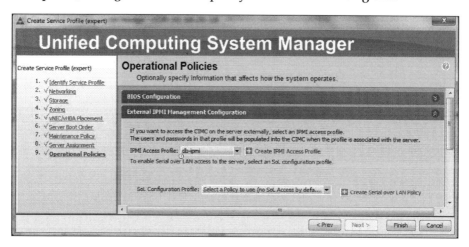

3. The next policy is **Management IP Address**. It is possible to create a management IP pool and IPs will be automatically assigned to the servers. The other option is to assign a static IP to the server management console. In this example, we selected the **Static** option for the **Management IP Address Policy** field:

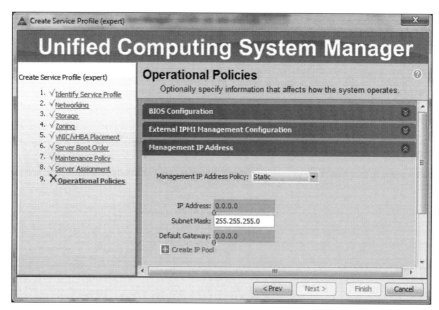

4. The next configuration is **Monitoring Configuration (Thresholds)**. It is possible to create a customized threshold policy with granular settings for server components. Mostly, a default policy is recommended, so this configuration can be skipped:

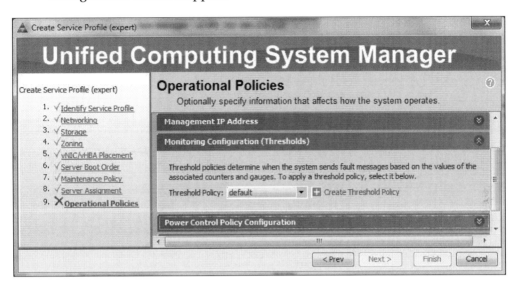

5. The next configuration is **Power Control Policy Configuration**, which determines the power allocation for the server. Typically, this policy can also be skipped unless it is a situation where power management is required. The default setting provides maximum power to the blades. For the server's power control, it is possible to create a new power policy or use an existing one:

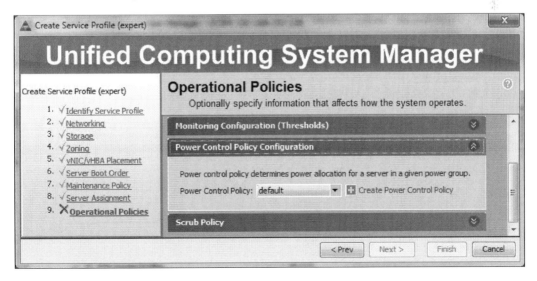

6. The last **Operational Policy** configuration is the selection of the server scrub policy. Options are to select an existing scrub policy or create a new scrub policy by clicking on the **+** sign:

7. Click on **Finish** to complete the service profile configuration.

Creating and applying a service profile template

UCS service profile template creation is an excellent feature. Service profile templates can be created once and deployed to any number of servers with similar hardware specifications. The procedure for creating a service profile template is exactly the same as the procedure for creating a service profile template in the expert mode. Only the initial steps are different as compared to the service profile in the expert mode and is shown in the following:

1. Log in to UCS Manager.
2. Click to expand the **Servers** tab in the navigation pane.
3. Click on the **Service Profiles Template** tab and expand **Root**.

4. Right-click on **Root** and on the pop-up menu that appears, click on **Create Service Profile Template**:

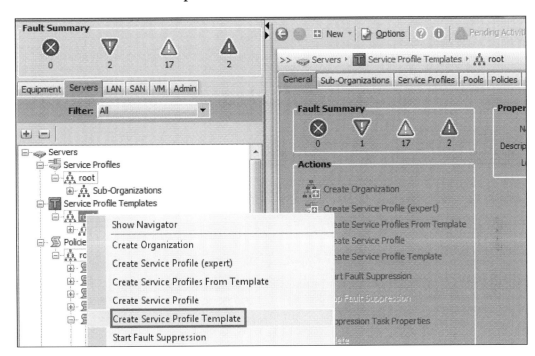

The next steps are exactly same which we followed while creating the service profile in the expert mode. Once the template has been configured, it can be used to create any number of service profiles using minimal effort. Perform the following steps to configure a service profile from an existing service profile template:

1. Click on the **Servers** tab in the navigation pane.
2. Click on the **Service Profiles** tab and expand **Root**.

3. Right-click on **Root** and on the pop-up menu that appears, click on **Create Service Profile From Template**:

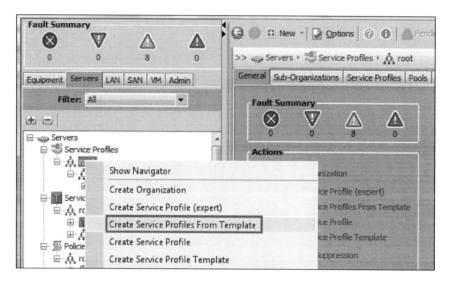

4. In the pop-up screen, enter values for **Naming Prefix** and **Number** to create a name for the new service profile, and select **Service Profile Template** from list of available templates:

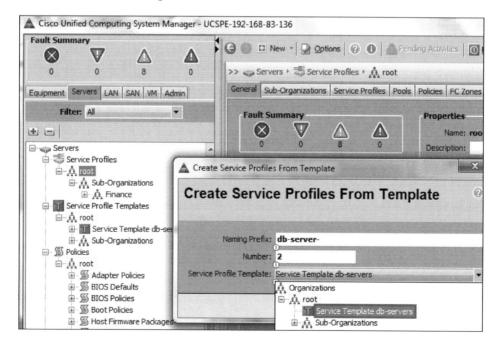

If you are using previous versions of UCS Manager including Version 2.0, pay special attention to the service profile naming as service profiles created with previous versions of UCSM cannot be renamed.

 It is now possible to rename a service profile after its creation in UCSM Version 2.1. In previous versions, it was not possible to rename a service profile, except by deleting and recreating with appropriate profile names.

Summary

In this chapter, we first acquired an understanding of the service profile and looked into various service profile creations options. We learned that expert mode service profile creation provides advanced configuration features, and also learned that creating service profile templates facilitate server provisioning. Then we looked into various policies that can be configured and later on, assigned to Blade Servers. We looked at policies such as BIOS, Adapter, Scrub, and QoS. Finally, we did a walkthrough of service profile creation using the expert mode, and utilized different UCS policies and settings to create a service profile that can be associated to a physical Blade Server, to provide the server with all configurations necessary for proper operation. We utilized the knowledge gained throughout the previous chapters and created a service profile that can provide the server with all the necessary characteristics.

In the next chapter, we will be looking into some common management tasks for managing and monitoring components, and advanced tasks such as role-based access control, authentication using external LDAP/AD, and multitenant environment considerations.

8
Managing UCS through Routine and Advanced Management

In this chapter, we'll cover some of the most common and advanced management tasks you'll perform with UCS Manager. These tasks include licensing extra ports, starting up, shutting down, blade power controls, locator LED, logging, the Call Home feature, organizational structure, role-based access, and configuring permissions in a multitenant environment. These routine management and operational tasks are crucial to understand in order to effectively design and administer Cisco UCS.

The tasks covered in this chapter do not fall into a single category and hence, are not located under a single tab in the UCS GUI Navigation pane. Most of the tasks are found in miscellaneous categories under the **Admin** tab in the Navigation pane, but other tasks are found on other tabs. For example, licensing configuration is under the **Admin** tab in the Navigation pane, but the option to get the host ID of the Fabric Interconnect is under the **Equipment** tab of the Navigation pane. It is therefore, necessary that you be very familiar with the UCS Manager GUI in order to find the pertinent information or configuration.

The list of topics that will be covered in the chapter is as follows:

- Licensing Cisco UCS Fabric Interconnect
- Startup and shutdown of Fabric Interconnect
- Controlling blade server power
- Status and Locator LED
- Configuring logging

- Configuring Cisco Call Home
- Organizational structure in UCS Manager
- Role-based access control
- Permissions in Multitenancy

Licensing Cisco UCS Fabric Interconnect

Cisco UCS Fabric Interconnect comes with default port licenses that are factory installed. Additional licenses can be purchased during the initial procurement or after delivery.

Each Fabric Interconnect provides the following licenses preinstalled:

- **Cisco UCS 6120XP**: Eight Ethernet ports enabled with preinstalled licenses and Fiber Channel ports on the expansion module.

- **Cisco UCS 6140XP**: Sixteen Ethernet ports enabled with preinstalled licenses and Fiber Channel ports on the expansion module.

- **Cisco UCS 6248**: Twelve unified ports enabled with preinstalled licenses. Expansion modules provide eight licenses which can be utilized on the expansion module or the main Fabric Interconnect.

- **Cisco UCS 6296**: Eighteen unified ports enabled with preinstalled licenses. Expansion modules provide eight licenses which can be utilized on the expansion module or the main Fabric Interconnect.

In order to purchase extra port licenses, you need to provide the host ID of the Fabric Interconnect to Cisco.

Use the following procedure to get the Fabric Interconnect host ID:

1. Log in to UCS Manager.
2. Click to expand the **Equipment** tab in the Navigation pane.
3. In the **Equipment** tab, click to expand **Fabric Interconnect**.
4. In the **Properties** area of the **General** area in the Work pane, note down the **serial number (SN)** of Fabric Interconnect.

 It is recommended to always have the same number of licenses on both Fabric Interconnects configured in **high availability (HA)**.

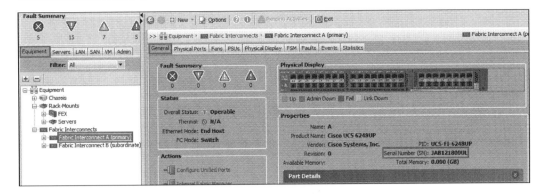

Once the license file is received from Cisco, it can be installed on Fabric Interconnect using the UCS Manager GUI or CLI, using the following steps:

1. In the Navigation pane, select **License Management** under the **Admin** tab.

2. Select the **General** tab under a Fabric Interconnect in the Work pane and select **Download License Files**.

3. In the pop-up window, browse for **Local File System** of the PC running the UCS Manager GUI session or provide details for **Remote File System** for **FTP, TFTP, SCP,** or **SFTP** sessions.

4. Repeat this task for all licenses for both Fabric Interconnects.

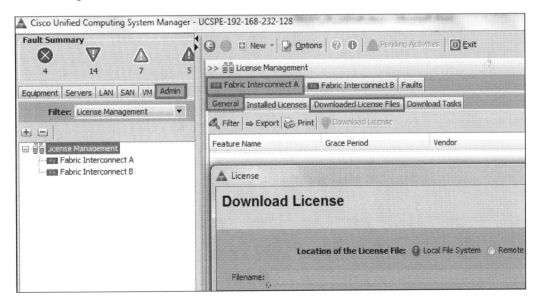

Startup and shutdown of Fabric Interconnects

UCS Fabric Interconnects are designed for continuous operation. In a production environment, there is no need to shut down or reboot Fabric Interconnects. Therefore, there is no power button on UCS Fabric Interconnects. In order to shut down UCS Fabric Interconnect, it is required to pull the power cable manually. Another option could be using smart PDUs that provide a remote control for the power of the electrical outlet.

In some rare cases, if it is required to reboot Fabric Interconnect, use the following procedure:

1. Log in to Fabric Interconnect using SSH.
2. Issue the following two commands:
   ```
   FI # connect local-mgmt
   FI # reboot
   ```

Controlling blade server power

UCS blade server chassis has a maximum of four power supplies. Each power supply is 2500 watts. Under normal conditions, UCS always has enough power to run all blade servers in the chassis. If required, power to each blade server can be capped. This may be required in a disaster situation where a limited amount of power is available.

When manual blade-level power capping is configured in the Global Cap policy, you can set a power cap for each blade server in a Cisco UCS domain.

Use the following procedure to enable the Global Manual Power policy:

1. Log in to UCS Manager.
2. Click to expand the **Equipment** tab in the Navigation pane.
3. In the main **Equipment** tab, click to expand **Equipment**.
4. Select **Global Policies** from the **Policies** tab in the Work pane.

5. In the **Global Power Allocating Policy** area, select **Manual Blade Level Cap** for the **Allocation Method**:

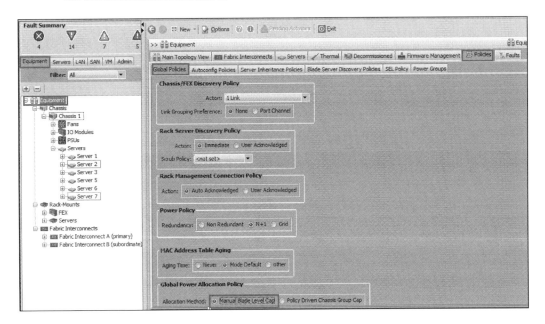

Once the global power policy is enabled for **Manual Blade Level Cap**, use the following procedure to allocate power to each blade:

1. Log in to UCS Manager.

2. Click to expand the **Equipment** tab in the Navigation pane.

3. In the **Equipment** tab, click to expand **Chassis**.

4. Expand the **Servers** tab and select **Server** in Navigation pane.

5. In the **General** tab of the selected server in the Work pane, select **Power Budget** for the server.

6. Select **Enabled** and define the power value for the blade in watts.

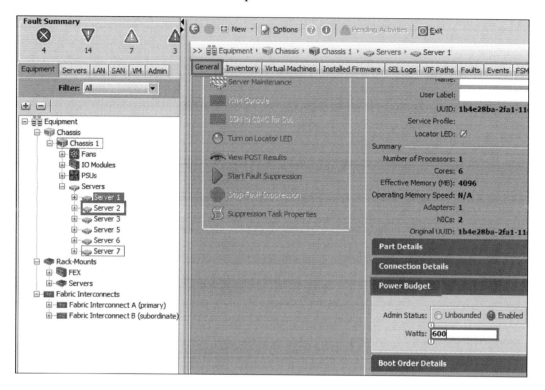

 Power capping only goes into effect if there is insufficient power available to the chassis to meet the demand. If there is sufficient power, the server can use as many watts as it requires.

Status and Locator LED

The following physical components of UCS have Status and Locator LED:

- UCS Chassis
- Blade Server
- UCS Fabric Interconnect

Status provides the overall operational state of the equipment and can be very useful in initial diagnostics. The status of a UCS component is available in the Work pane in the top-left corner under the **Fault Summary** area.

Locator LED on the other hand can be turned on in order to physically identify the equipment and is very useful for onsite troubleshooting. Suppose one of the Fabric Interconnects or one of the blade servers is faulty, you may help an onsite technician to physically identify (and maybe replace) the faulty components if Locator LED is remotely turned on by the administrator.

Please perform the following procedure for looking up the UCS component Status and turning on/off the Locator LED:

1. Log in to UCS Manager.

2. Click to expand the **Equipment** tab in the Navigation pane.

3. In the **Equipment** tab, click to expand **Chassis**.

4. In the **Status** area of the Work pane, the operational status of Fabric Interconnect is shown.

5. Click on **Turn on Locator LED** in the Work pane. This option is also available if you right-click on **Chassis**.

6. Click on **OK** on the pop-up message to confirm your action:

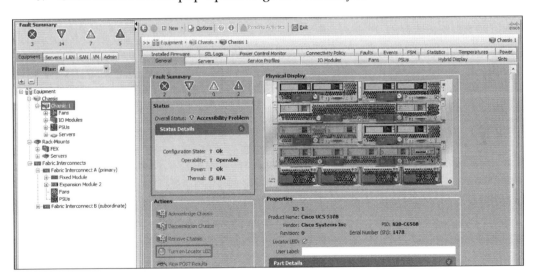

The preceding screen shows Status of the selected chassis. It also shows the option of turning on Locator LED. Once turned on, Locator LED will turn gray in UCS Manager and the text will change to **Turn off Locator LED**; now, Locator LED can be turned off from the same location:

Configuring logging

There are three major categories of the information collected by UCS Manager. These logs are accessible through the **Admin** tab in the Navigation pane.

Perform the following procedure to access the logs:

1. Log in to UCS Manager.

2. Click to expand the **Admin** tab in the Navigation pane.

3. In the **Admin** tab, click on **Faults, Events and Audit Log** to expand its content.

4. Click on the individual expanded tabs in the Navigation pane or individual horizontal tabs in the Work pane to expand the details of each category.

    ° **The Faults tab**: The **Faults** tab shows all the faults occurring on all UCS components. Individual faults are shown for each component when you are in the Components view and this tab provides details of all faults:

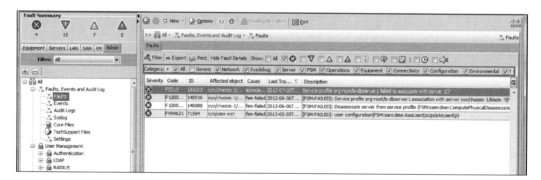

You may check or uncheck individual categories to filter the results.

- ○ **The Events tab**: Events are all the operations happening on all components such as a port configuration, a service profile association, and a VLAN configuration:

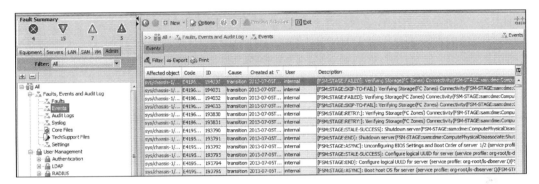

- ○ **The Audit Logs tab**: The **Audit Logs** tab provides the "audit trail", meaning which operations are carried out by which user. This log is helpful in establishing the accountability for the user actions:

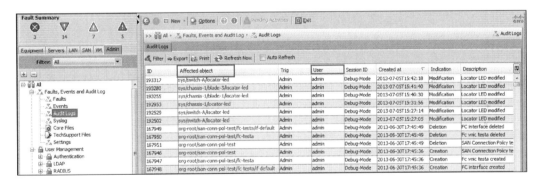

By default, **Faults, Events and Audit Log** are stored on the local UCS Fabric Interconnect. The default log settings are as shown in the following screenshot:

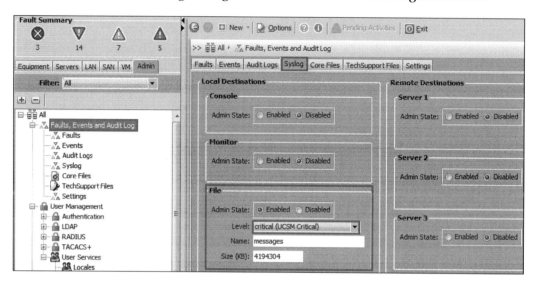

The default setting is to save all messages to a local file on Fabric Interconnect. In the **Level** section under **Local Destinations**, select the lowest message level and all the messages above that level will be automatically displayed.

It is also possible to show log messages on the **Console** or **Monitor** areas. The configuration option is the same, select the lowest level message and all messages above that level will be automatically displayed.

The following procedure shows how to direct the log message to the console:

1. Log in to UCS Manager.

2. Click on the **Admin** tab in the Navigation pane.

3. In the **Admin** tab, click on a **Faults, Events and Audit Log** to expand its content.

4. Click on individual expanded tabs in the Navigation pane or individual horizontal tabs in the Work pane to expand the **Syslog** category.

5. In the Work pane, under the **Console** area, click on **Enabled** to enable **Admin State**.

6. Select the message with the lowest state using the one of the three radio buttons **Emergencies, Alerts,** or **Critical**:

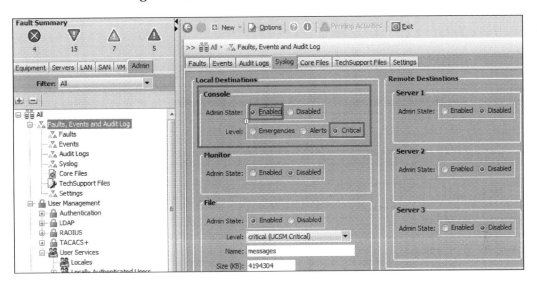

It is also possible to configure three remote Syslog Servers for the collection of UCS logs. Syslog Servers centralize the log collection.

Please use the following procedure to configure a remote Syslog Server:

1. Log in to UCS Manager.

2. Click on the **Admin** tab in the Navigation pane.

3. In the **Admin** tab, click on **Faults, Events and Audit Log** to expand its content.

4. Click on the individual expanded tabs in the Navigation pane or individual horizontal tabs in the Work pane to expand the **Syslog** category.

5. In the Work pane, in the **Remote Destinations** area, click on **Enabled** to enable **Admin State**.

6. Select the message with the lowest state using the drop-down menu for the messages. The above level messages will be automatically included.

7. Configure the hostname or IP for the remote Syslog server and select **Facility Level**:

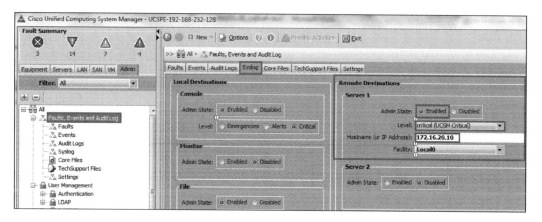

Configuring Cisco Call Home

The Call Home feature enables configuration of e-mail alert notifications for UCS errors and faults. The e-mail notifications can be configured for Cisco TAC (predefined) or any other recipient. This feature can be used to send a page message, an e-mail, or to generate a case with Cisco **Technical Assistance Center (TAC)**.

Cisco UCSM executes the appropriate CLI show command and the command output is attached to the message for Call Home messages.

Call Home messages are delivered in the following three formats:

- **Short text format**: Provides a short description, one or two lines of the fault that is suitable for pagers
- **Full text format**: Provides the complete message with detailed information
- **XML format**: The XML format enables communication with Cisco TAC

In the following example, we will configure Cisco Smart Call Home for UCS Call Home which will send the alert e-mails directly to Cisco TAC and to a network engineer.

1. Log in to UCS Manager.
2. Click on the **Admin** tab in the Navigation pane.
3. In the **Admin** tab, click on **Communication Management** to expand its content.
4. Click on **Call Home** under **Communication Management**.

5. In the Work pane, on the **General** tab, click on **On** under **Admin Area State**.

6. The screen will be extended for further configuration.

7. Configure **Contact Information** with the following details:

    ○ **Contact**

    ○ **Phone**

    ○ **Email**

    ○ **Address**

8. Configure the Cisco ID. The following information should be available from the CCO account:

    ○ **Customer ID**

    ○ **Contract ID**

    ○ **Site ID**

9. Configure the **From** e-mail address for the sender of the e-mail along with the **Reply To** e-mail address.

10. Configure the **SMTP** mail server with **IP/Hostname** and **Port** settings.

11. Click on the **Profiles** tab in the Work pane and edit the predefined **Cisco TAC-1** profile:

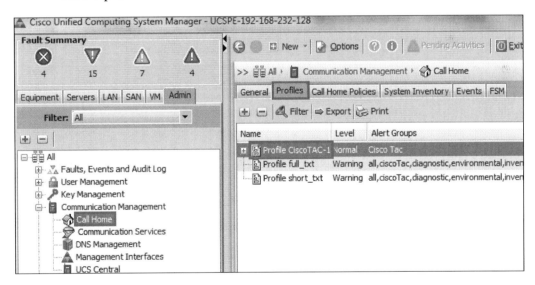

12. Add the e-mail recipient by clicking on the **+** sign in the pop-up window. The default e-mail format setting for the Cisco TAC profile is **Xml** and it cannot be changed. The severity level, however, can be changed:

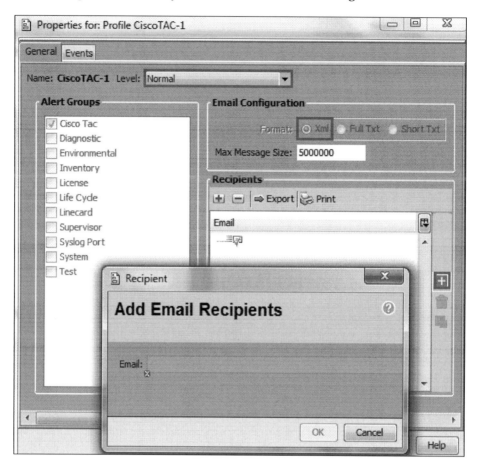

13. In the **Profiles** tab, edit the other predefined profile **full_text** and add the e-mail recipient. The default e-mail format is clear text and is grayed out. The severity level of messages can also be changed.

Apart from the predefined profiles, it is possible to create new profiles. Creating a new profile provides customization options such as severity level, mail format, and alert groups for all fields.

Organizational structure in UCS Manager

UCS organizational structure provides hierarchical configuration of the UCS resources. Organization can be created for policies, pools, and service profiles. The default organization for each category is Root. Based on the requirement, multiple suborganizations can be created under the Root organization. It is also possible to create nested suborganization under another suborganization. The hierarchical configuration into suborganizations has the following benefits:

- **Role-based Access Control (RBAC)**: For large setups, it is often required to delegate operational management to a team of professionals, and often with limited level of access to the resource, according to the role of the individual. Creating a suborganization and mapping appropriate user roles provides excellent security privileges and nonrepudiation.

- **Multitenancy**: For service providers, a suborganization's configuration provides the logical access isolation for the various clients who are sharing the physical UCS components. Unique resources to each tenant can be assigned related to the organizational structure. Combined with the RBAC configuration, a tenant's access privileges can be restricted to their organization only.

Please use the following procedure for creating suborganization under **Pools**. The procedure for creating suborganizations under the **Navigation** tab is similar, and once a suborganization is created under any tab, it will be available under all categories and resources:

1. Log in to UCS Manager.
2. Click on the **Servers** tab in the Navigation pane.
3. On the **Servers** tab click on **Pools** to expand its content.

4. Right-click on **Root** under **Pools** and click on **Create Organization**:

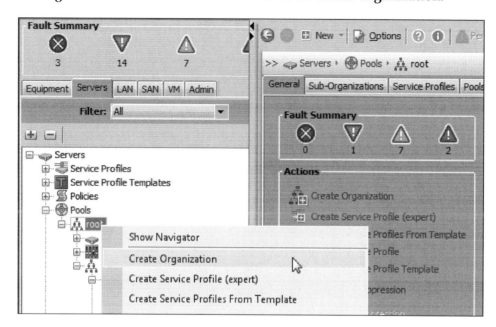

5. In the pop-up window, provide a name and description to the new organization and click on **OK**:

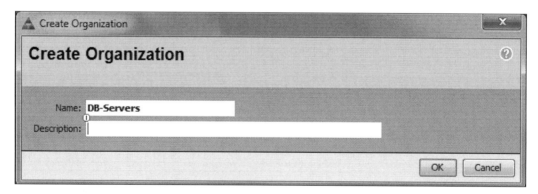

6. The new suborganization will be created under the **Root** organization.

Organizational inheritance

The policies, pools, and other resources configured under the root organization are available to all suborganizations. Root is the parent organization for all suborganizations. The resources configured under the suborganizations at the same level are not shared among the other suborganizations. A suborganization under another suborganization shares the resources of the parent.

Role-based Access Control

UCS Role-based Access Control (RBAC) provides granular control over the user security privileges. Combined with UCS organizations, RBAC delegates and controls the user access privileges according to the role and restricts user access within an organization boundary defined for the tenant in case of multitenancy.

Access privileges provide the users the capability to create, modify, or delete a specific type of configuration. UCS provides some predefined roles. **Roles** are a collection of different privileges. Hence, roles can be assigned to users according to their job requirement. For example, there's a built-in role called "read-only" that provides only read privileges to the user. This role can be assigned to any user to whom you do not want to provide any configuration capability.

In UCS, a user's authentication can be configured from various resources including the following:

- Local user
- LDAP (Active Directory, OpenLDAP, and so on)
- RADIUS
- TACACS+

Active Directory integration

We will now configure the LDAP authentication integration for UCS. We will integrate UCS Manager to Microsoft Active Directory Domain Controller. On the AD side, appropriate user groups should be created that can be used to provide mapping to UCS roles that provide privileges to the AD authenticated users accordingly.

Use the following procedure to enable Active Directory Authentication:

1. Log in to UCS Manager.
2. Click on the **Admin** tab in the Navigation pane.

3. On the **Admin** tab, click on **User Management** to expand its content.

4. Click on **LDAP** in the Navigation pane and click on **Create LDAP Provider** in the Work pane:

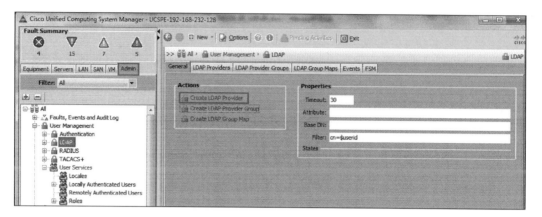

5. In the pop-up window, provide the following AD configuration details:

   1. Provide a DNS hostname or IP of the domain controller.

   2. Type in `lowest-available` in the **Order** field.

   3. Provide the **distinguished name** (**DN**) of the user with read and search permissions in the Active Directory into the **Bind DN** field. It is recommended to use the normal user account and not an administrator account for **Bind DN**.

   4. Provide a specification location of the AD where the search should start in the **Base DN** field. You may start from the root of AD for smaller organizations. For a large AD implementation, it is recommended to start the search where the AD users/groups are located.

   5. Type `389` in **Port** and leave **SSL** unchecked.

   6. Type `sAMAccountName=$userid` into the **Filter** field.

   7. Leave the **Attribute** field blank.

   8. Type in a password for the Bind user configured in step 3 and reconfirm the password.

9. Type in a **Timeout** value in seconds:

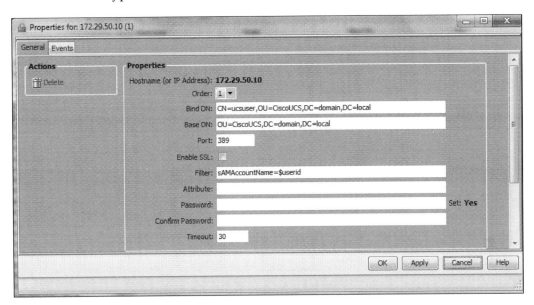

10. Click on **Next** and configure **Group Authorization** by clicking on the **Enable** button.

11. Leave the other two settings **Group Recursion** and **Target Attribute** with the default values.

12. Click on **Finish**.

13. Repeat the steps for the other domain controllers:

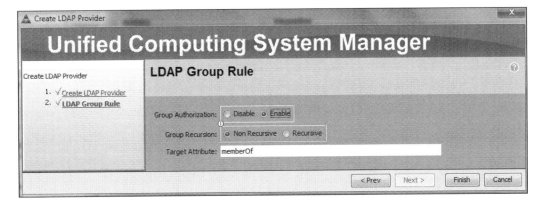

6. Create an LDAP Provider Group adding all domain controllers in the provider group and performing the following steps:

   1. Click on **LDAP** in the Navigation pane and click on **Create LDAP Provider Group** in the Work pane.

   2. In the pop-up window, assign a name for the LDAP Provider Group.

   3. Select domain controllers in the left-hand side pane and click on **>>** to add them to the group:

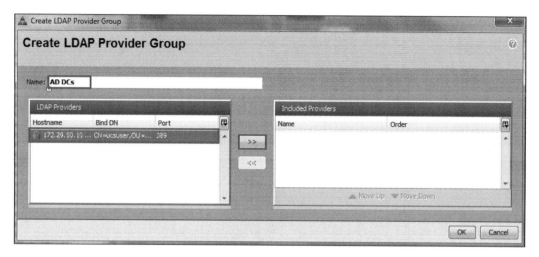

7. Create an LDAP Group Map for mapping AD users/groups to UCS local roles in order to provide access privileges. Perform the following steps to do so:

   1. Click on **LDAP** in the Navigation pane and click on **Create LDAP Group Map** in the Work pane.

   2. In the pop-up window, type in the LDAP Group DN of the AD user group to be mapped to a local role.

   3. Select the local UCS role from the **Roles** field.

4. Repeat the same procedure for adding all roles.

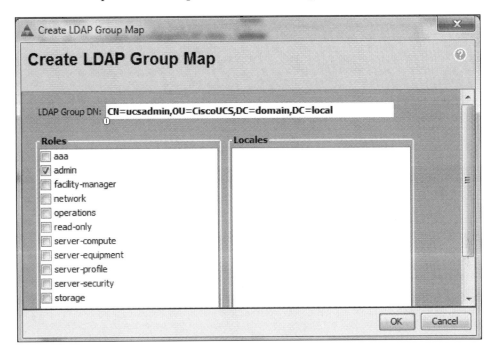

The next screenshot shows an example of some LDAP groups mapped to UCS roles. You can create different LDAP groups and map them to UCS local roles as per your environment.

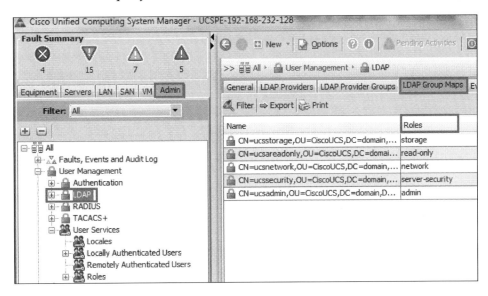

8. The last step for the Active Directory configuration is to define the authentication domain for UCS Manager:

1. Expand **Authentication** in **User Management** and right-click on **Authentication Domains** to create a new domain:

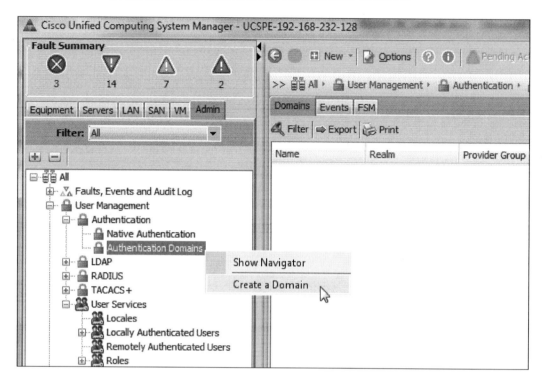

2. In the pop-up window, assign a name to the domain.

3. In the **Realm** field, select the **LDAP** radio button.

4. Select **Provider Group** from the drop-down menu and select **OK**:

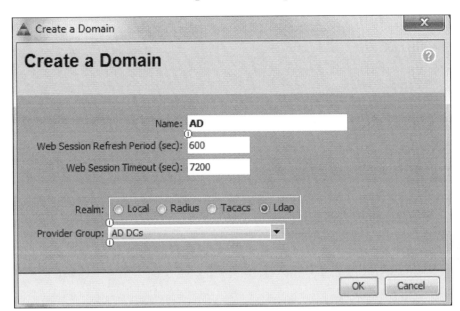

Predefined roles

UCS provides a number of predefined roles. These roles combine and provide different privileges as per organizational/team role roles of individual users. The built-in roles are as follows:

- **AAA Administrator**: This role provides the member with full access to a user configuration, roles assignment, and **Authentication, Authorization, and Accounting (AAA)** configuration and provides the read access to the rest of the system.

- **Administrator**: This role provides the member *complete* control to the UCSM. The default local admin account has this role by default, which cannot be changed.

- **Facility Manager**: This role provides the member with full access to power management operations through the **power-mgmt** privilege and provides read access to the rest of the system.

- **Network**: This role provides the member full access to the Fabric Interconnect infrastructure and network security operations and provides read access to the rest of the system.

- **Operations**: This role provides the member full access to systems logs, including the syslog servers and faults, and provides read access to the rest of the system.

- **Read-Only**: This role provides the read-only access to the system configuration with no privileges to modify the system state.

- **Server Compute**: This new role introduced in UCS 2.1 provides somewhat limited access to the service profiles, for example, a user cannot change vNICs or vHBAs configurations.

- **Server Equipment**: This role provides full access to physical-server-related operations and provides the read access to the rest of the system.

- **Server Profile**: This role provides full access to logical server related operations and provides the read access to the rest of the system.

- **Server Security**: This role provides full access to server-security-related operations and the read access to the rest of the system.

- **Storage Administrator**: This role provides full access to storage operations and provides the read access to the rest of the system.

It is also possible to create user-defined roles based on design requirements by adding the new role and assigning required individual privileges.

About UCS locales

UCS locales define the location of the user in the UCS organization hierarchy. A user without a locale assignment has access to the root organization. This means that the user has access to all suborganizations. Locales can be mapped to the suborganization, restricting the user access within the scope of suborganization. Locales can be created and then the user can be mapped to locales.

Perform the following steps to create a locale and restrict some users access to a suborganization:

1. Log in to UCS Manager.
2. Click to expand the **Admin** tab in the Navigation pane.
3. On the **Admin** tab, click on **User Management** to expand **User Services**.
4. Right-click on **Locales** in the Navigation pane and click on **Create New Locale**:

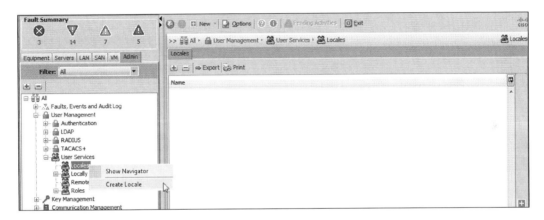

5. Assign a name for the locale and click on **Next**:

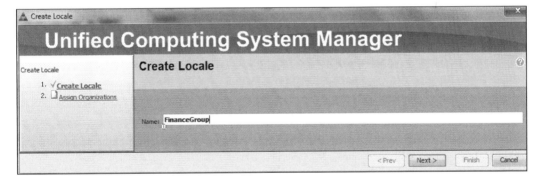

6. Expand **Organizations** in the left-hand side pane and drag-and-drop it to **Locale** in the right-hand side pane:

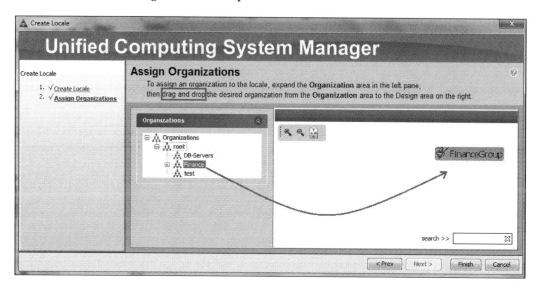

7. Click on **Finish**.

The new locale will be available which can be used by any locally or remotely authenticated users. Once the locale is assigned to the users/groups, the access will be limited to the suborganization.

To assign a locale to remote Active Directory authenticated users/groups, use the following procedure:

1. Log in to UCS Manager.
2. Click on the **Admin** tab in the Navigation pane.
3. On the **Admin** tab, click on **User Management** to expand **LDAP** content.
4. Select the existing AD groups and double-click on it to edit the settings.

5. A new option in the locale will be available which can be assigned:

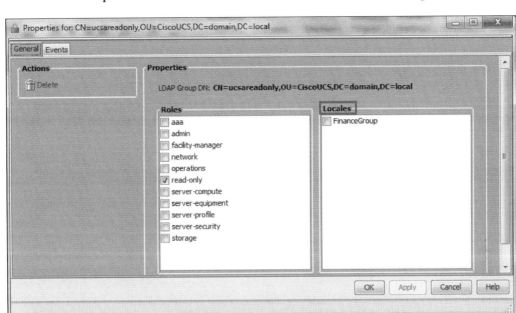

A UCS Manager admin user, which is configured as part of the initial configuration, can be used to log in to UCS Manager if the LDAP authentication is not available by selecting local authentication on the UCSM login screen.

Permissions in Multitenancy

Multitenancy is a requirement for service providers. A service provider can provide access to multiple tenants within the same UCS infrastructure with logical security isolation between tenants so that the resources provided to one tenant cannot be tampered by another.

UCS Multitenancy can be achieved with the following:

- Creation of a suborganization for each tenant
- Creation of locales to restrict user access to individual suborganizations

For example, we will create two tenants: Tenant 1 and Tenant 2.

Follow the steps defined in the *Organizational structure in UCS Manager* section of this chapter and create two tenants. Two organizational units defined as **Tenant1** and **Tenant2** are shown below in the screenshot:

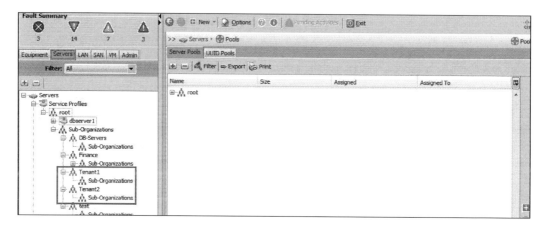

Follow the steps explained in the *Role-based Access Control* section of this chapter to create two locales for the suborganizations for the tenants:

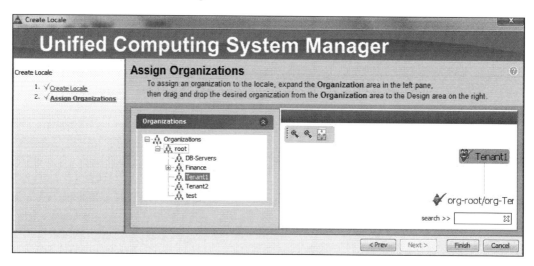

Create and map local users as explained in the *Role-based Access Control* section of this chapter:

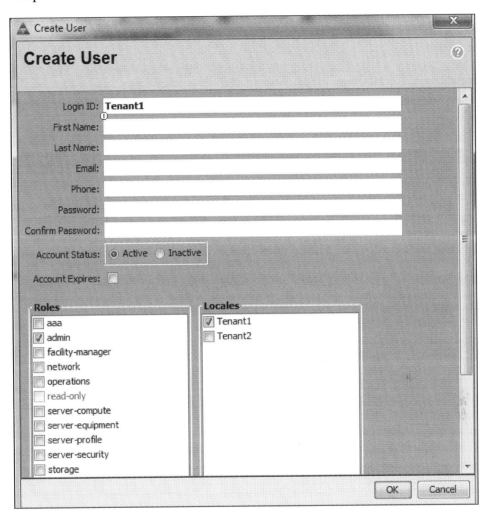

Summary

In this chapter, we learned about the miscellaneous and most common tasks along with some advanced management tasks you need to perform with UCS Manager. We started looking at how to obtain and configure extra port licenses for Fabric Interconnects. We learned that UCS Fabric Interconnects are designed for continuous operation and hence do not have a power button. It is however possible to reboot Fabric Interconnect, but only from CLI. We learned about a corner case requirement in a DR situation for how to control blade power usage. We learned about looking into the Status messages and turning on/off the Locator LEDs available on blades, blade chassis, and Fabric Interconnects. We covered what the default logging setting is and how we can configure a remote Syslog server. We configured the Call Home feature which can be used to inform/alert UCS management teams and Cisco Technical Assistance Center (TAC).

We finally learned about how we can configure organizational structure and role-based access control in UCS. We configured an external authentication using the LDAP configuration for Microsoft Active Directory and also mapped users to UCS locales. Combining user authentication, organization structure, and locales, it is possible to configure permissions for multitenant environments. UCS organizational design and the RBAC configuration provides the required security for authentication, authorization, and accountability to UCS in large-scale or multitenant UCS deployments where delegation of accesses with user nonrepudiation is required.

In the next chapter, we will learn about the integration of Cisco UCS within virtualized environments, mostly with VMware vSphere, which is the dominant hypervisor deployed in production environments and we will also look into Cisco Nexus 1000v Distributed Virtual Switch.

9

Virtual Networking in Cisco UCS

Cisco Nexus 1000v switch is a virtual machine that acts as an access switch. It is an intelligent software switch implementation based on IEEE 802.1Q standard for VMware vSphere environments, running the Cisco NX-OS software operating system.

The Nexus 1000v switch is a distributed layer 2 switch that is implemented as a virtual softswitch and runs Cisco's NX-OS.

In this chapter we will cover the following topics:

- Knowing about VN-Link
- Using the NX-OS
- Development of Nexus 1000v
- Nexus 1000v components
- VEM and VSM implementation
- **Virtual Ethernet Module (VEM)** data plane
- **Virtual Supervisor Module (VSM)** control plane
- Nexus 1000v and physical switches
- Deploying VSM
- Communication between VSM and VEM

Understanding IEEE 802.1Q

IEEE 802.1Q is the networking standard that supports **Virtual LANs (VLANs)** on an Ethernet network. The standard defines a system of VLAN tagging for Ethernet frames and the accompanying procedures to be used by bridges and switches in handling such frames. More information on this is available at http://en.wikipedia.org/wiki/IEEE_802.1Q.

Learning about VN-Link

VN-Link network services are available in VMware vSphere environments with the Nexus 1000v switch. Basically, it is a set of features and capabilities that enables VM interfaces to be individually identified, configured, monitored, migrated, and diagnosed so that they are consistent with the current network operational models. It replicates an operational experience similar to using a cable to connect a NIC with the network port of an access-layer switch.

Using the NX-OS

The Nexus 1000v switch offers the same Cisco NX-OS capabilities as the physical switch, which includes the following:

- **High availability**: Stateful failover is possible through synchronized, redundant VSMs

- **Management**: Standard management tools such as **Command Line Interface (CLI)**, **Simple Network Management Protocol (SNMP)**, XML API, and CiscoWorks **LAN Management Solution (LMS)** can be used

Changes in the datacenter

Moving from the physical to virtual, applications, network policies, and the **Network Administrator (NA)** and **Server Administrator (SA)** roles are the same. However, the network edge is now virtual and has moved into the host, that is, the ESXi server. This changes the distinct boundary between the SA and NA roles.

Where physical machines were once just plugged into a switch, and the switch port configured, the SA can now create and deploy multiple hosts in a fraction of time. And while the host lifecycle has changed significantly, the same management policies need to apply in both cases, which means that access lists, VLANs, port security, and many more parameters need to be consistent. The challenge for SAs is to take advantage of the flexibility of virtualization while conforming to organizational policy.

The challenge for NAs is to maintain control over the network traffic and the access ports that are running over hardware they don't directly control. Have a look at the following figure for more details:

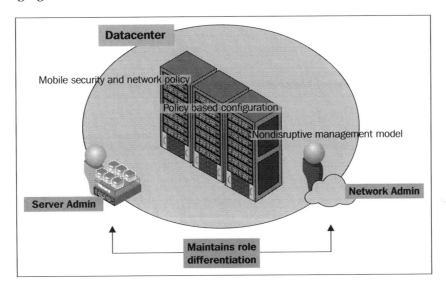

Specific benefits of the Nexus 1000v switch that help address these challenges are as follows:

- **Policy-based configuration**: This signifies a real-time configuration of network, storage, and security services. Server administrator's efficiency and flexibility can be rapidly improved using the policy-based configuration as it introduces a VM-centric management.

- **Mobile security and network policy**: When you perform a live migration such as vMotion, it moves the policy as well with the VM for a persistent network. In that way, vMotion won't be affected.

- **Nondisruptive management model**: Management and operations can come together in a single line for VMs' connectivity in the datacenter. Operational consistency and visibility is well maintained throughout the network.

Role differentiation

Nexus 1000v (N1KV) offers flexible collaboration between the server, network, security, and storage teams while supporting organizational boundaries and individual team autonomy. Essentially, it ensures that the traditional boundary between the SA and NA roles is maintained.

Role issues

Moving from the physical to virtual; applications, network policies, and the NA and SA roles are the same. However, the network edge is now virtual and has moved into the host, that is, the ESXi server. This changes the distinct boundary between the SA and NA roles. There is the added complication of VM lifecycles moving from months/years to weeks/day. So basically, port management is increasingly difficult. Have a look at the following figure for more details:

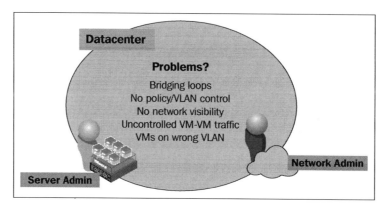

The following are some major problems with role issues:

* VMs can result in bridging loops on the network

* VMs could be on the wrong VLANs

* No insight into VM to VM communication is available

* The network admin has no visibility or policy/VLAN control

Development of Nexus 1000v

N1KV was developed jointly by VMware and Cisco. As such, it is certified by VMware to be compatible with VMware vSphere, vCenter, ESXi, and many other vSphere features.

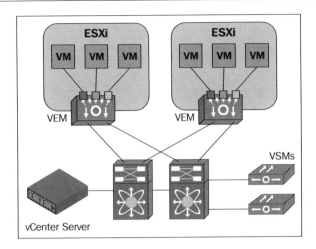

Virtual Ethernet interfaces

Cisco N1KV when enabled for VN-Link, operates on the basis of **virtual Ethernet (vEth)** interfaces. Once enabled for VN-Link, it maintains network configuration attributes, such as security and statistics for a given virtual interface across mobility events. vEth interfaces are comparable of physical network access ports. A mapping gets created between each vEth interface and the corresponding vNICs on the VM. You may ask me why you would need vEth interfaces. The main advantage of using these is that they can follow vNICs when VMs move to other ESXi hosts. Once you set up a VN-Link on N1KV switches, it enables transparent mobility of VMs across different ESXi hosts and physical access-layer switches, and it does so by virtualizing the network access port with vEth interfaces.

Learning about port profiles

Port profiles are nothing but a collection of interface configuration commands (same as physical switches) that can be dynamically applied at either physical or virtual interfaces on Cisco N1KV. So as an effect, if you make any change to a given port profile, it will be propagated immediately to all the ports that have been associated with it. For troubleshooting in a port profile, you have the flexibility to define a collection of attributes, such as VLAN, **private VLAN (PVLAN)**, ACL, port security, NetFlow collection, rate limiting, QoS marking, and even remote-port mirroring but only through **Encapsulated Remote SPAN (ERSPAN)**.

VN-Link can be implemented as a Cisco **Distributed Virtual Switch (DVS)**, running entirely in software within the hypervisor layer (N1KV) or in devices that support **Network Interface Virtualization (NIV)**, eliminating the requirement for software-based switching within hypervisors (Cisco UCS).

Nexus 1000v components

N1KV consists of VSMs and VEMs. While VEMs are software elements that reside inside the hypervisor, running as a part of the VMware ESXi kernel, the VSM is deployed as a virtual appliance. Have a look at the following figure for more details:

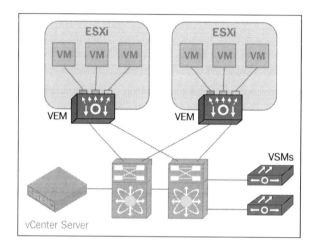

The highlighted components in the preceding figure are explained in the following sections.

The Virtual Ethernet Module

The VEM runs as a part of the VMware ESXi kernel. It uses the VMware **vNetwork Distributed Switch (vDS)** API to provide advanced networking capabilities to VMs.

The VEM provides advanced networking functions, such as **Quality of Service (QoS)**, security features, and monitoring features by taking configuration information from the VSM.

The Virtual Supervisor Module

Multiple VEMs create a single logical switch layer to the VSM. The VSM maintains configuration and pushes down the configuration to the VEMs. The administrator has the ability to define configurations on all VEMs being managed by the VSM from a single interface.

 The VSM can reside on a host that has exclusive network connectivity through Cisco N1KV. It can, therefore, manage its own network connectivity.

VEM implementation

The following are some important features of VEM:

- It is a virtual line card
- It is embedded in the vSphere host (hypervisor)
- It provides each VM with dedicated switch ports
- It has a switch in every host

Here, we run the ESXi package manager to show the VIB file used to implement the VEM. If you list the processes, you will also see the VEM data path agent, `vemdpa` that communicates with the VSM (running in the user mode).

Finally, the hypervisor driver (running in the kernel mode) performs packet switching.

 vCenter can operate without too much regard for the VEM. Typically, the only reason to go there (via SSH) is for troubleshooting purposes.

esxupdate is no longer supported but we can use it here to illustrate a point.

VSM implementation

The VSM acts as a control plane for the N1KVsolution, that is, it is responsible for the vCenter communication, programming, and management of VEMs. Unlike the VEM, which is a code running in the hypervisor, it is actually a VM on an ESXi server. It can also be deployed on a dedicated hardware appliance, such as Nexus 1010. VSMs are typically deployed as **High Availability (HA)** pairs. Have a look at the following figure for more details:

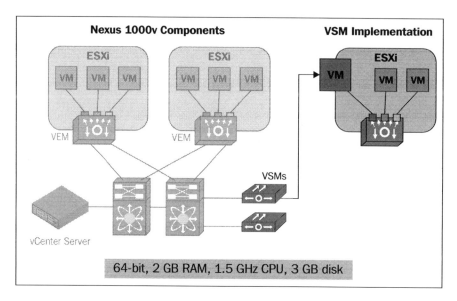

Please note that we can't have one VSM on Nexus 1010 and the other on the ESXi VSM.

- Control plane controls multiple VEMS
- Virtual machine running NX-OS

VEM data plane

There is a 1:1 mapping between hypervisor and VEM. VEM replaces the virtual switch by performing the following functions:

- Advanced networking and security
- Switching between directly attached VMs
- Uplinking to the rest of the network

You can install only one version of VEM on an ESXi host at any given point of time. Please have a look at the following figure for more details:

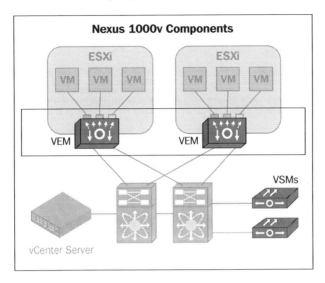

VEM functions

The following are the various functions of VEM:

- Advanced networking and security
- Switching between directly attached VMs
- Uplink to the rest of the network

Unlike conventional Nexus switches, each line card has its own **Media Access Control (MAC)** table that goes through the same process as conventional switches.

- **Ingress**: Traffic that comes inbound towards the interfaces of the N1KV switch
- **L2 Lookup**: A process that handles the packets after the parser engine has parsed the initial packet delivery
- **Egress**: Traffic goes out of the interfaces of the N1KV switch

VSM control plane

A VSM can be deployed either as a standalone or as an active/standby HA pair. It controls the VEMs and performs the following functions for the Cisco N1KV system:

- Configuration
- Management
- Monitoring
- Diagnostics
- Integration with the VMware vCenter

The following figure explains the various N1KV components and their relation. Essentially, it explains the relation between a VSM and VEM.

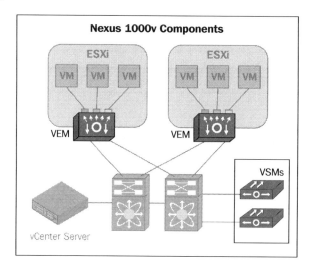

Nexus 1000v and physical switches

The VEM corresponds to a line card in a conventional physical switch while the VSM corresponds to a supervisor engine.

The physical switch chassis

In a hardware switch, the physical wiring that connects the **Supervisor Engine (SE)** and the individual line cards is known as the backplane. This is incorporated into the switch chassis. There are numerous types of modular switches which will have different configurations depending on their functions. However, all switches will have an SE and typically some Ethernet line cards.

Line cards

Other line cards include **Advanced Integrated Services Modules (AISMs)** that include firewall services, content switching, **Intruder Detection System (IDS)**, and **Wireless and Network Analysis Modules (WNAS)**.

Cisco N1KV uses local VEM instances to switch the traffic between VMs. Each VEM also interconnects the local VM with the rest of the network through the upstream access-layer network switch. VSM never forwards the packets. It runs the control plane protocols and configures the state of each VEM accordingly.

The N1KV backplane

The backplane function here is performed by the physical uplink switches, that is, the organization's own infrastructure. The number of line cards supported then is not determined by the physical capacity of the chassis, but by the VSM. Currently, up to 64 VEMs are supported by a single VSM or a HA pair.

 Obviously, you're limited to the type of cards that are feasible using this model. However, there are ways to enhance the functionality of N1KV using an appliance which allows other modules such as a firewall and **Network Access Module (NAM)**. Nexus 1010 is one such appliance.

In N1KV, there are two module slots. Either module can act as active or standby. As an effect, the first ESXi host will automatically be assigned to Module 1. The ports to which the virtual NIC interfaces connect are virtual ports on Cisco N1KV, where they are assigned a global number. Have a look at the following figure for more details:

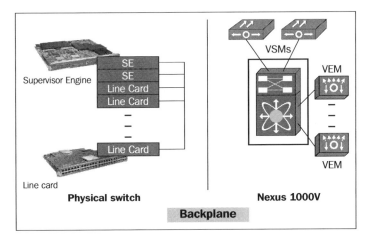

With the challenges presented by virtualization to the demarcation between host and network, N1KV allows the necessary collaboration between NAs and SAs.

Internal fabric helps the supervisors and line cards to communicate in a physical switch. On a similar note, N1KV uses external fabric that is provided by the upstream switches in the physical infrastructure.

The physical switch's backplane helps line cards to forward traffic to each other. However, N1KV does not have a backplane, thus a VEM cannot directly forward packets to another VEM. So, it has to forward the packet via some uplink to the external fabric, which then switches it to the destination.

Each VEM in Cisco N1KV is designed in order to prevent loops in the network topology, as using the **Spanning Tree Protocol (STP)** will deactivate all but one uplink to an upstream switch, hence preventing full utilization of the uplink bandwidth.

You can bundle the uplinks in a host in a port channel for load balancing and HA.

Nexus and vPath

Cisco vPath allows you to deploy network services like in a physical switch. It is embedded in every VEM. Essentially, it provides intelligent packet steering which means that policy lookup is decoupled from enforcement. For example, with the **Virtual Security Gateway (VSG)**, which is a virtualized Cisco firewall, once a policy decision is made at the VSG for a particular flow, it's up to vPath now to implement that policy for each packet in that flow; thereby freeing up the VSG.

The vPath is enabled at a port-profile level. When VSG policies are configured, flow is evaluated against the policy by the VSG, and then the policy decision is pushed for implementation to vPath. It stores that decision only for the duration of that flow. Once there is a **Reset (RST)** event or **Finish (FIN)** flag, the flow entry is removed from the vPath table. There is also an activity timer which can terminate sessions.

FIN and RST are TCP control bits (flags). FIN indicates that the client will send no more data, while RST resets the connection. **Virtual Wide Area Application Services (vWAAS)** is Cisco's WAN optimization technology used to improve application delivery in cloud environments. Have a look at the following figure for more details:

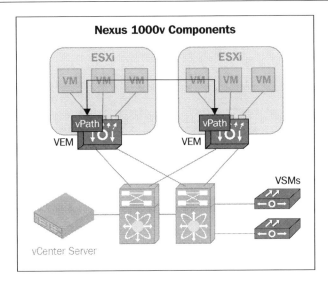

Performance advantages using vPath

vPath also provides performance advantages. Since only the initial packets of a flow need to go to the VSG, there is less packet steering going on. Subsequent policy enforcement is done by the local N1KV VEM in the kernel mode, so you get better performance overall.

HA is available, but if the service that vPath is directing to fails (for example, in the case of a firewall service where both firewalls are down), there is the option of failing "closed" or "open". It can stop all traffic, or can be configured to let everything through.

Deploying VSM

This is a good example to show how Nexus maintains the division between administrator roles while requiring collaboration at the same time.

1. Deploying VSM is the responsibility of an SA. The Cisco N1KV series is installed through a GUI installer when the OVA file is used.

2. Once the VSM deployment is done, NA finishes the installation of the Cisco N1KV switch. Once that job is done, the NA needs to open up the web interface of the Cisco N1KV. It needs to configure the VSM with the appropriate port-group VLAN and also perform the basic configuration of the Cisco N1KV series.

3. Once the communication gets established, the NA defines the port profiles to be used by the uplink interfaces, VMs, and other virtual interfaces. This is done via SSH to the N1KV switch.

4. Once the NA finishes defining the port profiles, the SA assigns the uplink port profiles to the appropriate physical NICs and then the port profile to VMs, providing network connectivity to the guest OS and migrating the VSM on its own port profile. If an SA uses the VMware update manager, the VEM code on each VMware ESXi server gets installed automatically. If the server administrator is not using the VMware update manager, the VEM has to be installed manually before the host is added.

VSM installation

For installing and configuring Cisco N1KV, you need three mandatory VM port groups in vCenter before installing and these are control, packet, and management. You can use just one VLAN for all of these but it is preferred to have them configured with separate VLANs.

First download the N1KV VSM at `http://www.cisco.com/go/1000veval` and then use the following procedure to deploy and install the VSM:

1. Unzip the Nexus1000v VSM ZIP file. Go to vCenter, click on the **File** menu, and select **Deploy OVF Template**.

2. Browse to the location of the unzipped file and double-click on the vsm folder. Click on **Browse...** to install the required folder, select the OVA file, and click on **Next** as shown in the following screenshot:

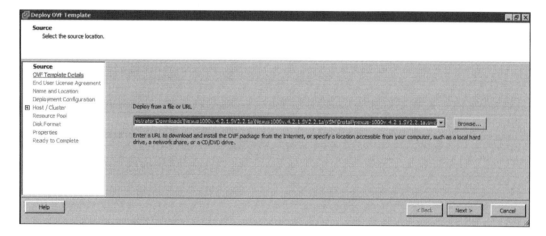

3. Click on **Next** twice.

4. Click on **Accept** for the **End User License Agreement** page and then click on **Next**.

5. Specify a name for the N1KV VSM and select the datacenter where you would like it to be installed. Then, click on **Next** as shown in the following screenshot:

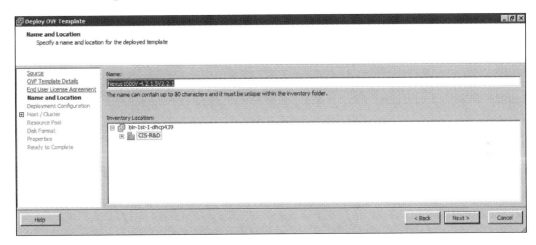

6. As this is the first installation, select **Nexus 1000v Installer** from the drop-down menu given for **Configuration**. This will also allow you to set up the Nexus switch via GUI. Then, click on **Next** as shown in the following screenshot:

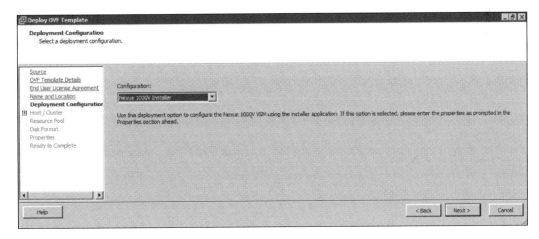

7. Select your **Datacenter** object again and click on **Next**.

8. Select the **Datastore** object to install the Nexus switch.

9. Choose **Thin Provisioning** for the virtual disk of Nexus and click on **Next**.

10. Under **Destination Networks**, select the networks that you had created earlier for **Control**, **Management**, and **Packet**. Then, click on **Next** as shown in the following screenshot:

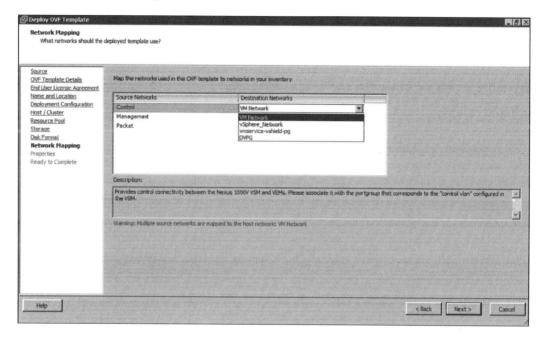

11. Enter the **VSM Domain ID, Nexus 1000V Admin User Password,** and **Management IP Address** values as shown in the following screenshot:

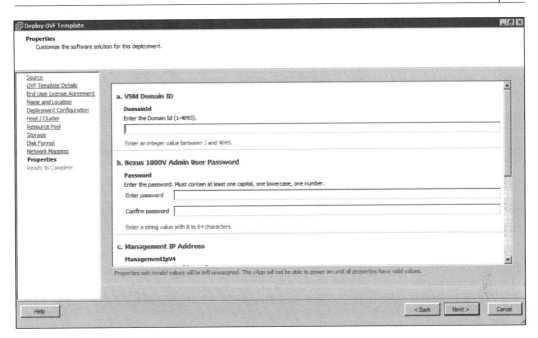

12. Specify the **Management Subnet Mask** and **IP Gateway** values too. Then, click on **Next**.

13. A summary of all your settings is then presented. If you are happy with these settings, click on **Finish**.

14. The deployment of the Nexus 1000v switch will then get started.

15. Once deployed, select the **Nexus 1000v** VM and click on **Power On** in the **Summary** screen.

16. Now, open your web browser and browse to the management IP address of your Nexus 1000v that you had set.

 If you are using Cisco Nexus 1000V Release 4.2(1)SV1(5.1) or later, the web mode of launching cannot be used as the installer is now defunct.

17. Click on **Launch Installer Application**. On a side note, this management station must have Java installed to run the application installer. Enter the VSM password that you had set in Step 11. Then, click on **Next**.

18. Enter your vCenter information that consists of **IP Address/Hostname**, **Port (https only)**, **User ID**, and **Password**. Then, click on **Next** as shown in the following screenshot:

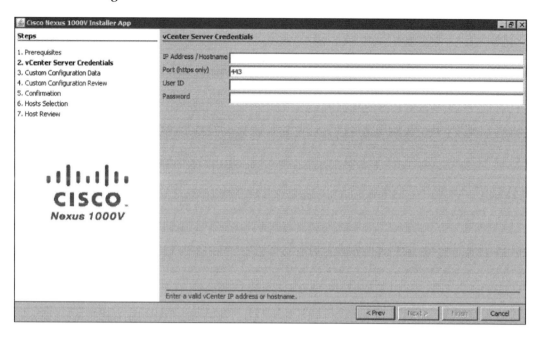

19. Choose your VMware cluster from the given list and click on **Next**.

20. From the drop-down menu, select the Nexus 1000v VM that you had created previously, choose **Advanced L2** and match the **Control**, **Management**, and **Packet** port groups to the ones you had created earlier. Then, click on **Next**.

21. Just make a note to select **Primary** as the **System Redundancy Role** value. Telnet can be enabled optionally. Then, click on **Next**.

22. You will see that a configuration summary is displayed. Click on **Next** to continue. The configuration of Nexus 1000v will now begin.

23. Select **No** at this stage so that we don't migrate the host and its networks across to the Nexus 1000v just yet. We will do it manually later on to have more control of the options. Then, click on **Finish**.

24. Once the installation is done, you will be presented with an installation summary. Then, click on **Close**.

25. The Cisco Nexus 1000v plugin is now installed in the vCenter server. You can verify this by opening vCenter and navigating to **Plug-ins | Manage Plug-ins**. You will see the plugin under **Available Plug-ins**.

26. You need to create a port profile of Ethernet type for the uplink management. For this, log in to the Nexus 1000v switch using SSH and type the following commands:

```
port-profile type ethernet system-uplink
    vmware port-group
    switchport mode trunk
    switchport trunk allowed vlan 1-1000
    mtu 9000
    no shutdown
    system vlan 1-1000
    state enabled
```

27. Move over to vCenter and add your ESXi host to the Nexus environment.

28. Open vCenter, click on **Inventory**, and select **Networking**.

29. Expand **Datacenter** and select **Nexus Switch**. Right-click on it and select **Add Host**.

30. Select one of the unused VMNICs on the host, then select the uplink port group created earlier (the one carrying the system VLAN data), and click on **Next**.

31. On the **Network Connectivity** page, click on **Next**.

32. On the **Virtual Machine Networking** page, click on **Next**. Please do not select the checkbox to migrate virtual machine networking.

33. On the **Ready to complete** page, click on **Finish**.

34. Finally, run the vemcmd show card command to confirm if the opaque data is now being received by the VEM.

35. Log in to your Nexus 1000v switch and type in show module to check whether your host has been added or not.

36. Log in to your ESXi server and type VEM Status. As you can see, VEM is now loaded on VMNIC.

Communication between VSM and VEM

There are two options for enabling communication between a VSM and a VEM: Layer 2 and Layer 3 (L2/L3). This is known as the **Software Virtual Switch (SVS)** mode.

Using Layer 2 connectivity

If the VSM and VEM are in the same Layer 2 domain, the best way to connect them is to use the Layer 2 connectivity mode which can be done through the following command line:

```
Nexus1000v(config-svs-domain)# svs mode L2
```

Using Layer 3 connectivity

If the VSM and the VEM are in different Layer 2 domains, the Layer 3 connectivity mode should be used. This can be achieved through the following command line:

```
Nexus1000v(config-svs-domain)# svs mode L3
```

The following figure explains the Layer 3 connectivity in detail:

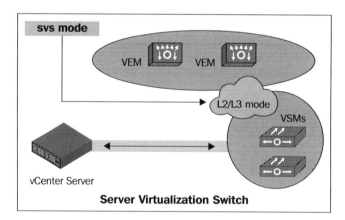

Using the Domain ID

The control information on a physical switch is normally transparent to the network module. This internal network is isolated by design. However, the N1KV control packets need to traverse the physical network between the VSM and the VEM.

Cisco N1KV uses the domain ID to identify a VSM and a VEM for ease of relating to one another, so that the VEM only receives the control packets intended for it and from the correct VSM. An SA defines this ID at the time of the VSM installation and becomes a part of the opaque data that is transmitted to vCenter.

This concept is depicted in the following figure:

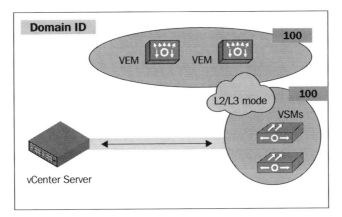

L2 mode

If you look at the following figure, you will see that two virtual interfaces are used to communicate between the VSM and the VEM:

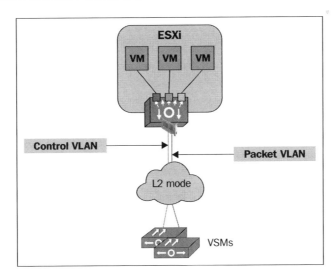

L3 mode

A VEM will use the VMkernel interface to tunnel the control and packet traffic to the VSM using **User Datagram Protocol (UDP)**. You can create a VMkernel interface per VEM and attach an L3 control port profile to it.

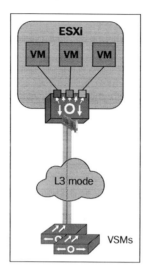

System VLANs and opaque data

You can add system VLANs as an optional parameter in a port profile. When you use the system VLAN parameter in a port profile, it helps the port profile to act as a special system port profile that is included in the N1KV opaque data. Interfaces which use this type of port profile, along with the members of one of the system VLANs, by default get enabled and forwarded. As a ripple effect, if the VEM does not have communication with the VSM, it still communicates when the ESXi host starts. This enables the use of critical host functions if the ESXi host starts but is unable to communicate with the VSM.

As a Cisco best practice, both the control and packet VLANs must be defined as system VLANs. Without this, they will not be included in the opaque data and therefore, the VEM will be unable to communicate with the VSM.

VSM to vCenter communication

Another important element of Cisco N1KV is VSM to vCenter communication.

The VSM connects via the management interface using a self-signed SSL certificate. It uses the vCenter API. Through this API, it can create port groups and pull data from the vCenter. The VSM can also store the DVS data in the vCenter database through this API.

It can also create dv-Port-Groups distributed virtual switch port groups in the vCenter and store the DVS data to be passed to ESXi hosts, which become members of the Nexus switch. It also gets useful information from the vCenter about its current structure.

Summary

In this chapter we introduced the Cisco N1KV virtual switch and outlined its implementation and features.

We identified functions of the N1KV components, installed those components, and identified their features too.

In the next chapter we will talk about the backup, restore, and HA of the Cisco UCS environment.

10
Configuring Backup, Restore, and High Availability

In this chapter, we'll learn how to back up and restore the UCS configuration. There are multiple UCS backup options which can be used either in disaster recovery scenarios to fully restore the Fabric Interconnects configuration and state or can be used to export the UCS configuration data to be imported to the same, or a different system. UCS configuration backups are in XML format and hence can be easily modified if required. We'll show different backup options and walk through creating and importing backup jobs from both the GUI and the command line.

In the second half of the chapter, we will learn about the Fabric Interconnect high-availability feature. This feature is for control plane functions only. From the data plane perspective, Fabric Interconnects actively participate in data flow and fabric failover can be configured at the vNICs level. For control plane, one Fabric Interconnect is configured as primary and the other as secondary in a cluster. Most of the high-availability configuration is possible from the GUI but there are some configurations and details which are only available through CLI. We will take a look into both GUI and CLI, for backup and high availability.

The following is a list of topics that will be covered in this chapter:

- Backing up the Cisco UCS configuration
- Creating UCS backup jobs
- Restoring backups using GUI
- Configuring high-availability clustering
- Fabric Interconnect elections
- Managing high availability

Backing up the Cisco UCS configuration

The following are the different options available for UCS data backup:

- **Full state backup**: Full state backup is the backup of an entire system in the binary format. It contains the system configuration, logical configuration, and the state of the system like assignment of pools, MAC addresses, FSM, faults, and so on. This type of backup can be used in a disaster recovery scenario to recover the whole configuration of a failed Fabric Interconnect. This type of backup cannot be imported to a different system. Full state backup is a snapshot of the system at a specific time. Any changes to the system render it obsolete. Any changes after the full state backup are lost if a system is restored from the backup.

- **System configuration backup**: System configuration backup consists of administrative settings such as username, RBAC, and locales in the XML format. This backup does not contain the system state and hence cannot be used to restore a system. This backup can be used to import system configuration settings to the original or a different Fabric Interconnect.

- **Logical configuration backup**: Logical configuration backup consists of administrative setting such as pools, policies, service profiles, and VLANs in XML format. This backup does not contain the system state and hence cannot be used to restore a system. This backup can be used to import system configuration settings to the original or a different Fabric Interconnect.

- **All configuration backup**: All configuration backup consists of System and Logical configuration backups in XML format. This backup does not contain the system state and hence cannot be used to restore a system. This backup can be used to import all configuration settings to the original or a different Fabric Interconnect.

UCS backup is non-disruptive and can be performed while the system is in production without any impact to the operating system running on the blade servers. A backup operation can be used to take a one-time backup or it can be scheduled to take a full state or all configuration backup using Backup and Export policy. Backups can be exported to multiple types of destinations including local filesystem (filesystem of the computer where UCS Manager is running), FTP, TFTP, SCP, and SFTP.

 UCS Manager Backup is not intended for taking Server Operating System level backup, which is running on the blade servers.

Creating UCS backup jobs

UCS backup job creation is done in the administrative configuration area of the UCS Manager GUI, or it could be accomplished using admin scope in the CLI mode. We will first walk through the graphical interface configuration and explain the various options and then we will walk through the command-line configuration.

Creating a manually run backup job using GUI

UCS backup jobs can be either run manually or can be programmed to run at specific schedules. We will first look at how to create a manual job. In order to create a manually run job, follow these steps:

1. Log in to UCS Manager.

2. Click on the **Admin** tab in the navigation pane.

3. Click on the **All** tab in the navigation pane and click on **Backup Configuration** in the work pane in the **General** tab.

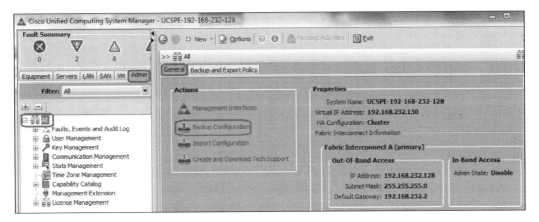

4. Click on **Create Backup Operation**.

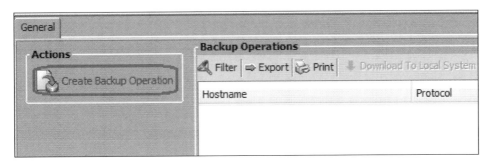

5. On the next pop-up screen, provide details for the backup job.

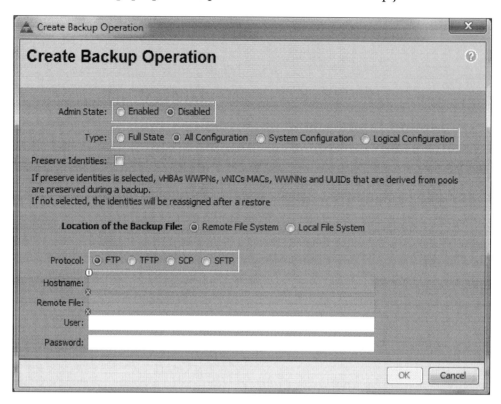

6. This table provides description for the configuration options available on the above screenshot:

Configuration	Description
Admin State	**Enabled**: The backup job runs immediately after the configuration is complete.
	Disabled: The backup configuration is completed but the job is not run immediately which could be manually run at a later time.
Type	Select the type of backup which could be **Full State**, **All Configuration**, **System Configuration**, and **Logical Configuration**.
Preserve Identities	A checkbox to preserve all identities derived from pools, including the UUIDs, MAC addresses, and WWNN and WWPN.

Configuration	Description
Location of the Backup File	**Local File System**: Backup is saved locally on the computer where UCS Manager is running. The screen changes to display the **Browse** button for storing the file.
	Remote File System: Backup is saved to a remote server using one of the protocols mentioned.
Protocol	For remote location, protocol selection could be **FTP**, **TFTP**, **SCP**, and **SFTP**.
Hostname	Remote server hostname or IP where the backup is stored.
Remote File	Remote filename with full path.
User	User having write permissions on the specified remote server.
	The **User** field will disappear for the **TFTP** selection.
Password	User password.
	The **Password** field will disappear for TFTP selection.

We will configure a local All Configuration backup as an example:

1. Select **Admin State** as **Disabled**.

2. Select **Type** as **All Configuration**.

3. Select the **Preserve Identities** checkbox.

4. Select **Location of the Backup File** as **Local File System**.

5. Select **Browse** and browse to the path of the local folder on the system where UCS Manager is running.

6. Click on **OK**.

7. In order to run the job at a later time, select the job and click on **Download to Local System**.

8. If it is required to delete a backup job, right-click on the job and select **Delete** as shown in the following screenshot:

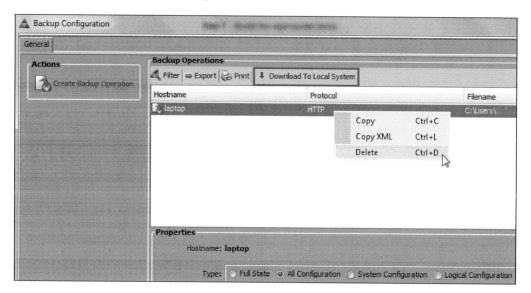

9. The same screen provides the status of the backup task in the form of Finite State Machine (FSM). Scroll down and expand **FSM Details**:

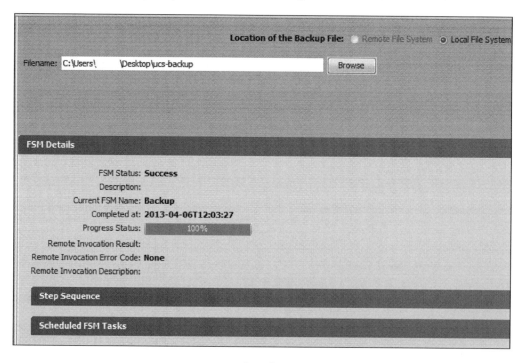

Creating a scheduled backup job using GUI

In order to schedule a backup job, it is required to configure Backup and Export Policy. Using this policy setting, it is possible to schedule a Full state backup or Full configuration backup export job on a daily, weekly, or biweekly basis. Follow these steps for configuration:

1. Log in to UCS Manager.
2. Click on the **Admin** tab in the navigation pane.
3. Click on the **All** tab in the navigation pane and click on **Backup and Export Policy** in the work pane.
4. Information to be entered here is identical to Backup job creation under the **General** tab except for **Schedule** which can be set as **Daily**, **Weekly**, or **Bi Weekly**.

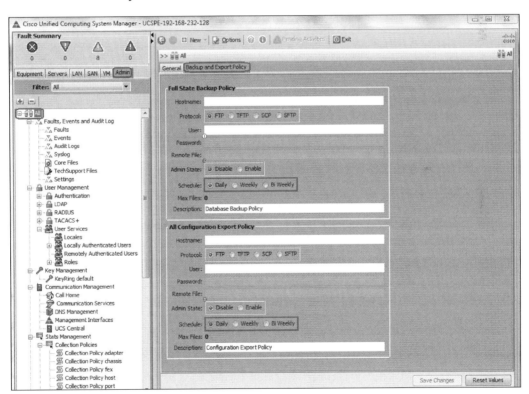

Creating a backup job using CLI

In order to perform the backup using CLI commands, follow these steps to create a weekly scheduled backup job to export a file using the SCP protocol to a remote server. Connect with FI CLI using SSH and run these scope commands:

1. Select organization scope:

   ```
   FI-A# scope org /
   ```

2. Select a backup policy:

   ```
   FI-A /org # scope backup-policy default
   ```

3. Select a remote hostname:

   ```
   FI-A /org/backup-policy # set hostname server
   ```

4. Select a protocol for the backup job:

   ```
   FI-A /org/backup-policy* # set protocol scp
   ```

5. Set the remote server username:

   ```
   FI-A /org/backup-policy* # set user username
   ```

6. Set a password:

   ```
   FI-A /backup-policy* # set password
   Password:
   ```

7. Select a remote server filename:

   ```
   FI-A /backup-policy* # set remote-file /backups/full-state1.bak
   ```

8. Select the admin state of the job to be enabled:

   ```
   FI-A /backup-policy* # set adminstate enabled
   ```

9. Select a schedule:

   ```
   FI-A /backup-policy* # set schedule weekly
   ```

10. Optionally add a description:

    ```
    FI-A /backup-policy* # set descr "This is a full state weekly backup."
    ```

11. Execute and save changes to the configuration:

    ```
    FI-A /backup-policy* # commit-buffer
    ```

Restoring backups using GUI

UCS restore job creation is also done in the administrative configuration area of the UCS Manager GUI or it could be accomplished using admin scope in the CLI mode. We will first walk through the configuration of the graphical interface and explain various options and then we will walk through the command-line configuration.

1. Log in to UCS Manager.

2. Click on the **Admin** tab in the navigation pane.

3. Click on the **All** tab in the navigation pane and click on **Import Configuration** in the work pane in the **General** tab as shown in the following screenshot:

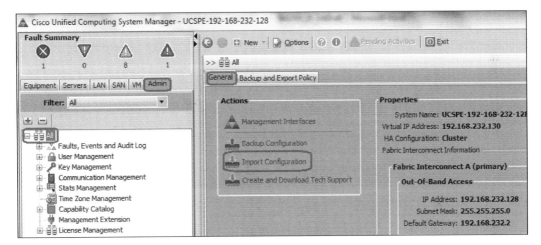

4. Click on **Create Import Operation**.

5. On the next screen, provide details for the backup job as follows:

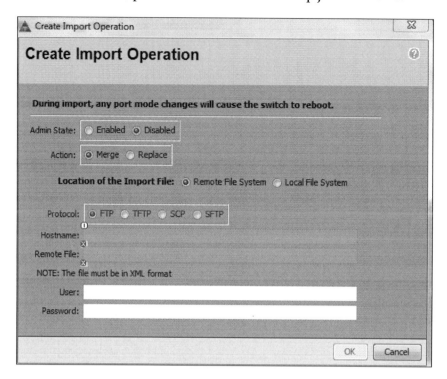

6. This table provides description for the configuration options available on the preceding screenshot:

Configuration	Description
Admin State	**Enabled**: Import job runs immediately after the configuration is complete.
	Disabled: Import configuration is completed but the job is not run immediately, which could be manually run at a later time.
Action	**Merge**: Merge into the existing configuration.
	Replace: Replace the existing configuration.
Location of the Import File	**Local File System**: Import is fetched locally from the computer where UCS Manager is running. The screen changes to display the **Browse** button for storing files.
	Remote File System: Import is fetched from a remote server using one of the protocols mentioned.
Protocol	For remote location, protocol selection could be **FTP**, **TFTP**, **SCP**, and **SFTP**.

Configuration	Description
Hostname	Remote server hostname or IP from where backup is restored.
Remote File	Remote filename with full path.
User	User having write permissions on the specified remote server.
	The **User** field will disappear for the **TFTP** selection.
Password	User password.
	The **Password** field will disappear for the **TFTP** selection.

We will restore from a local backup file as an example:

1. Select **Admin State** as **Disabled** (if to be run at a later time).

2. Select **Action** as **Merge** or **Replace**.

3. Select **Location of the Import File** as **Local File System**.

4. Click on **Browse** and browse to the path of the local folder on the system where UCS Manager is running.

5. Select the backup and Click on **OK**.

6. In order to run the job at a later time, select the job and click on **Import From Local System**.

7. If it is required to delete a backup job, right-click on the job and select **Delete**.

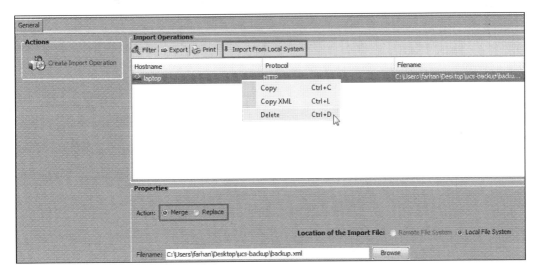

8. The same screen provides the status of the Import task in the form of Finite State Machine (FSM). To see the details, scroll down and expand **FSM Details**.

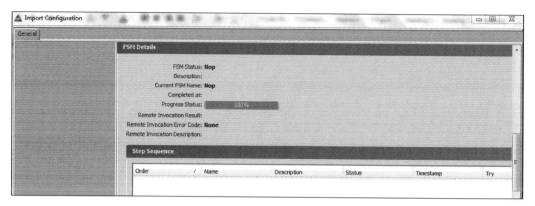

Configuring high-availability clustering

A UCS Fabric Interconnects pair can be configured in a high-availability cluster. In cluster configuration, FIs create primary secondary affiliation for control data traffic flow whereas data plane forwards simultaneously on both Fabric Interconnects. This means cluster control traffic flow is controlled only by primary node whereas network data can flow through both FIs under normal conditions. Fabric Interconnects are connected through dedicated Gigabit Ethernet UTP copper ports, which does not participate in the data plane. These interfaces are marked as **L1** and **L2**. L1 of one Fabric Interconnect should be connected to the L1 of the other Fabric Interconnect and similarly L2 should be connected to L2 of the peer. These links carry cluster heartbeat traffic.

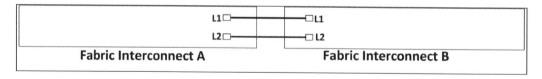

High-availability configuration requires three IP addresses. Both Fabric Interconnects require an IP address each, and the third IP address is the cluster IP for the management that floats between the peers A and B depending on which peer is primary.

Under normal conditions, both Fabric Interconnect peers must have the same hardware platform and software version. For example, a UCS 6248UP cannot be peered with 6296UP. However, this requirement may temporarily be allowed during an FI upgrade. Peers are upgraded one by one, which means that for a brief period, they can have different software and hardware.

Once cluster physical cabling is complete, both FIs go through the initial setup process. During the initial setup of the first Fabric Interconnect, it must be enabled for cluster configuration and it is configured as primary and assigned a cluster management IP. When the second FI is configured, it automatically detects the cluster peer and is configured as secondary.

Configuring the first Fabric Interconnect

Connect to the first Fabric Interconnect console using a serial connection. Configure the first Fabric Interconnect using the following steps:

1. Select the installation method:

   ```
   Enter the installation method (console/gui)? Console
   ```

2. Select the initial setup:

   ```
   Enter the setup mode (restore from backup or initial setup)
   [restore/setup]? Setup
   ```

3. Type in y to continue:

   ```
   You have chosen to setup a new switch. Continue? (y/n): y
   ```

4. Choose a complex password:

   ```
   Enter the password for "admin": password
   ```

5. Retype the password:

   ```
   Confirm the password for "admin": password
   ```

6. Choose creation of a new cluster by selecting yes:

   ```
   Do you want to create a new cluster on this switch (select 'no'
   for standalone setup or if you want this switch to be added to an
   existing cluster)? (yes/no) [n]: yes
   ```

7. A or B will be suffixed to the name defined in the next step:

   ```
   Enter the switch fabric (A/B): A
   ```

8. Enter the name of the Fabric Interconnect:

   ```
   Enter the system name: FI
   ```

9. Enter the Management IP address:

   ```
   Mgmt0 IPv4 address: 172.16.1.10
   ```

10. Enter the subnet mask:

    `Mgmt0 IPv4 netmask: 255.255.255.0`

11. Enter the address of the default gateway of the management network:

    `IPv4 address of the default gateway: 172.16.1.1`

12. Enter the shared IP of the cluster:

    `Virtual IPv4 address : 172.16.1.12`

13. Type in `yes` to configure the DNS:

    `Configure the DNS Server IPv4 address? (yes/no) [n]: yes`

14. Enter the DNS server IP address which is providing name services:

    `DNS IPv4 address: 8.8.8.8`

15. Type in `yes` to configure domain name:

    `Configure the default domain name? (yes/no) [n]: yes`

16. Enter the domain name of the company:

    `Default domain name: yourcompany.com`

17. After pressing *Enter*, the cluster configuration will be conformed with a summary of configurations. The following configurations will be applied:

    - Switch Fabric=A
    - System Name=FI
    - Management IP Address=172.16.1.10
    - Management IP Netmask=255.255.255.0
    - Default Gateway=172.16.1.1
    - Cluster Enabled=yes
    - Virtual IP Address=172.16.1.10
    - DNS Server=8.8.8.8
    - Domain Name=yourcompany.com

18. Type in `yes` to save changes:

    `Apply and save the configuration (select 'no' if you want to re-enter)? (yes/no): yes`

Configuring the second Fabric Interconnect

Connect to the second Fabric Interconnect console using a serial connection.
Configure the Fabric Interconnect using the following steps:

1. Choose the installation method:

   ```
   Enter the installation method (console/gui)? Console
   ```

2. If the physical cabling is done accurately, the secondary Fabric Interconnect
   will automatically be detected. Type y to configure it as secondary:

   ```
   Installer has detected the presence of a peer switch. This switch
   will be added to the cluster. Continue? [y/n] y
   ```

3. Use the same password as configured for the primary Fabric Interconnect:

   ```
   Enter the admin password of the peer switch: password
   ```

4. Enter the Management IP address:

   ```
   Mgmt0 IPv4 address: 172.16.1.11
   ```

5. Enter the subnet mask:

   ```
   Mgmt0 IPv4 netmask: 255.255.255.0
   ```

6. Save the configuration:

   ```
   Apply and save the configuration (select 'no' if you want to re-
   enter)? (yes/no): yes
   ```

 Note that the number of configuration steps of the secondary Fabric
Interconnect is far less than that of the primary Fabric Interconnect.
The secondary Fabric Interconnect automatically acquires all the
configuration information from the primary Fabric Interconnect.

If Fabric Interconnect was initially configured as standalone (a POC deployment),
it can be converted to be a cluster-aware configuration using the following steps.

Connect to the Fabric Interconnect using the Serial console or SSH connection.
Once connected, apply the following commands:

1. Connect to the CLI local management interface:

   ```
   FI-A# connect local-mgmt
   ```

2. Type in enable cluster with shared cluster IP:

   ```
   FI-A(local-mgmt)# enable cluster 172.16.1.12
   ```

3. Type in `yes` to configure clustering. Note that once a standalone Fabric Interconnect is converted to a cluster, it cannot be converted back to the standalone state:

   ```
   This command will enable cluster mode on this setup. You cannot
   change it back to stand-alone. Are you sure you want to continue?
   (yes/no) : yes
   ```

4. Once the standalone Fabric Interconnect is converted to the primary cluster peer, configure the second Fabric Interconnect following the same steps for the secondary Fabric Interconnects.

Fabric Interconnect elections

Fabric Interconnect elections are infrequent and may only occur under an equipment failure or user-forced conditions. A user-forced condition may occur during the firmware upgrade of the Fabric Interconnects. Firmware is upgraded on subordinate Fabric Interconnect first and after the reboot of the FI, it is converted to primary and then the firmware of current primary is upgraded. In order to force an election, connection to local-management interface using CLI is required:

1. `UCS-A# connect local-mgmt`

   This connects to the local management interface of the cluster.

2. `UCS-A (local-mgmt) #cluster{force primary|lead{a|b}}`

   The cluster lead command and cluster force primary command are two separate commands that can be used to start an election.

   The cluster force primary command can be used on the secondary Fabric Interconnect to make it primary. It can be used in critical situations where the primary Fabric Interconnect has failed.

   The `cluster lead a|b` command can be used on Fabric Interconnects to change the current cluster lead to peer A or peer B.

Managing high availability

The Fabric Interconnect cluster can be monitored from the UCS Manager GUI. The GUI provides information the primary and secondary peers and management IP. Perform the following steps to do this:

1. Log in to UCS Manager.

2. Click on the **Equipment** tab in the navigation pane.

3. Click on the **Fabric Interconnects** tab on the navigation pane and the work pane shows the high-availability status on the right-hand side pane.

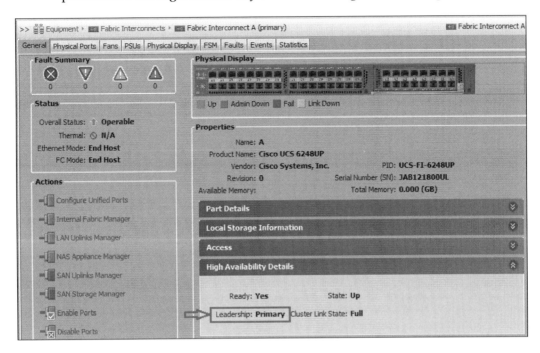

4. This figure shows that this is the active primary Fabric Interconnect because the **Leadership** status is indicated as **Primary**.

Fabric Interconnect IPs or the shared cluster IP (also known as VIP) can also be changed from the GUI. Follow these steps to configure the IPs:

1. Log in to UCS Manager.

2. Click on the **Admin** tab on the navigation pane.

3. Click on the **All** tab on the navigation pane and the **General** tab on the work pane.

4. Click on **Management Interfaces** on the work pane.

5. A new pop-up window will show all the IP settings:

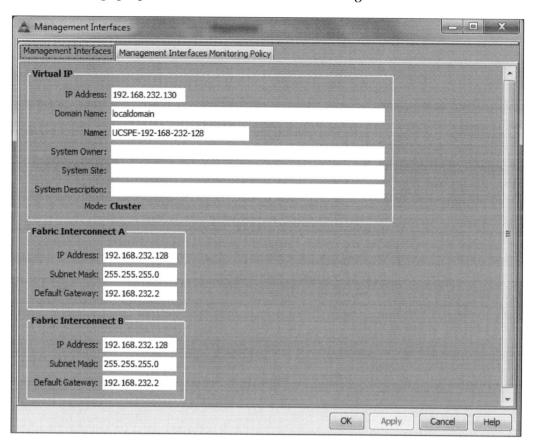

6. In the pop-up window, any of the IP addresses can be changed.
7. Cluster and Fabric Interconnect IP addresses can also be changed from CLI.
8. Cluster status can also be confirmed from CLI commands:

```
FI-A# show cluster state
```

This command provides the status summary of the cluster as follows:

```
A: UP, PRIMARY
B: UP, SUBORDINATE
HA READY
FI-A# show cluster extended-state
```

```
Cluster Id: 0x4690d6b6eafa11e1-0x8ed3547fee9ebb84


Start time: Mon Nov 12 12:00:16 2012
Last election time: Mon Nov 12 12:00:17 2012


A: UP, PRIMARY
B: UP, SUBORDINATE


A: memb state UP, lead state PRIMARY, mgmt services state: UP
B: memb state UP, lead state SUBORDINATE, mgmt services state: UP
   heartbeat state PRIMARY_OK


INTERNAL NETWORK INTERFACES:
eth1, UP
eth2, UP


HA READY
Detailed state of the device selected for HA storage:
Chassis 1, serial: FOX1622G490, state: active
Chassis 2, serial: FOX1616GSPV, state: active
```

Certain failure scenarios may impact the Fabric Interconnect high availability configuration. A number of techniques are used to avoid issues. These scenarios occur due to the network failure between L1, L2 dedicated network.

The Split-brain scenario

Under normal running conditions, one Fabric Interconnect (primary) serves as an active member and the other Fabric Interconnect serves as a standby. A Split-brain occurs when there is L1, L2 network failure between the primary and secondary Fabric Interconnects. Cisco developed the chassis midplane in such a way that there is EEPROM divided into sections, one for each Fabric Interconnect.

Fabric Interconnect A has the read/write access to one section of EEPROM through the chassis management controller and the read-only access to the other EEPROM.

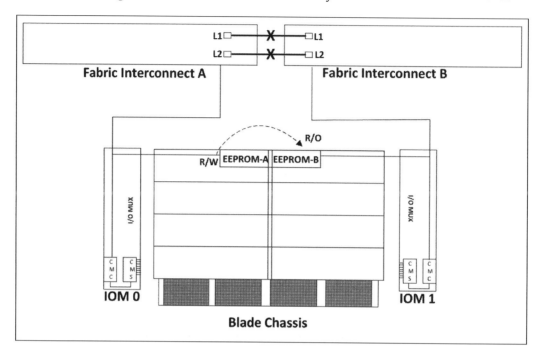

Partition in space

When the L1, L2 network between the two Fabric Interconnects is disconnected or fails, the primary FI continues to serve as primary; however, the secondary FI concludes that the primary FI is dead and tries to become primary. This is Split-brain partition in space because each Fabric Interconnect considers itself to be in control of the cluster.

When a partition in space is detected, both FIs immediately demote themselves, start the election process and start claiming chassis resources (known as quorum). The FI that claims more resources wins the election and stays in the cluster whereas the other FI aborts. When the link is restored, the second node can rejoin the cluster as a subordinate.

Partition in time

This condition may occur when one of the nodes stays down for a significant time period, in which configuration changes are made to the active node. Obviously, these changes are not available to the failed node. Now, if the primary node shuts down for some reason and the previously downed node is brought up alone in the cluster with an old database revision, there is a likely chance of configuration corruption. This condition is known as partition in time.

To resolve this Split-brain condition, each Fabric Interconnect writes a database version number to its section of EEPROM. Now when a Fabric Interconnect is brought alone in the cluster, it can still read the EEPROM database version and compare it to its own information. If the version number is same or higher, the FI can become the active member and if the version number is lower, the FI does not become the active member. This mechanism thus protects against applying an older version of the UCS configuration.

Summary

In this chapter, we learned about the different UCS backup and restore options available. Different types of backups are possible and the administrator may configure any combination of backup strategies according to requirement. It is possible to back up both to the local computer and remote server using various protocols. Backups can also be scheduled. Restore also has different options in terms of local or remote location and same selection of protocols as available for the backup jobs. We then learned about the Fabric Interconnect high-availability. We learned how high-availability is configured and managed. We looked at high-availability election and some high-availability failure conditions which result in the Split-brain condition and how various Split-brain conditions are resolved.

In the next chapter we will be discussing the common failure scenarios which will be very helpful in troubleshooting problems with UCS components.

11
Cisco UCS Failure Scenarios Testing

In this chapter, we will walk through the different types of failure scenarios that can occur in Cisco UCS. UCS solution components have excellent redundancy for critical equipment such as chassis and Fabric Interconnects. However, in an unexpected situation such as a physical component's failure, we should be able to identify the failed component and possibly conduct some troubleshooting before contacting Cisco TAC. The most common equipment that fails for the UCS are chassis/Fabric Interconnect power supplies, FAN units, IOMs and SFPs for both IOMs, and Fabric Interconnect ports. If proper failover is configured for the network adapters (vNICs) and proper connectivity is configured for the storage adapters (vHBAs), the majority of single component failures do not result in data or management traffic disruption.

UCS failures may also be related to configuration issues, firmware mismatches, temperature issues due to air flow obstruction, and physical cabling issues. In this chapter, we will look into how we can identify these issues from the UCS Manager GUI and also look into LEDs on UCS components.

The following are the topics that will be covered in this chapter:

- Port channel uplink failure and recovery on Fabric Interconnects
- Server downlink to Fabric Interconnect failure and recovery
- FEX IO modules—failure and recovery
- Fabric Interconnect devices—failure and recovery
- UCS chassis—failure, reporting, and recovery

- Fiber Channel single link failure and recovery on Fabric Interconnects
- Indicating status with LEDs
- Creating a tech-support file

In order to dive deep into various troubleshooting scenarios, we will first look at the network and storage connectivity from the mezzanine adapter to the northbound LAN or switch. Different types of ports are involved in this connectivity; they are as follows:

- **IOM Backplane ports**: IOM Backplane ports connect to the southbound server mezzanine card through midplane traces. First-generation 2100 series IOM FEXs provided 16 ports, whereas second-generation 2200 series IOM FEXs can provide a maximum of 32 backplane ports (IOM 2208).

- **IOM Fabric ports**: IOM Fabric ports connect to Fabric Interconnect for northbound connectivity. First-generation 2100 series IOM FEXs provided four fixed ports, whereas second-generation 2200 series IOM FEX have four/eight ports for 2204 and 2208 respectively.

- **Fabric Interconnect server ports**: UCS Fabric Interconnect has a fixed unified port module. The unified ports configured as server ports provide southbound connectivity to the UCS chasses IOM module fabric ports.

- **Fabric Interconnect uplink ports**: UCS unified ports configured as uplink ports provide northbound connectivity to upstream Nexus switches.

- **Fabric Interconnect FC**: UCS unified ports configured as fiber channel ports provide SAN connectivity. Ethernet ports are counted from start to finish, whereas FC ports are counted from finish to start. Port reconfiguration between Ethernet and FC requires a reboot of the FI or expansion module.

- **Fabric Interconnect FCoE ports**: UCS unified Ethernet ports can also be configured as Fiber Channel ports over Ethernet (FCoE) ports for SAN connectivity using the FCoE protocol.

The following diagram shows the different ports for both IOM modules
and Fabric Interconnects:

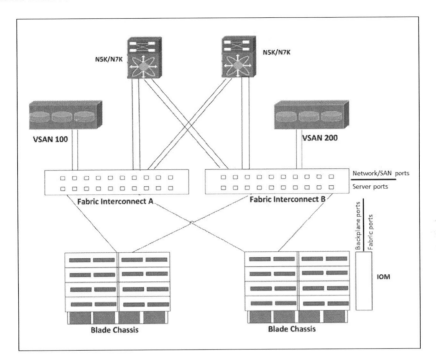

Port-channel uplink failure and recovery on Fabric Interconnect

Fabric Interconnects can connect to northbound Nexus switches either directly or
using a port channel. Port channel configuration, which not only load-balances
bandwidth utilization but also avoids unnecessary reconvergence in the case of
partial link failures, is recommended as multiple uplink ports can be aggregated.

Use the following procedure to verify northbound port channel configuration and
operational state:

1. Log in to UCS Manager.
2. Click on the **LAN** tab in the Navigation pane.

3. In the **LAN Cloud** tab, expand **Fabric A** and **Port Channels**.

4. In the Work pane, the **Status** of **Port Channels** is shown in the **General** tab as follows:

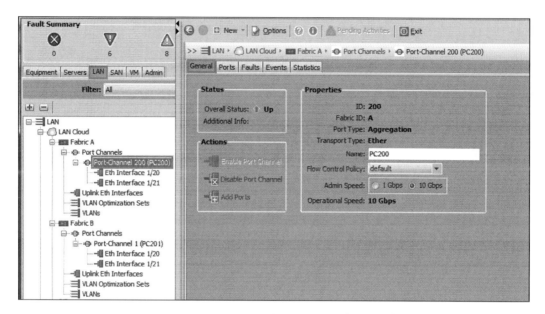

5. The **Ports** tab shows member ports and the **Faults** tab shows any faults as shown in the following screenshot:

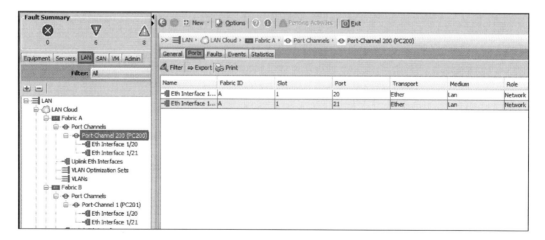

The following screenshot shows the error message that gets displayed when
a port channel cannot be brought up due to a mismatch in speed between the
Fabric Interconnects and uplink Nexus ports:

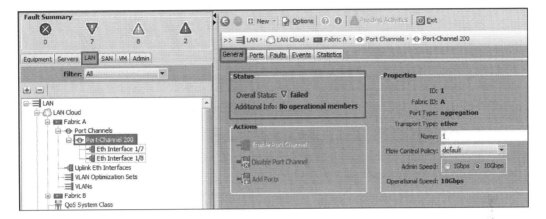

Some other common upstream port channel issues and recommended solutions
are as follows:

Issue	Recommended solution
Port channel does not come up.	Verify cable connectivity and look for any physical SFP failure
	Verify that there is no protocol or speed mismatch between the connected ports
	Verify individual connectivity by removing the port channel configuration
Port channel member failure. The error message in GUI is membership-down.	Verify cable connectivity and look for any physical SFP failure
	Verify any speed mismatch and correct the issue

Server link to Fabric Interconnect failure and recovery

For blade server and Fabric Interconnect connectivity, there are two connections involved between the server mezzanine card, IOM backplane ports, IOM fabric ports, and Fabric Interconnect server ports. These connections are as follows:

1. The connection between the blade server mezzanine card and IOM backplane port that connects the blade server to the IOM in the chassis.

2. The connection between the IOM fabric port and Fabric Interconnect server port that connects the IOM in the chassis to the Fabric Interconnect.

Connectivity failure can happen due to a mezzanine card, IOM ports, or Fabric Interconnect server ports. We will now look at different port failure scenarios.

Identifying a mezzanine adapter failure

The first requirement is to identify and isolate the source of the issue, which can be the server mezzanine card, IOM card ports, or Fabric Interconnect server port. To determine that the issue is with the server mezzanine card and not with the IOM or Fabric Interconnect ports, physically have a look at the server motherboard LED's status at the front of the server as follows:

- If the Network link LED at the front of the blade server is off, the adapter will not be able to establish the network link

- The Network link LED will be green if one or more links are active

The Network link LED for the UCS Blade B22 M3 is shown in the following illustration:

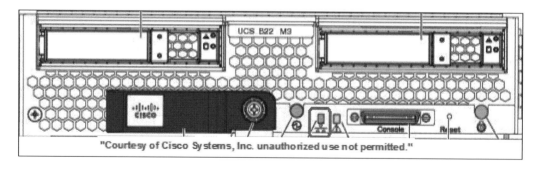

"Courtesy of Cisco Systems, Inc. unauthorized use not permitted."

Once the physical connectivity is verified by the LED indicator status, you can also look into the UCS manager for any issues related to the server adapter.

Use the following procedure to determine the type of server mezzanine adapter errors being experienced:

1. Log in to UCS Manager.

2. Click on the **Equipment** tab in the Navigation pane.

3. In the **Equipment** tab, expand the desired server in the desired chassis.

4. Expand the desired adapter, and the **Overall Status** of the **Adapters** will be shown in the work pane.

5. This is a quick view for looking at any adapter errors on that server. In order to see the details of the errors, click on the **Faults** tab in the work pane that will provide all the error messages related to the adapter as shown in the following screenshot:

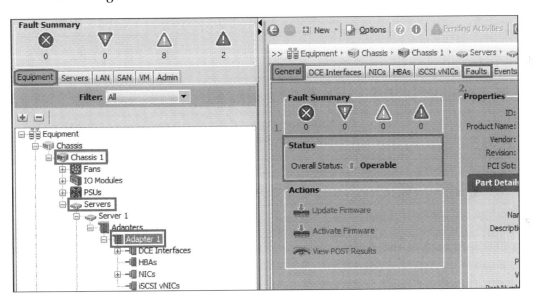

Common mezzanine adapter error messages

The following is a list of some common adapter issues and recommended solutions to troubleshoot and fix adapter issues. This information is an excerpt from the *Cisco UCS Faults and Error Messages Reference* guide available on the Cisco website at `http://www.cisco.com/en/US/docs/unified_computing/ucs/ts/faults/reference/UCS_SEMs.html`.

Some other common mezzanine adapter error messages and recommended solutions are as follows. For a detailed list of UCS error messages, follow the preceding link:

Issue	Recommended solution
The adapter is reported as "inoperable" in Cisco UCS Manager.	For a new installation, verify that the adapter is compatible with the Blade Server.
	In case of a UCS Manager firmware upgrade, verify that the adapter has the required firmware version to work with the version of Cisco UCS Manager.
	Verify that the adapter is seated properly in the slot on the motherboard. Reseat to ensure good contact, reinsert the server, and rerun the POST.
	Verify that the adapter is the problem by trying it in a server that is known to be functioning correctly and that uses the same adapter type.
The adapter is reported as degraded in UCS Manager.	Reseat the Blade Server in the chassis.
The adapter is reported as overheating	Verify that the adapter is seated properly in the slot. Reseat it to assure good contact and re-run the POST.
	Verify if there are any Server/Chasses airflow issues and correct these issues.

FEX IO modules – failure and recovery

IOM provides southbound connectivity to servers using Backplane ports and northbound connectivity to Fabric Interconnects using Fabric Ports. When a service profile is successfully associated with the server, the Backplane port's status shows as **Up**.

Use the following procedure the look into the status of IOM Backplane and Fabric Ports:

1. Log in to UCS Manager.
2. Click on the **Equipment** tab in the navigation pane.

3. In the **Equipment** tab, expand the desired server in the desired chassis.

4. Expand the desired IO Modules by expanding **IO Modules**, and the status of **Backplane Ports** and **Fabric Ports** will be shown in the Work pane.

5. The following screenshot shows the **Backplane Ports** statuses that are connected to the server's mezzanine card:

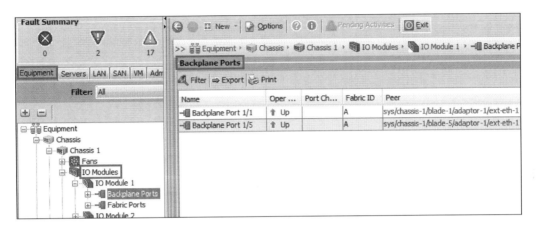

6. The following screenshot shows the **Fabric Ports** statuses that are connected with Fabric Interconnect server ports:

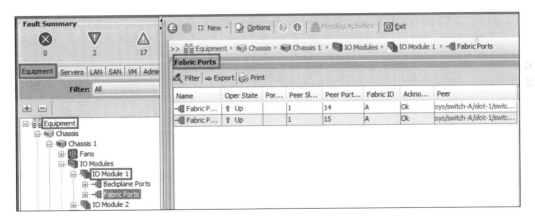

It is also possible to configure a port channel for the IOM Fabric Ports connected to Fabric Interconnect. This configuration is different as compared to the north switch port channel, and this port channel is configured using the **Chassis/FEX Discovery Policy** section as shown in the following screenshot:

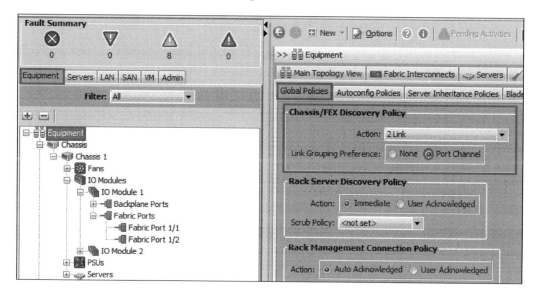

Common IOM error messages

This information is an excerpt from the *Cisco UCS Faults and Error Messages Reference* guide available on the Cisco website at http://www.cisco.com/en/US/docs/ unified_computing/ucs/ts/faults/reference/UCS_SEMs.html.

A list of some of the common IOM FEX issues and recommended solutions to troubleshoot and fix these issues is as follows. For a detailed list of UCS error messages, follow the preceding link.

Issue	Recommended solution
The IOM port fails	• For this fault, generate a tech-support file for Cisco UCS Manager and the chassis or FEX module • Contact Cisco TAC

Issue	Recommended solution
The IOM shows "insufficient-resources"	• Verify the VIF namespace size and its usage • Delete all vNICs on the adapter above the maximum number • Add additional fabric uplinks from the IOM to the Fabric Interconnect and re-acknowledge the chassis • If the preceding actions did not resolve the issue, generate a tech-support file and contact Cisco TAC
The IOM shows "satellite-connection-absent"	• Verify that the Fabric Interconnect server port is configured and enabled • Verify that the links are plugged in properly, and re-acknowledge the chassis • If the preceding actions did not resolve the issue, generate a tech-support file and contact Cisco TAC
The IOM displays "satellite-mis-connected"	• Make sure that each I/O module is connected to only one Fabric Interconnect • Verify that the links are plugged in properly, and re-acknowledge the chassis • If the preceding actions did not resolve the issue, generate a tech-support file and contact Cisco TAC
The IOM displays "equipment-removed"	• Reinsert the IOM module and wait a few minutes to see if the fault clears • If the preceding action did not resolve the issue, generate a tech-support file and contact Cisco TAC
The IOM shows unsupported connectivity	• Verify that the number of links in the chassis discovery policy are correct • Re-acknowledge the chassis • If the preceding actions did not resolve the issue, generate a tech-support file and contact Cisco TAC

Fabric Interconnect server port failure

For troubleshooting connectivity issues, it is also necessary to look into the status of the Fabric Interconnect ports where the IOM Fabric Ports are connected. These Fabric Interconnect ports are configured as **Server** ports.

Use the following procedure to have a look at IOM Backplane and Fabric Ports:

1. Log in to UCS Manager.
2. Click on the **Equipment** tab in the navigation pane.
3. In the **Equipment** tab, expand the desired Fabric Interconnects.
4. Change the **General** tab to the **Ethernet Ports** module, and the **Overall status** of the Backplane and Fabric Ports will be shown in the work pane.
5. In the **Filter** bar, uncheck **All** and check the **Server** checkbox to display server ports only. Ports status and any adapter errors on that server port will be displayed on the screen as shown in the following screenshot:

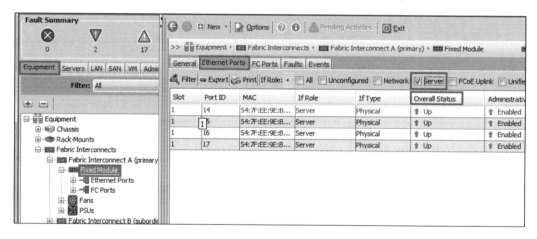

If there are some errors, the **Overall Status** tab in the Work pane will indicate the issue, for example, **Link down** in case of a physical SFP failure.

Rectifying the Global Chassis Discovery Policy configuration error

In *Chapter 3, Configuring Cisco UCS Using UCS Manager*, we discussed and configured Global Chassis Discovery Policy, which dictates the number of physical connections from the UCS chassis expected by the UCS Manager software to acknowledge the chassis. UCS Manager generates an error if IOM connectivity with the Fabric Interconnect is not compliant with Global Chassis Discovery Policy.

The following screenshot shows an **Unsupported Connectivity** error due to a misconfigured Chassis Discovery Policy. In order to rectify this issue, configure the Global Chassis Discovery Policy according to the number of physical links (one, two, four, or eight) connected from the IOM to the Fabric Interconnect using the steps provided in *Chapter 3, Configuring Cisco UCS Using UCS Manager,* and re-acknowledge the chassis.

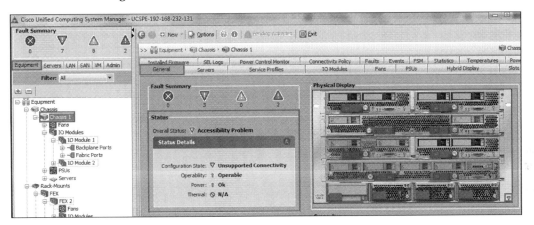

Fabric Interconnect device failure and recovery

UCS Fabric Interconnects are deployed in a cluster configuration from the control plane perspective. A Fabric Interconnect pair is in active/standby configuration. The active Fabric Interconnect is called primary and the standby Fabric Interconnect is called subordinate.

All control plane communication is handled by the primary Fabric Interconnect that manages the main configuration database. The main configuration database is stored on the primary and replicated on the subordinate Fabric Interconnect. The primary sends updates to the subordinate when configuration changes occur through dedicated Ethernet links called L1/L2.

In a situation where the Fabric Interconnect running the primary instance fails, the subordinate Fabric Interconnect takes the role of primary instantaneously. Access to UCS Manager stops, and you need to log out and log back in. In a split-brain situation where both Fabric Interconnects try to come online as the primary, the Fabric Interconnect database version gets checked, and the Fabric Interconnect with the higher database revision number becomes the primary. We discussed a split-brain situation in *Chapter 10, Configuring Backup, Restore, and High Availability,* and learned that the UCS chassis midplane has been designed such that it is helpful in resolving split scenarios.

If the dedicated communication links L1/L2 between two Fabric Interconnects fail, the Fabric Interconnects have special access to Blade chassis for communicating the heartbeat. In this situation, the role of the Fabric Interconnects will not change; primary will remain primary, and subordinate will remain subordinate. However, any configuration changes made on primary will not be reflected on the secondary database until the dedicated Ethernet links are restored.

The following procedure should be used to replace a failed Fabric Interconnect:

1. Upgrade the firmware of the replacement Fabric Interconnect to the same level as the running Fabric Interconnect with the following steps:

    1. Connect the new Fabric Interconnect to the management network (do not connect the L1 and L2 cables).

    2. Convert the new Fabric Interconnect into an SSH, and run through the setup wizard by configuring the Fabric Interconnect as a standalone.

    3. Update both UCS Manager and the Fabric Interconnect firmware code to the code running on the existing cluster member.

    4. Once the upgrades are complete, verify that the running and startup versions match those of the existing cluster member.

2. Once the firmware is updated, use the following commands to erase the configuration on the standalone Fabric Interconnect:

    ```
    UCS # connect local-mgmt
    UCS # erase configuration
    UCS # yes (to reboot)
    ```

3. Connect the L1 and L2 cables between the Fabric Interconnect.

4. Erase the configuration; this will cause the setup wizard to run again on the new Fabric Interconnect and detect the presence of a peer Fabric Interconnect. When prompted for the detection of a peer Fabric Interconnect, type y to add the new Fabric Interconnect to the existing cluster. Save the configuration and reboot.

5. Log in to the UCS Manager, or use the following command line to verify the cluster state:

```
UCS # connect local-mgmt
UCS # show cluster state
Cluster Id: 0x633acf7e9b7611e1-0x9587147fbb1fc579
A: UP, PRIMARY
B: UP, SUBORDINATE
HA READY
```

Sometimes, it may also become necessary to change the current primary Fabric Interconnect in the cluster. One such situation is during a Fabric Interconnects firmware upgrade, where it is necessary to switch the cluster lead while upgrading code on the primary cluster.

Use the following command to change the cluster lead:

```
UCS # cluster lead a
UCS # cluster force primary
```

Either of these two commands can be used to make **Fabric-A** the primary Fabric Interconnect:

```
UCS # show cluster state (if done quickly, you'll see the status
  of SWITCHOVER IN PROGRESS)
```

Note that Fabric Interconnects have redundant power supply and fan units so they can avoid a complete failure. With this built-in redundancy, it is very rare that Fabric Interconnects will go down completely. The redundant parts of Fabric Interconnects are hot swappable and can be changed without any disruption.

Common error messages with Fabric Interconnect

This information is an excerpt from the *Cisco UCS Faults and Error Messages Reference* guide available on the Cisco website at http://www.cisco.com/en/US/docs/unified_computing/ucs/ts/faults/reference/UCS_SEMs.html.

Some other common error messages with Fabric Interconnects and recommended solutions are as follows. For a detailed list of UCS error messages, follow the preceding link:

Issue	Recommended solution
Management entity degraded Management entity down	• Verify that both L1 and L2 links have proper connectivity between the Fabric Interconnects • If the preceding action did not resolve the issue, generate a tech-support file and contact Cisco TAC
Management entity Election failure	• Verify that the initial setup configuration is correct on both the Fabric Interconnects and the L1/L2 links are properly connected • Convert SSH to CLI and run the "cluster force primary" in the `local-mgmt` command on one Fabric Interconnect • Reboot the Fabric Interconnects • If the preceding actions did not resolve the issue, generate a tech-support file and contact Cisco TAC
HA not ready	• Verify that the initial setup configuration is correct on both the Fabric Interconnects and the L1/L2 links are properly connected • Verify IOM connectivity • If the preceding actions did not resolve the issue, generate a tech-support file and contact Cisco TAC
Version incompatible	• Upgrade the Cisco UCS Manager software on the subordinate Fabric Interconnect to the same release as the primary Fabric Interconnect • If the preceding action did not resolve the issue, generate a tech-support file and contact Cisco TAC
Equipment inoperable	• Reseat the failed equipment, such as FANs, power-supply, or SFP

UCS chassis failure, reporting, and recovery

The UCS 5100 Series chassis is a critical component of the UCS solution and is fully redundant. The redundant components of the UCS chassis are as follows:

- Eight FANs for proper airflow
- Four power supplies for power redundancy
- Two redundant IOM module slots for northbound connectivity
- Redundant midplane traces for data and management traces

It is very rare that the UCS chassis will fail completely. The most common failure suspects for the UCS chassis are components such as FAN modules, power supplies, IOM modules, or Blade Servers inserted into the chassis. All UCS chassis components are hot pluggable, so in the case of a failure, the failed component can be replaced without disruption.

Common failure messages for UCS Chassis

This information is an excerpt from the *Cisco UCS Faults and Error Messages Reference* guide available on the Cisco website at `http://www.cisco.com/en/US/docs/ unified_computing/ucs/ts/faults/reference/UCS_SEMs.html`. For a detailed list of UCS error messages, follow the preceding link.

Some common failure messages for UCS chassis and their recommended solutions are as follows:

Issue	Recommended solution
Server identification problem	• Remove and reinsert the server card
	• Re-acknowledge the server
	• If the preceding actions did not resolve the issue, generate a tech-support file and contact Cisco TAC
Port failed	• Re-insert the IOM module
	• If this did not resolve the issue, contact Cisco TAC

Issue	Recommended solution
Equipment inoperable	• Re-acknowledge the chassis that raised the fault
	• Physically unplug and replug the power cord to the chassis
	• Verify that the I/O modules are functional
	• If the preceding actions did not resolve the issue, execute the `show tech-support` command and contact Cisco Technical Support
	• This error message may also appear for the FAN and power supply units
Unsupported connectivity	• Verify that the number of links in the Chassis Discovery Policy is correct
	• Re-acknowledge the chassis
	• If the preceding action did not resolve the issue, generate a tech-support file and contact Cisco TAC
Equipment unacknowledged	• Verify the connectivity state of the I/O module links
	• Re-acknowledge the chassis
	• If the preceding actions did not resolve the issue, execute the `show tech-support` command and contact Cisco Technical Support

Single fiber channel failure and recovery on Fabric Interconnects

In virtualized environments, SAN connectivity is very crucial for hypervisors as a shared SAN is a critical component for advanced virtualization features, such as migrating and then running virtual machines between different hosts. A problem with the connectivity of the SAN array can also cause issues with the SAN boot.

SAN could be connected to Fabric Interconnects directly or through a northbound Nexus, MDS, or third-party switch. Proper connectivity between Fabric Interconnects and SAN storage processors or Fabric Interconnects and SAN fabric switches is necessary. SAN connectivity is also configured as redundant. However, unlike Ethernet, where a northbound vPC that is using a cross switch connection can protect against a complete switch failure, the connectivity between SAN switches and Fabric Interconnects can only be a straight connection. It is, however, possible to create a Fiber Channel port channel for protection against a single port failure.

Use the following procedure to look into SAN connectivity (the screenshot is showing direct attached FCoE storage):

1. Log in to UCS Manager.

2. Click on the **SAN** tab in the navigation pane.

3. In the **SAN** tab, expand the Fabric Interconnects in the **Storage Cloud** expand list.

4. Expand **Storage FCoE Interfaces**, and the status of the SAN connectivity will be shown in the work pane as follows:

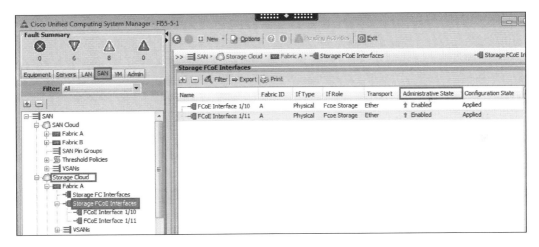

5. The following screenshot shows a port connectivity issue in the form of **membership-down**; this means that the physical connectivity between the Fabric Interconnect and its storage is down:

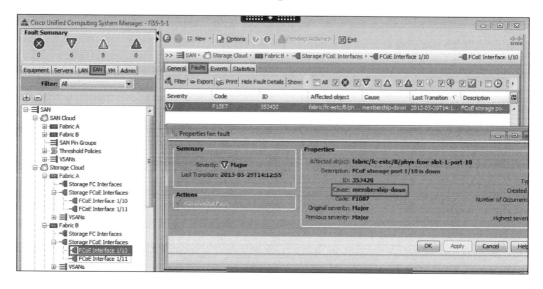

In order to mitigate the risk of Fiber Channel single link failures, Fiber Channel port channels or Trunking can be established to ensure uninterrupted connectivity. Refer to *Chapter 5, Configuring SAN Connectivity*, that discusses the procedure for the creation of a Fiber Channel port channel for storage connectivity.

Indicating a status with LEDs

UCS chassis and components have different colored LEDs and flashing patterns. Looking at the LED's status can also help identify various issues. All UCS components, including chassis, IOMs, power supplies, FAN units, Blade Servers, and Fabric Interconnects have different LED indicators that can provide information about the component's location, faults, or operational status. Locator LEDs are blue in color, operational status LEDs are usually green or a blinking green color, and faults are identified with solid, amber-colored LEDs. UCS chassis and Blade Servers have some buttons as well; these can be pushed to turn the locator LED on/off.

The following table describes how to interpret the LED indicators on various UCS components:

LED status	Interpretation
Off	Not connected. No power.
Green	Normal operation.
Blinking green	Normal traffic activity.
Amber	Booting up, then running diagnostics or a minor temperature alarm.
Blinking amber	Failed component or major temperature alarm.
Locator LED (blinking blue)	Locator feature enabled.

Creating a tech-support file

In the case of an equipment failure, use the following procedure to create a tech-support file for Cisco TAC:

1. Log in to UCS Manager.

2. Click on the **Admin** tab in the navigation pane.

3. In the **Admin** tab, click on the **All** expandable list.

4. In the work pane, click on **Create and Download Tech Support** as shown in the following screenshot:

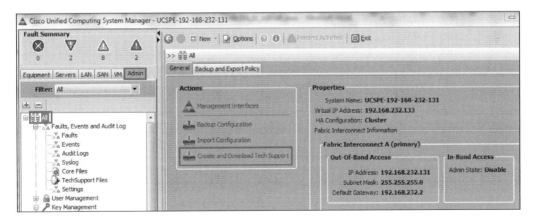

5. In the pop-up window that opens, select the desired option to create the tech-support file and browse to a local location on the PC to save the file as shown in the following screenshot:

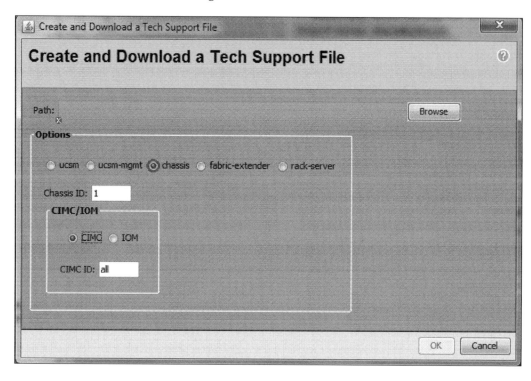

Summary

In this chapter, we walked through some failure scenarios that are mostly related to connectivity issues or physical components, such as power supplies, FANS, or SFP failures. We looked at how to acquire information for troubleshooting and identify failed components or misconfiguration that results in a connectivity failure. We looked into the issues related to network connectivity with northbound port channels. We also looked into complete connectivity, from mezzanine adapters to IOM Backplane ports, to IOM Fabric Ports, to northbound Fabric Interconnect server ports. We also looked into Fiber Channel connectivity issues.

We then looked into a complete Fabric Interconnect or Blade Server chassis failure. We discovered that as there are redundant parts in both Fabric Interconnects and chassis, it is very rare that complete equipment will fail. We looked into the most common failures, such as SFPs, power supplies, and FAN units. We also looked into IOM connectivity and some possible failure scenarios. We learned about various LEDs on the UCS and how we can use these LED indicators to identify a possible issue with a UCS component.

In the next chapter, we will be looking at the integration of some third-party applications, such as VMware vCenter extension and EMC Unified Infrastructure Manager, and Cisco tools, such as UCS Power Tools and goUCS.

12
Third-party Application Integration

Cisco UCS has all the capability to get integrated with third-party applications. In this chapter we will show you three application integrations. The aspects of those integrations are as follows:

- Integration with EMC Unified Infrastructure Manager (UIM) for provisioning
- Integration with VMware vCenter Server
- Integration with Cisco UCS PowerTool

Understanding the challenges in Infrastructure

As you support your growing business, what challenges do you face when asked to create an infrastructure that is ready to support a virtual application or test beds for a new line of business request?

- When there are too many highly technical people involved, in a provisioning process, it wastes time
- These guys can take weeks/months to deliver the infrastructure for a new service, which will certainly delay the rollout and impact the bottom line business
- Normal human tendency is to make mistakes in manually-intensive processes, which becomes costly and also takes time to determine the issue
- You may be unaware of the changes that may take the infrastructure configuration out of compliance, and this significantly leads to hardware issues in future

If you have ever faced this problem, EMC **Unified Infrastructure Manager (UIM)** is the solution for you. In the next section, we will go through the UIM and its benefits.

Going deep with UIM

UIM is a purpose-built service for Vblock Infrastructure Platforms that has centralized interaction with element managers to define available resource "pools" and then view their capacity through a single dashboard. It creates policy-based, automated, converged infrastructure provisioning templates that can be used on any Vblock platform.

A UIM service offering is a template that you can create in anticipation of the applications that will be deployed on your Vblock platform. Once created, the templates are placed into the UIM/P catalog, ready for provisioning and activation when needed. Service offerings contain all except components needed to have a complete foundational infrastructure such as storage, compute, network, and operating system.

UIM/Provisioning provides administrators with a tool to provision the VCE Vblock system from one location. Compute, storage, and SAN components are discovered into UIM. The discovered resources can then be provisioned with UIM, making it a simplified approach to end-to-end provisioning.

A base configuration is required for provisioning to occur. As an example, the UCS must be configured with a number of policies, Fabric Interconnect connectivity, and so on. Storage must have the RAID groups and/or pools. The following diagram shows the overall architecture of UIM and its component connectivity diagram:

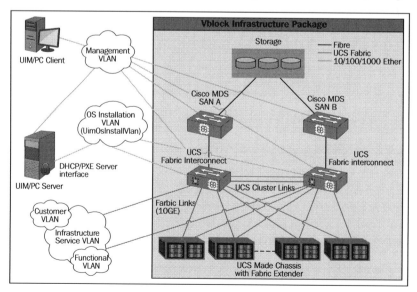

UIM is designed to discover the Vblock components, attempting to simplify the Vblock system into a single entity, create infrastructure services for automated provisioning of the Vblock system, and integrate the provisioned ESXi clusters with vCenter.

Understanding the discovery mechanism of UIM

The **discovery mechanism** is designed to pull and import the device data from all Vblock components into a single database. UIM utilizes HTTP(S) to communicate via the XML API to the UCS.

A list of items is required for the discovery of a Vblock system. Each Vblock system must have a unique name. The **Description** field is optional but is displayed on the **Vblock** tab, so if there is a good business use to distinguish Vblock systems, it is a useful entry.

The high-level results of the discovery will be displayed within the **Results** screen. Details about the blades, storage, and network can be viewed on their respective tabs in the **Administration** view. For example, storage details can be seen in the **Storage Pool** tab.

When discovery finishes you will see a blade pool that identifies all UCS blades with chassis, slot, model, CPU, and memory. Also, it discovers network profiles that identify attributes from UCS to associate vNICs with VLANs, QoS, and adapter policies.

The following screenshot is an example of the **Discovery** screen for a Vblock 300. The only optional items on this screen are **Description** and the **Use SSL** checkboxes. By default, all VCE builds would use SSL for UCS communication.

Once all of the details have been entered, clicking on **Add and Discover** will automatically start the discovery. Clicking on **Add** will only add the Vblock system to the list, but will not begin the discovery:

The following screenshot is an example of the discovery results in the **Details** view. As you can see, **UCS**, **Network**, **Storage**, and **SAN** information are shown.

This is just the high-level. The details can be seen in the **Blade Pool**, **Storage Pool**, and **Network Profiles** tabs:

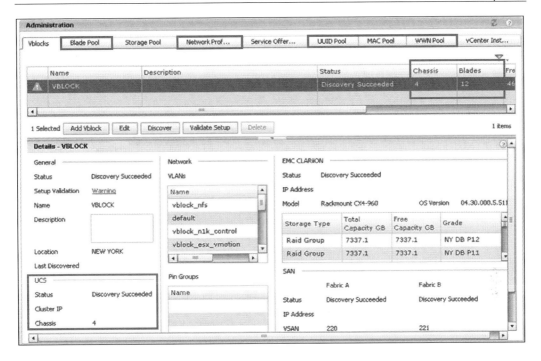

The following is a list of the details that are pulled from the UCS in the Vblock system:

- UCSM version
- # of chassis
- # of blades
- Blade location
- Blade model
- Blade CPU
- Blade memory
- All S/N info
- VLANs created
- QoS
- Adapter policies
- PIN groups

Learning about the UIM service life cycle

An **infrastructure service** is a cluster of servers packaged together with the network and storage resources required to enable the cluster. Unified Infrastructure Manager/ Provisioning Center provides **Infrastructure as a Service (IaaS)** for Vblock systems:

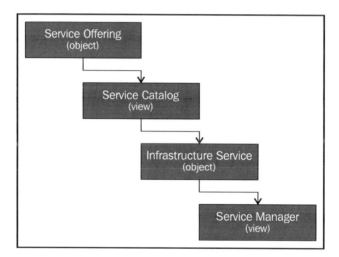

This lifecycle shows the overview of the service lifecycle as it pertains to an infrastructure service. It starts off as a generic template. The catalog displays a list of all templates (offerings). Based on the current need, selecting the proper template (offering) will allow the administrator to create the desired infrastructure service for provisioning.

As mentioned before, **Service Offering** is a template. Within the template, there are minimum and maximum allocations that can be used. For example, you can have a template that allows a minimum of 2 and a maximum of 8 blades.

Service offering also identifies whether an OS will be installed with the infrastructure service, and if yes, then which OS. It might be a good idea to have duplicates of each service offering, one with and one without OS, in case the option is needed.

Anyone creating an Infrastructure Service will be bound to the resource restrictions defined in the service offering.

The following is an example of what a completed service offering may look like. Notice the minimum and maximums in the **Servers** section. There is also a default number that can be used to minimize infrastructure service creation. This example shows a range of 1-12 servers, with a default of 1. When the infrastructure service is created, there will be 1 server, and any more servers needed will require a click of the **Add** button. If 4 will be the normal number of servers, 4 should be the default value:

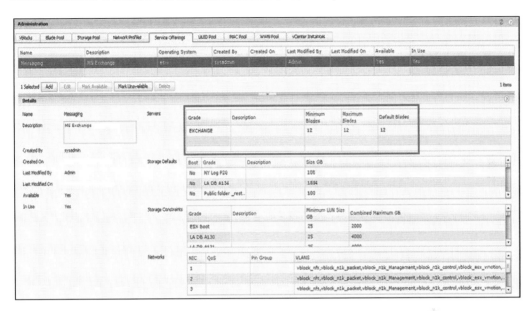

Service offerings cannot be created until the Blade Pool and Storage Pool objects are graded. The grade can be considered similar to a **class of service**. The way the pools are graded completely depends on the business requirements for the Vblock system.

Methods of grading are as follows:

- **Performance factor**: CPU speed or amount of available memory (blades)
- **Resource configuration**: Half-width versus full-width (blades)
- **BU/Customer allocation**: Finance group purchased the resource
- **Cluster-specific**: Granular selection of components for each vCenter cluster

Since this is a virtualized environment, these well-known identifiers need to be configured on each component as the provisioning occurs. The pool should be a unique pool, not overlapping with any other system.

Each pool will be completely consumed before moving on to the next pool. For instance, if you create a pool of 100 addresses for the first UUID pool, that pool will be completely used before moving to the second pool that you create.

For the WWPN and MAC pools, you can create separate pools for A and B sides, allowing easy identification of where the address resides.

All pools are created as global or Vblock-specific pools. This comes into play more when there are multiple Vblock systems managed by one UIM instance.

To recap the service offering, it is just a template. The details of each server and datastore can be edited before provisioning. For example, the hostname, IP address, datastore name, and so on.

Now let us move to the integration of UCS Manager with VMware vCenter Server.

Integrating VMware vCenter server with UCSM

Do you use Cisco UCS servers in your VMware virtualized environment and use different management tools to manage the blades and your virtual environment?

Then you should start using Cisco UCS Manager Plugin for VMware vCenter that can manage all your virtual and physical servers in a single management pane in your vCenter.

Cisco UCS vCenter integration plugin brings capabilities of UCS Manager into vCenter and you can use your vCenter to manage all your Cisco blades. The result is a single pane of glass for VirtualCenter users to get both physical and virtual infrastructure information for a given hypervisor.

Before you start the integration of UCSM with VMware vCenter, you first need to check the following prerequisites for this setup:

- vSphere Enterprise Plus License
- Support for Pass Through Switching (PTS)
- Minimum Cisco UCSM release of 1.2 (1d)
- VLANs configured in UCSM for exposing it to your VMs
- Datacenter object created in vCenter Server to contain the PTS DVS

You can either use the automated wizard to integrate vCenter Server in UCSM or you can also choose the manual integration method.

If you use the wizard, you will perform the following steps:

1. Install a plugin on vCenter Server.
2. Define DVS.
3. Define a port profile and a port profile client.
4. Apply a port profile to VMs.

Configuring vCenter with UCSM

Let us start looking at the configuration steps for UCS Integration in vCenter Server.

1. Log in to the UCS Manager.
2. From the main page, click on the **VM** tab:

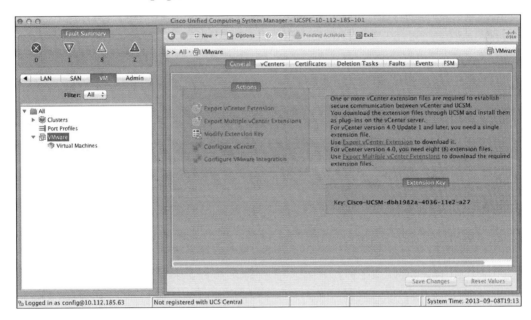

3. Click on **Export vCenter Extension**.

4. Choose a location to save and click on **OK**:

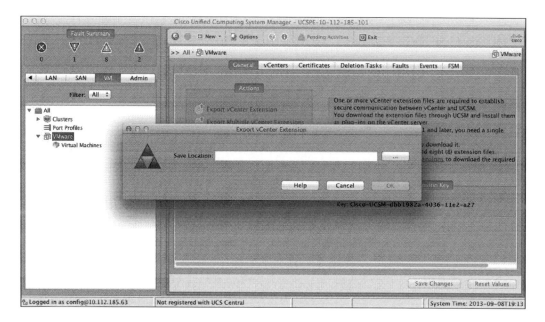

5. After exporting the XML file, copy this to VMware vCenter Server.

6. Log in to the vCenter Server.

7. From the **Plug-Ins** menu, choose **Plug-In Manager**.

8. Right-click on the **Plug-In Manager** window and select **New Plug-In**.

9. In the **Register Plug-In** window, click on the **Browse** button and select the XML file you copied to the server.

10. After installing the extension XML file, click on the **Register Plug-In** button in the **Register Plug-In** window.

11. Once the plugin registration process is done, return to the UCS Manager window.

12. Click on **Configure VMware Integration**.

13. Click on **Next**.

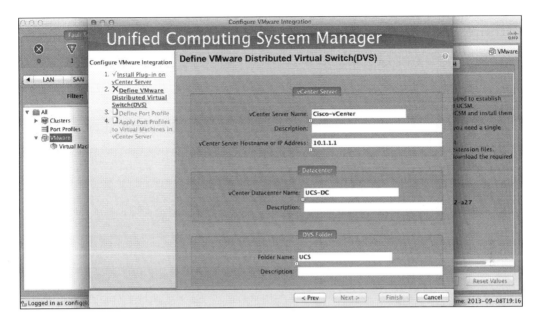

14. In the **vCenter Server** area, complete the fields to define the connection to VMware vCenter.

15. In the **Datacenter** area, complete the fields to create the datacenter in VMware vCenter.

16. In the **DVS Folder** area, complete the fields to create a folder to contain the distributed virtual switch in VMware vCenter.

17. In the **DVS** area, complete the following fields to create the distributed virtual switch in VMware vCenter.

18. Click on **Next.**

19. In the **Port Profile** area, complete the fields to define the port profile.

20. In the **VLANs** area, do the following to assign one or more VLANs to the port profile:

    1. In the **Select** column, check the checkbox in the appropriate row for each VLAN that you want to use in the port profile.

    2. In the **Native VLAN** column, click on the radio button in the appropriate row for the VLAN that you want to designate as the native VLAN.

21. In the **Client Profile** area, specify the information on those fields to create a profile client for the port profile.

22. Click on **Next.**

23. Review the text on the page in the **Configure VMware Integration** wizard.

24. Click on **Finish.**

Cisco UCS Manager connects to the vCenter Server, creates the specified DVS, and applies the port profiles.

Integration with Cisco UCS PowerTool

Did you ever face a challenge in managing multiple UCS systems? Did you encounter problems in maintaining an overarching system that maintains resource pools, users, and policies, and so on?

If yes, you need automation in place, and Cisco UCS PowerTool is a good choice.

You can use UCS PowerTool to monitor event streams and to export entire UCS configuration. Using UCS PowerTool, you can manage the following objects:

- Service profiles
- Servers
- Chassis
- Fabric Interconnects
- Configuration operations

Cisco UCS PowerTool is a Windows PowerShell tool that provides functionalities for managing your Cisco UCS. It has more than 1700 commandlets to let you better manage your UCS platform as a module.

The latest version that you get is 1.0.1. You can download it from `http://software.cisco.com/download/type.html?mdfid=283850978&flowid=25021`.

Installing PowerTool is pretty much similar to the way you install any Windows-based application. So, let us see how to use it.

Connecting your UCS Manager using PowerTool

The first thing you have to do is to connect to a UCS Manager. To do that, double-click on the PowerTool icon to open up the PowerShell window and run the following command:

```
Connect-UCS <IP Address of UCSM>
```

It will immediately ask you for the username and password of UCSM as shown in the following screenshot:

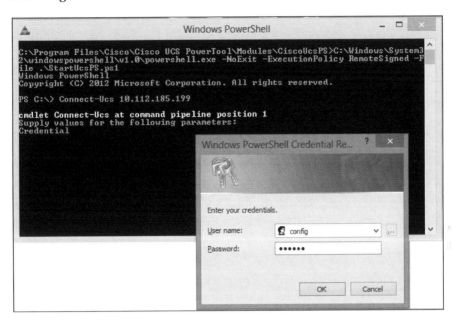

Once it authenticates, you it will show the details of the UCS System as shown in the following screenshot:

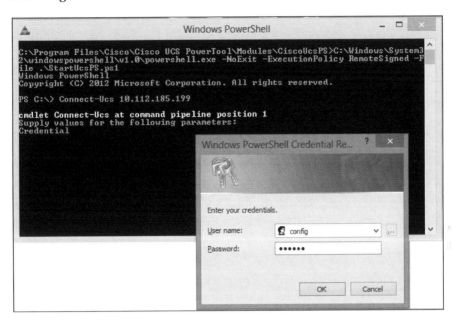

One of the main tasks using this PowerTool is to see how to use the commandlets and how to get more help around this. Cisco really did a good job in bringing all of the commandlets help within the PowerTool. Let me show you an example of it. If you want to get help on the `Get-UcsBlade`, run the following command:

`Get-Help Get-UcsBlade`

You will see a full blown output of what you can do with the specified commandlet as shown in the following screenshot:

If you want to get some examples of the commandlet you want to use, you should add -examples at the end of the get-help command. The following is an example output of the command:

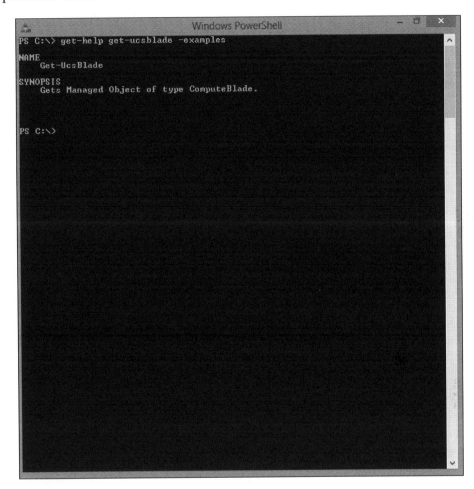

If you want to get the status of the UCS Chassis, run the following command:

```
Get-UcsChassis
```

The following screenshot is the example output of the command:

Similarly, if you want to get the statistics of the UCS Chassis, such as, Input Power, Output Power and so on, run the following command:

`Get-UcsChassisStats`

A sample output should look like the following screenshot:

So, you can see how easily you can manage your UCSM through PowerTool. But this is not the end; there is something which will give you tremendous help in building your script for your future task automation.

If you want to automate what you do through GUI without the knowledge of all of the commandlets, wouldn't that be great? Yes, of course! Cisco has thought about this and provided a wizard to help us understand what the backend command looks like, if you perform any frontend operation through GUI.

To do that, run the following command from the PowerTool prompt:

```
ConvertTo-UcsCmdlet
```

At this point, open up the GUI and perform any task. This tool will capture those frontend operations and will generate the backend commands on your screen.

Summary

In this chapter, we have discussed EMC UIM/Provisioning and VMware vCenter Integration aspects with UCS Manager. We have seen how efficiently UCS Manager can manage third-party applications and provide us with a better way to manage compute in the real world.

So you see throughout the book that Cisco Unified Computing System (UCS) provides unique features for the contemporary datacenters. Cisco UCS is a unified solution that consolidates computing, network, and storage connectivity components along with centralized management.

This book is a hands-on guide to take you through deployment in Cisco UCS. With real-world examples for configuring and deploying Cisco UCS components, this book will prepare you for practical deployments of Cisco UCS datacenter solutions.

If you want to learn and enhance your hands-on skills with Cisco UCS solutions, this book is certainly for you.

Index

IOM ports, configuring 115
license file, installing 223
port-channel uplink failure 299
port-channel uplink recovery 299
rebooting 224
SAN, connecting to 133-136
server port failure 308
server ports, configuring 114
shutting down 224
starting up 224
uplink ports configuration,
    learning 104-106
FI-specific VLAN configuration 107
functions, Cisco UCSM
identity and resource pools 68
policies 68
service profile 68
templates 68

G

Global Chassis Discovery Policy
about 308
configuration error, rectifying 308
global configuration policies
about 81
Chassis/FEX Discovery Policy 81
DNS Server 83
MAC Address Table Aging 82
Power Policy 82
SNMP 84, 85
Time Zone Management 84
Global VLAN configuration 107
grading
methods 327
Graphical User Interface (GUI)
about 67
used, for creating scheduled
    backup job 281
used, for restoring backups 283-286
Gratuitous Address Resolution Protocol
    (GARP) 110
grid redundant mode 35

H

hardware settings
configuring 56, 57

HBAs 149
high-availability clustering
configuring 286
high availability (HA)
about 222, 252, 258
managing 290-293
high availability management
partition, in space 294
partition, in time 295
Split-brain scenario 293

I

identity and resource pools 150
identity pools
conventions 162
IEEE 802.1Q
about 252
Wiki URL 252
infrastructure
challenges 321
Infrastructure as a Service (IaaS) 326
infrastructure service 326
Ingress 259
initiator 126
Input Output Module (IOM) 68
installation, UCS chassis components
about 35
blade server installation 36
installation, VSM 264-269
Intelligent Platform Management Interface.
    See **IPMI**
Internet Small Computer System Interface.
    See **iSCSI**
IOM Backplane ports 298
IOM Fabric ports 298
IOM modules
about 19
Cisco 2104XP IOM card 21
Cisco 2204XP IOM card 20
Cisco 2208XP IOM card 20
features 19
IOM ports
configuring 115
IOMs
southbound connectivity,
    configuring to 113

Thank you for buying

Implementing Cisco UCS Solutions

About Packt Publishing

Packt, pronounced 'packed', published its first book "Mastering phpMyAdmin for Effective MySQL Management" in April 2004 and subsequently continued to specialize in publishing highly focused books on specific technologies and solutions.

Our books and publications share the experiences of your fellow IT professionals in adapting and customizing today's systems, applications, and frameworks. Our solution based books give you the knowledge and power to customize the software and technologies you're using to get the job done. Packt books are more specific and less general than the IT books you have seen in the past. Our unique business model allows us to bring you more focused information, giving you more of what you need to know, and less of what you don't.

Packt is a modern, yet unique publishing company, which focuses on producing quality, cutting-edge books for communities of developers, administrators, and newbies alike. For more information, please visit our website: www.packtpub.com.

About Packt Enterprise

In 2010, Packt launched two new brands, Packt Enterprise and Packt Open Source, in order to continue its focus on specialization. This book is part of the Packt Enterprise brand, home to books published on enterprise software – software created by major vendors, including (but not limited to) IBM, Microsoft and Oracle, often for use in other corporations. Its titles will offer information relevant to a range of users of this software, including administrators, developers, architects, and end users.

Writing for Packt

We welcome all inquiries from people who are interested in authoring. Book proposals should be sent to author@packtpub.com. If your book idea is still at an early stage and you would like to discuss it first before writing a formal book proposal, contact us; one of our commissioning editors will get in touch with you.

We're not just looking for published authors; if you have strong technical skills but no writing experience, our experienced editors can help you develop a writing career, or simply get some additional reward for your expertise.

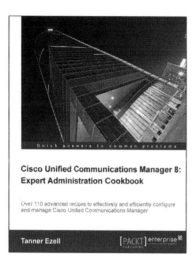

Cisco Unified Communications Manager 8:
Expert Administration Cookbook

Over 110 advanced recipes to effectively and efficiently configure and manage Cisco Unified Communications Manager

Tanner Ezell

Cisco Unified Communications Manager 8: Expert Administration Cookbook

ISBN: 978-1-84968-432-3   Paperback: 310 pages

Over 110 advanced recipes to effectively and efficiently configure and manage Cisco Unified Communications Manager

1. Full of illustrations, diagrams, and tips with clear step-by-step instructions and real-time examples.

2. Master call admission control and the technologies associated with it, which is an important aspect of any unified communications deployment to ensure call quality and resilience.

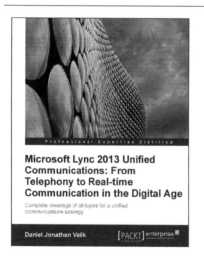

Microsoft Lync 2013 Unified
Communications: From
Telephony to Real-time
Communication in the Digital Age

Complete coverage of all topics for a unified communications strategy

Daniel Jonathan Valik

Microsoft Lync 2013 Unified Communications: From Telephony to Real-time Communication in the Digital Age

ISBN: 978-1-84968-506-1   Paperback: 224 pages

Complete coverage of all topics for a unified communications strategy

1. A real business case and example project showing you how you can optimize costs and improve your competitive advantage with a Unified Communications project.

2. The book combines both business and the latest relevant technical information, so it is a great reference for business stakeholders, IT decision makers, and UC technical experts.

Please check **www.PacktPub.com** for information on our titles

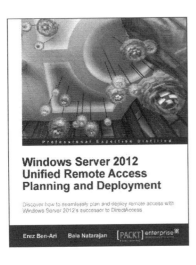

Windows Server 2012 Unified Remote Access Planning and Deployment

ISBN: 978-1-84968-828-4   Paperback: 328 pages

Discover how to seamlessly plan and deploy remote access with Windows Server 2012's successor to DirectAccess

1. The essential administrator's companion for the successor to DirectAccess.

2. Get to grips with configuring, enabling, and deploying Unified Remote Access.

3. A quick start guide to have you up and running with Windows Server 2012 URA in no time.

GNS3 Network Simulation Guide

ISBN: 978-1-78216-080-9   Paperback: 154 pages

Acquire a comprehensive knowledge of the GNS3 graphical network simulator, using it to prototype your network without the need for physical routers

1. Develop your knowledge for Cisco certification (CCNA, CCNP, and CCIE), using GNS3.

2. Install GNS3 successfully on Windows, Linux, or OS X.

3. Work your way through easy-to-follow exercises showing you how to simulate your test network using Cisco routers, Ethernet switches, and Virtual PCs.

Made in the USA
Lexington, KY
07 April 2014